AMERICA'S
Best RECIPES

AMERICA'S
Best RECIPES

STATE FAIR
Blue Ribbon Winners

*Over 250 Mouthwatering Family Recipes
from State Fairs Across the Country*

ROSEMARY &
PETER HANLEY

GALAHAD BOOKS
NEW YORK

To Kate
We couldn't have done it
without you.

First Galahad Books edition published in 1998.

Galahad Books
A division of BBS Publishing Corporation
386 Park Avenue South
New York, NY 10016

Galahad Books is a registered trademark of BBS Publishing Corporation.

Published by arrangement with Rosemary A. and Peter C. Hanley.

Library of Congress Catalog Card Number: 97-77426
ISBN: 1-57866-013-0

Printed in the United States of America.

TABLE OF CONTENTS

AMERICA'S
Best RECIPES

1

SOUPS, SALADS, DRESSINGS, APPETIZERS AND SNACKS

SOUPS

FRANK HALL — PALMER LAKE, COLORADO

When we got in touch with the 1981 "Queen of the Kitchen" at the Colorado State Fair, he was in boot camp at Fort Dix, New Jersey. Frank Hall picked up this top honor at the 1981 Colorado State Fair by "placing" in eleven of fifteen different categories and by accumulating more points than the other 210 contestants. Frank is proud of that fact because many of the other competitors were home economists. He never studied cooking, but began competing as a 4–H member. He attributes his cooking skills to his mother, who "taught me everything I know."

Frank is now studying Military Intelligence and will soon be off to Germany. But if you think his absence will give you a better chance at being selected "Queen of the Kitchen" we should warn you that Frank's brother Tom took those honors in 1982.

Following is Frank's blue ribbon recipe for Duchess Soup. His Broccoli Soufflé can be found on page 49 and his Green Chili is on page 50.

DUCHESS SOUP
Yield: 2 servings

- 4 Tablespoons butter
- 4 Tablespoons flour
- ½ teaspoon salt
- ½ teaspoon white pepper
- 2 cups milk
- ½ cup shredded American cheese
- ½ cup shredded Swiss cheese
- ¼ teaspoon paprika
- ¼ to ½ cup dry white wine
- ¼ cup finely chopped celery
- ¼ cup finely grated carrots

Melt the butter over low heat. Stir in the flour. Season with salt and white pepper. Gradually add the milk. Cook, stirring constantly, until thickened. Remove from heat and add the cheeses and paprika. Stir until the cheese is melted. Stir in the white wine and vegetables. Blend well and serve immediately.

BLUE RIBBON WINNER, COLORADO STATE FAIR

KITTY MARINO — SYRACUSE, NEW YORK

At the New York State Fair winning the blue ribbon for Macaroni and Cheese is difficult enough. But when your chief competitors are your ex-husband and your mother, it can be downright traumatic. Yet, Kitty Marino's unusual recipe not only won the blue ribbon (her ex took second, her mom third), it took the grand prize over thousands of entries. We can thank Kitty's younger sister for encouraging her to enter her Harvest Stew in the fair competition eight years ago. That year Kitty won her first blue ribbon and got "hooked" on state fairs. Since then she has entered every year, accumulating twenty-nine ribbons, three of them in the Grand Prize competition. She creates all her own recipes, trusting only her own instincts and creativity and her "ESP."

Below is Kitty's blue ribbon Homemade Bean Soup. On page 34 you will find the blue ribbon Macaroni and Cheese that beat out her mother's and ex-husband's.

HOMEMADE BEAN SOUP
Yield: About 6 servings

- 1 large package navy beans
- 1 ham bone (with ample ham for removing and adding to soup)
- 2 onions
- 1 Tablespoon fresh garlic, minced
- 2 green onions
- 2 carrots
- 1 large boiled potato
- 2 stalks celery
- ½ teaspoon coarsely ground black pepper
- Salt to taste
- ½ teaspoon garlic powder

Soak the beans overnight. Boil for 1 hour in a covered pot (water 3 inches above beans). Add more water during cooking if necessary. Add the ham bone. Sauté the onions, garlic and green onions and add to soup. Remove 1 cup of the beans from pot and mash with boiled potato. Add to soup. Add spices to taste. Add carrots and celery. Cover and continue cooking 1½ hours, stirring often. Remove the ham bone and slice the meat off the bone. Add to soup. Simmer an additional ½–¾ hour.

BLUE RIBBON WINNER, NEW YORK STATE FAIR

AGNES ADAMS, ALEXIS HUSTON, DOROTHY ZELLER, WINNIE OSBORNE — SYRACUSE, NEW YORK

Blue ribbons are a family tradition in Syracuse, New York, but the only four-star kitchen in town belongs to Agnes Adams and her three daugh-

ters, Alexis Huston, Winnie Osborne and Dorothy Zeller. This is one of the many instances where we found multiple family members winning blue ribbons. What makes it so unique is that they have won in so many different categories. You can literally put together a blue ribbon meal using the prize-winning recipes from this outstanding family. You can try the recipes for Winnie's Hearty Vegetable Soup and Agnes's Three Bean Salad in this chapter. On pages 79–80 you will find Dorothy's Pumpernickel and Marmalade-Oatmeal Breads. Alexis's Brioche is on page 81 and Winnie's Tamale Pie can be found on 44.

WINNIE OSBORNE — SYRACUSE, NEW YORK

HEARTY VEGETABLE SOUP
Yield: 6½ quarts

    4 quarts water
    1 Tablespoon salt
    4 cups thinly sliced cabbage
1½ cups chopped onion
    6 carrots, pared and cut in 3-inch pieces
¾ cup chopped celery
¼ cup chopped green pepper
    1 can tomatoes, undrained
½ package (10 oz. size) frozen lima beans
½ package (9 oz. size) frozen cut green beans
½ package (10 oz. size) frozen peas
    1 can whole-kernel corn, drained
    1 pared potato, cubed
    2 Tablespoons chopped parsley
    1 can tomato paste
½ teaspoon ground cloves
    1 teaspoon sugar
    2 teaspoons salt
½ teaspoon pepper

Bring 4 quarts of water and 1 tablespoon of salt to a boil in a very large kettle. Add the cabbage, onions, carrots, celery, green peppers and tomatoes. Bring back to boiling, then simmer, covered, for 30 minutes. Add all the remaining ingredients and simmer, covered, for 3½ hours. If desired, refrigerate overnight and reheat when ready to serve by slowly heating the soup to boiling.

BLUE RIBBON WINNER, NEW YORK STATE FAIR

CAROLYN E. JENDREK, CAROLYN J. JENDREK BLAIR — BALTIMORE, MARYLAND

Mrs. Carolyn E. Jendrek is a secretary for a plastic surgeon in Baltimore, Maryland. The plastic surgeon's name is Carolyn J. Jendrek, her daughter.

The senior Carolyn Jendrek and her husband, John, a retired attorney, have raised quite a family. In addition to Carolyn junior, the surgeon, there are three other children. Paul, the oldest, has a Ph.D. in chemistry and is a lieutenant colonel in the Air Force. Their second son, Ed, is a veterinarian and their youngest, Mark, is a schoolteacher who is presently planning to enter law school.

Both Carolyn Jendreks manage to find the time to compete and win at the Maryland State Fair. Last year was a busy time in the Jendrek household. Carolyn J. Jendrek Blair gave birth to her first child, a son, Christopher Blair, on Halloween. Now when you visit the doctor's office, you will have the good fortune of meeting three generations of the Jendrek family.

Carolyn senior's Blue Ribbon Convenience Dinner consists of five family favorites. This category required that five separate items make up a complete dinner. Maryland judges consider not just the quality of each item, but also how they complement each other. Below you will find Carolyn's winning menu. In addition, you can find Carolyn junior's Peach Marmalade on page 300, and Carolyn senior's Apricot Jam and Grape Conserve on page 301 and her Beef Jerky on page 278.

CAROLYN E. JENDREK — BALTIMORE, MARYLAND

CONVENIENCE DINNER

Tomato–Mushroom Soup (below)

Turkey Chow Mein (page 57)

Seafood and Wild Rice (page 58)

Snow Peas (page 58)

Black Raspberry Cobbler (page 166)

TOMATO–MUSHROOM SOUP

Yield: 10–12 servings

    3 quarts ripe tomatoes
    1 pint beef stock
    2 small onions, chopped
    4 stalks celery, chopped
    ½ teaspoon thyme
    ½ teaspoon oregano
    1 clove garlic, minced
    1 Tablespoon chopped parsley
    1 pound sliced mushrooms

Cook and sieve 3 quarts of tomatoes. This yields about 2 quarts of puree. Simmer the puree with all the remaining ingredients except the mushrooms for ½ hour. Add the mushrooms. At this point you may either continue cooking for about 30 minutes and serve, or pour into sterilized jars and process 30 minutes at 10 pounds pressure.

BLUE RIBBON WINNER, MARYLAND STATE FAIR

CHRISTY MESSER — SHREVEPORT, LOUISIANA

At thirteen years of age, Christy Messer is a typical all-American teenager. She is active in the 4–H Club, where she participates in the Junior Leadership program. She is also looking for after-school employment and hoping that Christmas will bring a telephone to her room.

Christy's mother is a registered dietician and a home economist for the Louisiana Cooperative Extension Service. She is clearly the inspiration behind Christy's cooking skills and blue ribbon success.

MICROWAVE CORN CHOWDER
Yield: 3–4 servings

   3 slices raw bacon, diced
   ¼ cup finely chopped onion
   1 can (16 oz.) cream-style corn
   ¼ cup hot water
   1 cup milk
   ½ teaspoon salt
   ¼ teaspoon pepper
   Finely chopped parsley for garnishing

Place the bacon and onion in a deep 2-quart heat-resistant non-metallic casserole. Heat, covered with paper towel, on highest setting for 3 minutes. Combine the remaining ingredients, except the parsley. Blend until smooth. Heat, uncovered, on "Roast" for 7 minutes or until the soup is heated to 160 degrees. Stir occasionally. Allow soup to stand before serving. Garnish with parsley.

BLUE RIBBON WINNER, LOUISIANA STATE FAIR

MILDRED MOTT — UNION, MISSISSIPPI

Mildred Mott attributes all her success to God. She thanks Him for the many talents He has given her.

One of those talents is cooking and we are pleased that Mildred shared her favorite recipes with us. All are blue ribbon winners at the Mississippi State Fair.

Mildred manages to do all her work herself. This includes the plowing on her thirty-acre farm, a chore that she has handled since the death of her husband, nine years ago.

In spite of the hard work she enjoys tilling the soil, planting seeds and watching them grow. She then jars and freezes the fruits of her labor and selects the best to compete at the state fair.

Mildred Mott not only gave us her two favorite blue ribbon winners, her soup (below) and her special relish (page 269), but also inspired us with her special strength.

VEGETARIAN VEGETABLE SOUP
Yield: About 7 quarts

1½ quarts water
2 quarts peeled, cored, chopped tomatoes (about 12 large)
1½ quarts cubed, pared potatoes (about 6 medium)
1 quart green lima beans
1 quart cut corn, uncooked (about 9 ears)
1½ quarts ¾-inch-sliced carrots (about 12 medium)
2 cups 1-inch-sliced celery
2 cups chopped onions
Salt to taste

Add water to the vegetables; boil for 5 minutes, and immediately pour into hot quart jars, leaving 1-inch head space. Add ½ teaspoon of salt to each quart and adjust caps. Process 1 hour and 25 minutes, at 10 pounds pressure.

Note: Use any mixture of vegetables liked in soup. Process the length of time needed for vegetables requiring the longest processing time.

BLUE RIBBON WINNER, MISSISSIPPI STATE FAIR

SALADS

THE PARKER C. FOLSE FAMILY — DALLAS, TEXAS

Parker Folse of Beaumont, Texas literally learned how to cook at his mother's bedside. When Mrs. Folse became ill during Parker's senior year in high school, his mother taught him her recipes so that he could handle the cooking responsibilities for the family.

Years later, Parker moved to Dallas and began attending the Great State Fair of Texas. In 1965, while touring the automotive pavilion, he was attracted by a lovely model who was demonstrating cars for General Motors. He managed to get her name and strike up a conversation. Parker was hooked. He visited the automotive pavilion every night of the fair and married the lovely lady less than a year later.

The Folses are truly a state fair family.

Parker's culinary interests grew over the years and in 1969 he was encouraged by friends to enter his first state fair cooking contest. That year he entered five jars of preserves and pickles and waited up till 1:00 A.M. to check the list of winners published in the first edition of the morning newspaper.

Every one of his recipes had won a blue ribbon.

Parker, his wife, Lois, and their two daughters, Donica and Micheau, have become regular contestants and it is believed that they have won more food contests than any other family at the Texas State Fair. Parker alone has won more than five hundred ribbons including over two hundred blue ribbons and fourteen Best of Show.

Lois Johnson Folse also comes from a state fair family. Every year for the past sixty-one years her family has held a family reunion on the fairgrounds. Their annual picnic has become a tradition and they are often joined by their many friends who work at the fair.

The tradition will be carried on by the Folse children, Donica and Micheau, who are regular competitors at state fair events. Donica has already won fifteen blue ribbons and Micheau has won ten.

We think you'll enjoy a number of the Folse family recipes. Following are Captain Joe's Seafood Sauce and Salad, Parker's Green Salad and Fruit Salad with Poppy Seed Dressing. Throughout the book you'll find additional favorite blue ribbon winners from Parker, Lois, Donica and Micheau.

PARKER C. FOLSE, JR. — DALLAS, TEXAS
Yield: About 6 servings

CAPTAIN JOE'S SEAFOOD SAUCE AND SALAD

This recipe was given to Parker by Captain Joe of New Orleans, Louisiana. He is a steamship pilot and a superb chef, who has traveled the seas throughout the world. His cooking skills have won him a reputation of preparing only the best recipes. It is with his good wishes for happy dining that he shares this marvelous seafood sauce. Parker uses it as a topping for shrimp, crab and seafood salads, as well as a dip for seafoods and chips.

Shortly after receiving this recipe, Parker used it over a shrimp and crabmeat salad and entered it in the State Fair of Texas Salad Contest. It won "Best of Show."

SEAFOOD SAUCE
1 medium white onion, finely chopped
2 medium green onions with ⅓ of the green top, finely chopped
1 pint mayonnaise
4 dashes Tabasco sauce
4 dashes Worcestershire sauce
2 heaping teaspoons fresh horseradish, grated
2 heaping teaspoons Dijon-style mustard
1 heaping teaspoon yellow prepared mustard
Salt and pepper to taste

Combine all the ingredients in a bowl and mix well, beating with a wooden spoon. Refrigerate and let stand for at least 2 hours before using. This will keep for a month in the refrigerator.

SEAFOOD SALAD
1 pound fresh cooked crabmeat
1 pound boiled shrimp, shells removed and deveined
1 head curly leaf lettuce, torn into bite-sized pieces
½ green pepper, thinly sliced
2 green onions, finely chopped
1 avocado, peeled and sliced

½ cup ripe olives
12 cherry tomatoes
 2 hard-cooked eggs, sliced lengthwise into fourths
 1 pimiento, thinly sliced

Select an attractive serving bowl and arrange the broken lettuce pieces in it. Scatter the shrimp and crabmeat onto the surface and garnish with the remaining ingredients. Chill thoroughly. Pour a generous amount of Captain Joe's Seafood Sauce over the salad just prior to serving.

BLUE RIBBON WINNER, BEST OF SHOW, TEXAS STATE FAIR

PARKER'S GREEN SALAD
Yield: 15–20 servings

DRESSING
 ½ cup fresh lemon juice
1½ cups olive oil
 1 Tablespoon crushed dried oregano
 2 cloves garlic, peeled and left whole
 1 teaspoon salt

Place all the ingredients into a pint jar, tighten lid, and shake well. Let marinate overnight. Reshake just before using. Will keep refrigerated indefinitely.

THE SALAD
Any assortment of salad vegetables will do, but here is one that Parker suggests.
 2 large heads of Romaine lettuce, torn into pieces
 2 large heads of leaf lettuce, torn into pieces
 4 medium tomatoes, sliced in wedges
 4 green onions, chopped
 1 bell pepper, chopped
 2 cucumbers, sliced

20 Italian sweet peppers
2 small cans whole anchovies
1 cup ripe green olives
1 cup ripe black olives
¼ pound Feta cheese, crumbled
½ cup almond slivers
¼ cup grated Parmesan cheese
Salt and freshly ground black pepper to taste

Toss all lettuce and chilled vegetables together. Add the Feta cheese, almonds, and salad dressing and toss to coat all ingredients. Add salt, pepper and Parmesan cheese and toss to barely mix. The lettuce pieces, green onions, bell peppers and cucumbers may be placed in plastic bags and stored overnight in the refrigerator. Do not slice the tomatoes or add olives, anchovies, almonds and cheese until just before tossing the salad. It would take an enormous salad bowl to accommodate this much salad at once, so it should be divided into two or three bowls.

BLUE RIBBON WINNER, TEXAS STATE FAIR

FRUIT SALAD WITH POPPY SEED DRESSING
Yield: 6–10 servings

POPPY SEED DRESSING
1¼ cup honey
1 Tablespoon dry mustard
1 teaspoon salt
¾ cup red wine vinegar
¼ cup grated onion
1 pint safflower oil
2 heaping Tablespoons poppy seeds
½ teaspoon ground coriander

Place the honey, dry mustard, salt, red wine vinegar and grated onion into a mixing bowl and stir together. Use an electric mixer and slowly add the oil while beating on medium speed. When it is all combined and nicely thickened, add the coriander and poppy seeds and beat a few minutes longer. Pour into jars and refrigerate. Restir before using.

THE SALAD
1 lemon
1 cup water
1 or 2 bananas, peeled and sliced into ¼-inch rounds
2 oranges, peeled and sliced into ¼-inch rounds
1 apple, partially peeled, cored and sliced
1 cup fresh green grapes
1 cup purple grapes, seeded
8 plums, pitted and quartered
1 pint fresh strawberries, stems removed
2 pears, peeled and sliced
1 cantaloupe or other similar melon, cut from rind into chunks
2 peaches, peeled and sliced

Make a solution of the juice of 1 lemon and 1 cup of water. Soak the bananas, apples and pears in this liquid to prevent their discoloring. Place the fruit in a large glass bowl lined with curly lettuce leaves and pour the poppy seed dressing over the salad. If served individually, then place fruit on top of a curly lettuce leaf centered on a salad plate and pour dressing over it.

Note: Any fruits available may be used in place of those not in season. Exotic fruits such as kiwi, pineapple, and mangos may be used.

BLUE RIBBON WINNER, TEXAS STATE FAIR

THREE BEAN SALAD
Yield: 8–10 servings

1 can yellow string beans, drained
1 can green string beans, drained
1 can red kidney beans, drained
1 medium onion, diced
2 medium green peppers, diced
1 can tomato soup, undiluted
½ cup salad oil
1 cup sugar
¾ cup vinegar
½ teaspoon each salt and white pepper
1 teaspoon mustard

Mix the beans, onions and peppers together. In a separate bowl, combine the remaining ingredients and blend until smooth. Pour the sauce over the beans and refrigerate overnight. Serve in a bowl lined with crisp lettuce leaves.

BLUE RIBBON WINNER, NEW YORK STATE FAIR

NANCY LEPRELL — DALLAS, TEXAS

Nancy LePrell first learned of the Texas State Fair cooking contest in 1981 while reading a friend's premium book. Until that time she had never even attended a state fair.

She was immediately attracted to the "Italian Contest" because of her Sicilian heritage but hesitated to enter because she really didn't feel her cooking was good enough to win. Nonetheless, at the insistence of her friends, she decided to enter three of the four categories.

Nancy was surrounded by her family and friends as the judging began. It lasted almost four hours and proved to be the "the longest time" of her

*life. But the wait was worth every minute when Nancy learned to her sur-
prise that she had won a blue ribbon for her Bensadano Salad as well as
for her Eggplant Sicilian Style.*

*These recipes are truly special. The Bensadano Salad went on to win
"Best of Show" and the Eggplant (page 30) is prepared from a recipe that
has been in Nancy's family for five generations. Her great-great-grand-
mother used to prepare it in her native Sicily.*

BENSADANO SALAD
Yield: 4–6 servings

DRESSING
½ cup olive oil
¼ cup wine vinegar
2 teaspoons salt
2 teaspoons pepper
2 Tablespoons grated cheese

THE SALAD
1 can (8 oz.) artichoke hearts (drained)
1 can (4 oz.) black olives, pitted (drained)
1 small head lettuce
½ cup provolone cheese (diced in 1-inch chunks)
8 thin slices hard salami (sliced in ¼-inch strips)

Two hours before serving combine all ingredients for the dressing
in a medium bowl. When well blended, add the artichokes and
olives, and marinate in refrigerator until serving time. Five minutes before serving chop the lettuce in a large bowl. Add the
cheese and salami; next add the marinated vegetables and dressing. Toss and serve.

BLUE RIBBON WINNER, BEST OF SHOW, TEXAS STATE FAIR

DRESSINGS

JANE FRISCH — LINCOLN, NEBRASKA

The Frisches have raised four children of their own and two foster children and are now the proud grandparents of eight. Although they are retired, they are certainly not inactive.

Jane Frisch is President of the Board of St. Monica's Home, an Episcopal Church-sponsored halfway house for alcoholic women. Church-related activities have always have been an important part of Jane's life.

The Frisches also love plants and gardening and are accredited rose show judges. They grow and show about two hundred roses of their own each year.

Fresh from the Frisches' garden is Jane's own recipe for green onion dressing.

GREEN ONION DRESSING
Yield: 4 cups

    1 cup unflavored yogurt
2½ cups mayonnaise
    2 Tablespoons lemon juice
  ½ teaspoon salt
  ½ teaspoon dill seed
  ¾ cup thinly sliced green onion
  ¼ cup chopped ripe tomato, peeled and seeded

Combine the yogurt, mayonnaise, lemon juice, salt and dill seed until smooth. Add the onion and tomatoes. Store in a glass jar in the refrigerator.

BLUE RIBBON WINNER, NEBRASKA STATE FAIR

MARY ANN EATON — DANVERS, MASSACHUSETTS

Mary Ann Eaton has been attending the Topsfield Fair in Massachusetts since she was a child.

But her interest in the cooking competition didn't begin until 1979, when she and her sisters decided to compete against each other in the chocolate cake contest. That year Hershey began sponsoring a special chocolate competition at the Topsfield Fair.

Mary Ann and her sisters Nancy and Susan are true fair folk. In 1982 they participated at the Three County Fair, the Rochester, New Hampshire, Fair, the Deerfield, New Hampshire, Fair and, of course, at Topsfield in Massachusetts.

The family's biggest win of the year probably came when Nancy's "singing" roosters took first, second and third place in the cock crowing contest at the Three County Fair. It must have been a sight to see the three sisters rolling down the Massachusetts Pike in Nancy's fire-engine-red Ford truck loaded down with baked goods, decorated cakes and the four roosters (Moe, Larry, Curley and Cadbury).

In 1981 Mary Ann's husband, Quentin, began keeping bees. Anticipating great flows of honey, Mary Ann began experimenting with cooking with honey. The two recipes, offered below and on page 256, are the products of that experience and are both blue ribbon winners at the 1981 Topsfield Fair.

Mary Ann, Quentin, Nancy, Susan and assorted other relatives and friends are a wonderfully unpredictable group. If you travel the New England fair circuit, you are sure to come across them in beekeeping, cock crowing or crocheting. If not there, look at the swine show or in baked goods or maybe over at decorated cakes. You'll be sure to recognize them by the telltale fire-engine-red Ford truck.

HONEY FRENCH DRESSING
Yield: About 1½ cups

½ cup salad oil
½ cup vinegar
½ cup honey
½ Tablespoon salt

Mix the first two ingredients, add the remaining ingredients, and beat vigorously.

BLUE RIBBON WINNER, TOPSFIELD STATE FAIR

ALICE ROWAN WAUGH — MARLINTON, WEST VIRGINIA

Alice Rowan Waugh began her teaching career in 1930 in a one-room schoolhouse on the top of a mountain ten miles outside of Marlinton, West Virginia. She used to ride a horse or walk down the mountain every weekend to visit her parents at their general store in Marlinton. Those were the difficult Depression years and Alice remembers holding box suppers to raise money for the Spruce Flat school library.

Alice's teaching career spanned forty-three years. In 1973 she retired as principal of the Marlinton Elementary School.

Now seventy-two years of age, she enjoys competing at the West Virginia State Fair. Cooking has always been her hobby and she remembers becoming a competitor many years ago in a General Foods contest at the Pocahontas County Fair. Over the years she has won many blue ribbons for her cooking skills. Jokingly she said she can't understand why she's still single since she always heard that "the way to a man's heart is through his stomach." Once, when a student asked why she wasn't married, she answered, "Because I didn't realize my last chance was my last chance."

We could have talked for hours with Alice, she is so representative of the nice people you meet at state fairs. We're very pleased to provide her recipe for Boiled Salad Dressing.

BOILED SALAD DRESSING
Yield: About 2 cups

    2 Tablespoons flour
    1 teaspoon salt
    1 cup sugar
    1 egg, well beaten
    ¾ cup vinegar
    1 Tablespoon butter
    ¼ teaspoon prepared mustard
    Cream or milk, as needed
    Mayonnaise
    Paprika (optional)

Ground celery seed (optional)
Sour cream, to taste

Mix the flour, salt and sugar. Add the beaten egg and beat well. Heat the vinegar to boiling; add the sugar mixture and cook until thick, stirring constantly. When done, remove from heat; add the butter and mustard. When cold, put in a container and refrigerate. When ready to use, thin the dressing with cream or milk and some prepared mayonnaise and mix until proper consistency to blend with salad ingredients.

This dressing is especially good with potato salad, cole slaw and chicken salad. For fresh garden vegetable salad, season with generous amounts of paprika, ground celery seed and some sour cream. Basic dressing will keep indefinitely when refrigerated. Also freezes well.

BLUE RIBBON WINNER, WEST VIRGINIA STATE FAIR

VERNA WIGDAHL — WEST ALLIS, WISCONSIN

Verna is truly a state fair pro . . . she has been winning blue ribbons at the Wisconsin State Fair since 1966. She especially likes to enter new categories because it "makes the challenge greater." She also thinks that the cooking contests give valuable experience and that you can learn important things about taste, texture and appearance.

Verna's husband, Truman, is a retired industrial carpenter. They have two daughters who are also good cooks. One lives near by in West Allis and the other, a hairstylist, lives in Florida.

The blue ribbon recipe that Verna has provided works well both as a salad dressing and also as a dip for fresh vegetables.

SEA GREEN SALAD DRESSING
Yield: About 2½ cups

1 teaspoon prepared mustard
1 cup salad oil

½ cup sugar
¼ cup cider vinegar
1 egg
1 teaspoon celery seed
1 medium onion
¼ cup snipped green onion tops
½ teaspoon prepared horseradish

Place all the ingredients into a blender. Blend until smooth. Refrigerate.

BLUE RIBBON WINNER, WISCONSIN STATE FAIR

APPETIZERS AND SNACKS

CASSIE MARCOM — CARY, NORTH CAROLINA

Cassie Marcom entered the North Carolina State Fair at the urging of her best friend and next-door neighbor, Betty Griffin. Betty had won her first blue ribbon (page 251) and wanted Cassie to share in the excitement, just as they have shared so many other things over the years. A former member of 4–H and the Future Homemakers of America, Cassie started cooking thirty-three years ago as a new bride and now has the honor of being Betty's favorite chef. But sharing is the key word in the Marcom–Griffin friendship. Betty's daughter Denise and Cassie's son Ricky carry this family tie into the second generation as best friends. Below is Cassie's recipe for Cheese Straws, which are served as snacks or hors d'oeuvres at the Marcom home.

CHEESE STRAWS
Yield: 16–18 dozen

1 pound very sharp grated cheese
¾ pound margarine
4 cups plain flour

1 teaspoon salt
¼ teaspoon paprika

Grate the cheese. Cream the margarine and cheese with your hands or an electric mixer until very soft. Sift the dry ingredients and add, a little at a time, to the cheese and margarine mixture until all is thoroughly mixed. Put mixture in a cookie press and press out in lines about 12 inches long. Cut each into pieces about 3 inches long. Bake at 375 degrees for 15 minutes, checking frequently so straws do not burn.

BLUE RIBBON WINNER, NORTH CAROLINA STATE FAIR

LOIS JOHNSON FOLSE — DALLAS, TEXAS

HAPPY HOUR MUSHROOMS
Yield: 36 mushroom caps

36 medium-size fresh mushrooms
3 Tablespoons melted butter
1 stick softened butter
⅔ cup grated Monterey Jack cheese (4-ounce wedge)
1 clove garlic, finely chopped
2 Tablespoons red table wine
2 Tablespoons soy sauce
1 teaspoon onion powder
⅓ cup crushed Fritos corn chips (1¼ ounces by weight)

Remove the stems from the mushrooms and wash and dry the caps. Brush them with the melted butter and set aside. Combine the soft butter, grated cheese and chopped garlic in a bowl. Add the remaining ingredients and stir together to form a paste. Fill the mushroom caps with the mixture, mounding the top neatly. Place on a baking sheet about 5 inches beneath the oven broiler and broil for about 3 minutes or until the stuffing is bubbling and lightly browned. Serve while hot. These may be prepared well in advance and refrigerated until needed. Allow to come to room temperature 30 minutes before broiling.

BLUE RIBBON WINNER, BEST OF SHOW, TEXAS STATE FAIR

LOIS AND PARKER FOLSE — DALLAS, TEXAS

SUNSHINE SOUFFLE

Yield: 16 2½-inch squares

This should be assembled a day in advance and baked just prior to serving.

```
   7  slices white bread with crust left on
   1  stick butter, softened
   5  eggs
1½  cups whole milk
   1  teaspoon Dijon-style prepared mustard
  ½  teaspoon turmeric
  ¼  teaspoon thyme, crushed
   1  Tablespoon onion flakes
  ¼  teaspoon garlic powder
  ¼  teaspoon cayenne pepper
   4  ounces grated sharp cheddar cheese
```

Several hours or the night before serving time, butter a 9×9-inch ovenproof casserole or tin. Spread both sides of the 7 slices of white bread with 1 stick of the softened butter and place them into the dish, overlapping them where necessary. Beat the eggs in a mixing bowl until they are frothy and continue beating while adding the milk, mustard and seasonings. Pour the liquid over the bread slices. Scatter the grated cheddar cheese over the surface and refrigerate for several hours or overnight.

Bake in a preheated 350-degree oven for about 35 minutes or until set. Cut into squares and serve while hot. Easy, but delicious.

BLUE RIBBON WINNER, TEXAS STATE FAIR

CHRISTY CULP — SMITHTON, MISSOURI

Christy Culp plays the piano for her high school chorus as well as for the Lake Creek Methodist Church. She also plays the clarinet and has the fourth of seventeen chairs in her school band.

But music isn't her only talent. She also belongs to the science and math clubs at Smithton High and is active in the Homemakers of Tomorrow.

Christy is also a member of 4–H, which is where she learned to cook and sew. Her inspiration for state fair competition came from her great-aunt, Lulu May Finley, who still competes at the age of eighty-two. Christy is certainly following in her footsteps. In 1981 she won the "Bake it with Lard" contest sponsored by the Missouri Porkettes.

The Culps live on a 187-acre farm on which her father raises corn, wheat and hay. Her mother works as a secretary for an insurance company in Sedalia.

Below is Christy's Gold'n Nut Crunch recipe, which won the blue ribbon at the Missouri State Fair.

GOLD'N NUT CRUNCH
Yield: 6½ cups

    1 can (12 oz.) mixed nuts or 1 jar (12 oz.) dry roasted peanuts
    ¼ cup oleo, melted
    ¼ cup grated Parmesan cheese
    ¼ teaspoon garlic powder
    ¼ teaspoon ground oregano
    ¼ teaspoon celery salt
    4 cups Golden Graham cereal

Preheat oven to 300 degrees. Mix the nuts and oleo in a medium bowl until well coated. Add the cheese, garlic powder, oregano, celery salt and cereal. Toss until well coated. Spread on an ungreased jelly roll pan 15½×10½×1 inches. Bake, stirring occasionally, for 15 minutes. Store in an air-tight container.

BLUE RIBBON WINNER, MISSOURI STATE FAIR

2

MAIN COURSES

ROBERT VASQUEZ — ALBUQUERQUE, NEW MEXICO

Robert Vasquez is certainly one of the premier chili makers in America. His recipe for Carne Adovada Burrito Casserole is a frequent award winner. It has won first prize at the Hatch Chile Festival, which is noted as the chile capital of the world. In 1980 it took first place and won a blue ribbon for Best of Show at the New Mexico State Fair.

Mr. Vasquez is active in the International Chile Society, the Saint Vincent de Paul Society and the West Mesa Little League and American Legion baseball teams. He has recently been selected to compete in the Chile Cookout sponsored by Circus Circus Hotel in Las Vegas, Nevada. If he wins there he will go on to compete in the national competition in California.

CARNE ADOVADA BURRITO CASSEROLE
Yield: 8–10 servings

CARNE ADOVADA
10 pods red chile
1 cup water
¼ teaspoon monosodium glutamate (MSG)
Garlic salt to taste
5 pounds lean pork

Mix, in a blender or by hand, the red chile pods, water, MSG and garlic salt to make a medium paste. Prepare two-thirds of the meat by slicing very thinly (easier if meat is partially frozen). Save the remainder of the meat for green chile salsa (below). Marinate the sliced pork in red chile sauce at least 2 hours. In a frying pan, cook the marinated meat slowly, being careful not to scorch. Do not simmer, but cook until liquid has evaporated and meat is well done. Allow to cool before burritos are prepared.

TORTILLAS

1½ cups white flour
½ teaspoon baking powder
⅛ teaspoon salt
1 Tablespoon (heaping) unmelted lard
½ cup water

Mix into dough the flour, baking powder, salt, lard and water. If the dough is sticky, add extra flour, 1 teaspoon at a time, until smooth. Let stand for 5 minutes. Separate and form into a dozen small balls. Roll out into round tortillas and fry on an unoiled iron skillet or griddle on high heat until lightly browned. Turn and brown on other side. Cool.

GREEN CHILE SALSA

Lean pork (remaining third of 5 pounds)
2 Tablespoons white flour
3 Tablespoons meat drippings
14 pods green chile, cooked, peeled and chopped
1½ cups water
¼ teaspoon monosodium glutamate (MSG)
Garlic salt to taste
Salt to taste
1 pound cheddar cheese, grated
Lettuce, tomato and onions

Cube the meat and fry in a medium-size pan without oil. When the meat is brown, push to one side of the pan and brown the flour in the drippings, being careful not to burn the flour. When browned, mix in the meat, chile and water (do not make too thin). Bring to a boil and add MSG, garlic salt and salt to taste. Lower heat and simmer for 15–20 minutes.

TO MAKE BURRITO CASSEROLE

Spread the cool carne adovada over the cool tortilla. Fold the ends of the tortilla in on four opposite sides and then fold in the middle (to keep the meat from spilling out). Place side by side in a large pan. Sprinkle 1 pound grated cheese over burritos and place in oven, preheated to 350 degrees, just long enough for the cheese to start melting. Pour green chile sauce over the top and serve immediately, before the tortillas get soggy. Garnish with chopped tomatoes, shredded lettuce and chopped onions, if desired.

BLUE RIBBON WINNER, BEST OF SHOW, NEW MEXICO STATE FAIR

JOHN AND EVA WIESNER — SYRACUSE, NEW YORK

We were particularly impressed with the number of husband-and-wife teams who enter state fair competitions. John and Eva Wiesner of Syracuse, New York, are just such a couple.

John is a relatively new contestant and won his first blue ribbon at the 1982 New York State Fair, for his Chuckwagon Beef Stew recipe. Eva specializes in the baked goods categories. You'll find her delicious blue ribbon Coconut Custard Pie recipe on page 190.

JOHN WIESNER — SYRACUSE, NEW YORK

CHUCKWAGON BEEF STEW
Yield: 6–8 servings

- 5 or 6 slices bacon, cut in half
- 2 pounds lean beef, cut into bite-size cubes
- 6 Tablespoons seasoned flour
- ½ pound small pearl onions
- 2 cloves garlic, finely chopped

1 can (8 oz.) tomato sauce
1 can (10½ oz.) beef broth
1 cup dry red wine (or sherry)
6 carrots, sliced
6 medium potatoes, cut in ½-inch pieces
2 stalks celery, chopped
2 green peppers, chopped in ½-inch pieces
2 red peppers, chopped in ½-inch pieces
10 fresh mushrooms, sliced
3 bay leaves

Use a heavy kettle large enough to contain the finished stew. Crisp the bacon in the kettle; remove the bacon, drain and reserve. Shake the cubed beef with the flour in a plastic bag or other container. Brown the beef in bacon fat in the kettle. Add more bacon fat if required — or you may substitute a little vegetable oil. Add onion, garlic, broth, sauce, wine. Cook approximately 1½ hours. Add remaining ingredients. Simmer for 1 hour. Garnish with reserved bacon strips, if desired.

BLUE RIBBON WINNER, NEW YORK STATE FAIR

NANCY LEPRELL — DALLAS, TEXAS

EGGPLANT SICILIAN STYLE
Yield: 6–8 servings

2 medium eggplant (about 3 pounds)
2 cans (28 oz.) tomato puree
1 can (6 oz.) tomato paste
1 pound ground beef
2 teaspoons salt
2 teaspoons pepper
½ cup sugar
1 teaspoon parsley

1 Tablespoon oregano
1 cup water
1 cup olive or regular cooking oil
1 cup grated cheese (Romano or Parmesan)

Three hours before cooking, slice the eggplant in ¼-inch strips. Layer crosswise on a 9-inch dish, alternating with 2 teaspoons salt. Set aside to drain excess water.

Brown the beef in a 2-quart saucepan. Combine the remaining ingredients (except oil and cheese) with the beef and cook for 2 hours over low heat.

Drain off excess water from the eggplant and pat dry with paper towel. Brown in 2 tablespoons of oil over medium heat. Drain on paper towel, continue until all is cooked. Preheat oven to 350 degrees. In a 9-inch square pan place sauce to cover the bottom of the pan. Place eggplant to cover bottom, sprinkle with ¼ cup cheese. Continue to layer, finishing with sauce. Bake for 45 minutes.

BLUE RIBBON WINNER, TEXAS STATE FAIR

CATHY ZORDAN — EVANSTON, ILLINOIS

Between being the director of a preschool, a licensed real estate agent, a teacher of children's cooking classes, getting her college degree and raising three children, Cathy Zordan found time to enter the Illinois State Fair. When you grow up in a family where the father owns five restaurants, "cooking is in your blood," according to Cathy. Food preparation was a major topic of conversation around Cathy's house. With this advantage, and Cathy's "can-do" attitude, she decided to compete at the Illinois State Fair. Even discovering that her two dogs had devoured her elaborate entry (over fifty separate pieces!) for the Gingerbread House category on the night before the deadline left Cathy undaunted. On her very first attempt in state fair competition she won eleven ribbons, with three in the Grand Prize category.

MICROWAVE SEAFOOD QUICHE

Yield: 1 pie, 4–6 servings

    3 eggs
    1 cup whipping cream
    1 cup half and half
 1½ Tablespoons flour
    1 cup Monterey Jack cheese
    ½ cup sliced green onions
    ½ cup diced cooked shrimp
    ½ cup diced cooked crab meat
    ¼ cup cooked bay scallops
    1 baked pie shell (*recipe follows*)

Beat the eggs in a blender. Add the cream and half and half and flour. Blend. Place the cheese, seafood and onions in the pie shell. Add the egg mixture, stirring to blend well. Microwave on high for 10 minutes. Serve with a salad.

    PIE CRUST (for 2 crusts)
    2 cups flour
    ⅔ cup shortening
    1 egg
    ¼ cup ice water
    1 teaspoon salt
    1 Tablespoon lemon juice

Combine the flour and shortening. Add the egg, salt, water and lemon juice. Work to form a ball. Roll out half of the dough and place in a 9-inch glass pie plate. Place wax paper over shell, and weight down with beans or rice.

Microwave on high for 3 minutes. Remove beans and paper, then microwave on high for 3 minutes more.

BLUE RIBBON WINNER, ILLINOIS STATE FAIR

STUFFED FLANK STEAK
Yield: 6–8 servings

1 flank steak (about 1½ lbs.)
1 package Good Seasons Italian salad dressing, made with olive oil
2 Tablespoons soy sauce

STUFFING
1 cup shredded zucchini
½ cup shredded carrots
1 cup dry stuffing mix
½ teaspoon Italian seasoning
4 Tablespoons melted butter
½ cup chopped onions
½ cup diced green pepper
½ teaspoon salt
¼ cup red wine

Marinate the meat in dressing and soy sauce. Pat the meat dry with a paper towel. With a sharp knife, butterfly the meat. Pound the meat on both sides until it is ¼ inch thick. Mix the stuffing ingredients and spread over the meat. Roll, starting at the long side, jelly roll fashion, and tie with strings in several places. Pour wine into the reserved marinade. Baste the meat with the marinade. Place in roasting pan and bake in a preheated 350-degree oven for 40 minutes, basting once. Let rest for 10 minutes before cutting.

BLUE RIBBON WINNER, ILLINOIS STATE FAIR

BEVERLY SHANSTROM — PUEBLO, COLORADO

When Beverly Shanstrom's husband started to spend his vacation working at the Colorado State Fair, she decided, "If you can't lick 'em, join 'em." And so she entered her first competition. That first entry ten years ago took a blue ribbon and since then there has been no stopping Beverly.

At least until last year when her eleven-year-old daughter, Krista, beat her in the Jelly category and Beverly had to settle for a red ribbon.

Now twelve 12 and a champion like her mother, Krista enjoys "creating" in the kitchen. She and her mother compete at the fair, where they often finish first and second. We think you'll enjoy Beverly's Stuffed Pepper Arroz. Even Krista couldn't take the blue ribbon away from her mother on this one.

STUFFED PEPPER ARROZ
Yield: 4–6 servings

    1 large can red chili sauce with pork
    2 regular cans Mexican rice
    2 to 3 medium green peppers, halved and cleaned
    1 cup shredded cheddar cheese
    ½ cup sliced black olives

In a baking dish, place the cleaned pepper halves. Combine rice, cheese, and olives. Mix well and fill each pepper half. Pour hot red chili sauce over them. Bake in 350-degree oven for 1 hour. Serve with tossed green salad and warm sopapillas.

BLUE RIBBON WINNER, COLORADO STATE FAIR

KITTY MARINO — SYRACUSE, NEW YORK

MACARONI AND CHEESE DISH
Yield: 5–6 servings

    6 Tablespoons margarine
    ½ cup flour
    1 teaspoon salt

¾ teaspoon pepper
1 teaspoon dry mustard
1 small grated onion
4 cups milk
2 cups grated sharp cheddar cheese
2 Tablespoons grated cheese
2 cups grated extra-sharp cheddar cheese
5 to 6 cups small elbow macaroni, cooked
1 fresh large tomato, sliced
3 slices crumbled cooked bacon
   Breadcrumbs
1 teaspoon margarine

Melt the margarine over low heat. Over low heat, stir in the flour, salt, pepper and dry mustard. Cook until smooth, stirring constantly. Add the grated onions. Remove from heat. Gradually stir in the milk. Bring to a boil over medium heat, stirring constantly. Boil and stir for 1 minute. Remove from heat. Stir in the cheese until melted. If necessary, return to low heat to melt the cheese. Combine the cheese sauce and macaroni. Grease the casserole dish; turn half of the macaroni into dish. Add 4 slices of tomato. Sprinkle a little crumbled bacon over tomato. Add rest of macaroni, sprinkle a little more bacon, place 3 large slices of tomato on top. Cover lightly with buttered breadcrumbs, dot with margarine. Add remaining 2 tablespoons grated cheese. Bake at 350 degrees for 45 minutes.

BLUE RIBBON WINNER, NEW YORK STATE FAIR

COLLEEN BARDELL — RIDOTT, ILLINOIS

"Use only the best ingredients and never cut corners" is Colleen Bardell's cooking philosophy. Though Colleen had never entered a state fair before, she saw an ad for contestants in her local Ridott, Illinois, paper and decided to give it a try. Colleen's real cooking career began when she bluffed her way into a job as the cook for a sorority house in Albuquerque. There she learned to experiment in the kitchen, changing typical college fare into a gastronomic delight. Once, when Colleen served a meal to the

students, they all rose from their seats to give her a standing ovation. Here she combines plums and oranges with pork, to create an entree that won her a blue ribbon on her first try at state fair competition.

MANDARIN PORK RIBS
Yield: 8 servings

        3   plums, canned or fresh
        1   can (6 oz.) mandarin oranges with juice
        3   Tablespoons brown sugar
        ⅓   cup chili sauce
            Dash liquid smoke
            Dash garlic salt
        ½   teaspoon salt
            Dash white pepper
            Dash Worchestershire sauce
        2   Tablespoons soy sauce
        ¼   teaspoon minced fresh ginger
     3½ to 4 pounds pork ribs, lean and meaty
            Parsley
            Orange slices, peeled

Puree the first eleven ingredients and simmer for 10 minutes. Set the prepared sauce aside. Preheat oven to 325 degrees. Remove any excess fat from the ribs. Place on a rack in a roasting pan with a small amount of water in the bottom. Cover and bake for 2 hours. Uncover and remove any excess water that has accumulated in the bottom of the pan while baking. Continue baking uncovered for about 15 minutes on each side, basting frequently with prepared sauce. Ribs should be crispy and glazed. Serve on a large heated platter. Garnish with parsley and peeled orange slices.

BLUE RIBBON WINNER, ILLINOIS STATE FAIR

DREAMY CRAB CASSEROLE
Yield: 2–4 servings

WHITE SAUCE
- 2 Tablespoons butter
- 2 Tablespoons flour
- 1 cup milk
- 2 Tablespoons white wine
- ⅛ teaspoon nutmeg

Melt the butter in a small saucepan over medium heat. Add the flour, stirring constantly, and cook it for 3 minutes. Do not let it brown. Add the milk and wine. Stir and cook until the sauce thickens. Set aside.

THE CASSEROLE
- 2 Tablespoons butter
- 6 mushrooms, sliced
- ⅓ cup bell pepper, finely chopped
- 2 Tablespoons parsley, finely chopped
- 1 clove garlic, finely chopped
- 2 Tablespoons onion, chopped
- ¼ cup mayonnaise
- 1 egg, separated
- 2 teaspoons Worcestershire sauce
- 1 teaspoon Dijon-style mustard
- 1 Tablespoon lemon juice
- 1 teaspoon salt
- ⅛ teaspoon cayenne pepper
- ½ teaspoon tarragon leaves, crushed
- 1 pound fresh lump crab meat
- 2 Tablespoons capers
- 2 Tablespoons breadcrumbs
- 2 Tablespoons grated Parmesan cheese
- 1 Tablespoon butter

Melt the butter and fry the mushrooms, bell peppers, parsley, garlic and onion until they are softened. Do not brown. Set aside. Combine the white sauce with the mayonnaise, egg yolk, Worcestershire, mustard, lemon juice, salt, pepper, and tarragon. Combine and add the fried vegetables, capers, and crab meat. Beat the egg white until stiff and stir it in. Place all ingredients in a buttered casserole and sprinkle the breadcrumbs and Parmesan cheese over the top and dot it with butter. Bake in a 400-degree oven for 12 minutes.

BLUE RIBBON WINNER, TEXAS STATE FAIR

PARKER FOLSE, JR. — DALLAS, TEXAS

EL CHILI BRAVO!
Yield: Serves 6

- 2 pounds chili meat, cut into ½- to ¾-inch cubes
- 1 large Spanish onion, chopped
- 6 cloves of garlic, minced or pressed through garlic press
- 1 smoked ham hock (cut from bone and ground fine, including rind)
- 1 jalapeno pepper, fresh or canned, chopped, including seeds
- 1 can (16 oz.) tomatoes or 1 pound fresh tomatoes, peeled and chopped
- 4 Tablespoons chili powder
- 1 heaping teaspoon cayenne pepper
- 2 Tablespoons ground comino (or cumin)
- 1 teaspoon oregano
- 1 Tablespoon ground coriander
- ½ cup red wine
- 2 Tablespoons honey
- 2 Tablespoons catsup
- Salt to taste
- Hot water

Use a heavy black iron kettle with lid (Parker believes this deepens and enriches the color of the chili). Place the kettle over high heat and add the chili meat and onion. Reduce heat and sear until lightly browned. Add the garlic and ground ham hock. Stir and toss until all the ingredients are browned. Add all the remaining ingredients and enough hot water to cover. Cover the kettle, and reduce heat low enough to keep kettle bubbling. Cook for 2 hours and be sure to stir occasionally and add water as needed. Don't let it burn on the bottom or become too dry. Thin to desired consistency with water. Serve hot.

BLUE RIBBON WINNER, BEST OF SHOW, TEXAS STATE FAIR

VEAL PARMIGIANA
Yield: 4 servings

MARINARA SAUCE
- ¼ cup butter
- ¼ cup olive oil
- 1 medium onion, chopped finely
- 3 garlic cloves, mashed
- ¾ cup chopped parsley
- 3 pounds canned tomatoes
-   Grind of black pepper
- ½ teaspoon salt
- 1 Tablespoon oregano
- 1 bay leaf
- 1 small can anchovies, chopped
- ¼ cup tomato paste

Melt the butter with the olive oil in a saucepan and sauté the onion and garlic for 5 minutes. Add the parsley and cook for another few minutes. Drain the tomatoes and chop them. Add them to the pan along with the salt, pepper, oregano and the bay leaf. Simmer for 30 minutes and add the anchovies and tomato paste.

Stir together and remove from the heat. This is a good basic tomato sauce to serve not only with this dish, but also as a topping
for macaroni and spaghetti. Makes over 1 quart of sauce.

VEAL PARMIGIANA
2 pounds veal, sliced thinly
1 egg, beaten
½ cup flour
¾ cup breadcrumbs
¼ cup olive oil
¼ cup melted butter
3 green onions, chopped finely
2 cups of the Marinara Sauce
4 slices prosciutto ham
4 slices mozzarella cheese
  Salt to taste
  Grinds of black pepper
  Parmesan cheese, grated

Cut the veal into 4 uniform slices and pound them quite thinly.
Beat 1 large egg in a small bowl. Dip the veal into flour to coat it,
then into the egg, and then press each cutlet into the breadcrumbs. Melt half the butter with the olive oil in a skillet and
sauté the breaded cutlets on each side for 6 to 7 minutes per side.
Mix the green onions into the remaining butter and reserve. Pour
enough Marinara Sauce into the bottom of a baking dish to coat it
evenly and lay the cutlets on top of it. Cover them with more
sauce. Place a slice of prosciutto on top of each cutlet and cover
with the green onions–butter mixture. Top this with a slice of
cheese and more sauce. Sprinkle with salt and pepper and grated
Parmesan cheese. Bake in a 375-degree oven for 20 minutes and
serve while hot.

BLUE RIBBON WINNER, TEXAS STATE FAIR

SWEET AND SOUR PORK
Yield: 4 servings

THE MEAT
1 pound lean pork loin
1 Tablespoon soy sauce
1 egg yolk
4 Tablespoons cornstarch
Cooking oil for deep frying

Slice pork into thin strips about the size of the little finger. Mix the soy sauce, egg yolk and 1 tablespoon of the cornstarch together. Coat the pork pieces with this and let marinate for about 20 minutes. Coat the marinated pork pieces with the remaining cornstarch. They will become sticky and will adhere to one another. Separate them and fry them quickly in very hot cooking oil until they are browned, about 3 minutes. Remove from oil and drain. This can be done in advance and reserved until final preparation time.

SWEET AND SOUR SAUCE
3 Tablespoons vinegar
3 Tablespoons sugar
3 Tablespoons catsup
¼ teaspoon salt
1½ teaspoons cornstarch

Mix the above ingredients together and reserve in a cup.

FINAL PREPARATION
3 Tablespoons cooking oil
½ teaspoon minced garlic
1 hot pepper (optional), finely chopped
1 green bell pepper, seeded and cut into ½-inch squares
3 pineapple slices, cut into 1-inch pieces

In a wok or other frying pan bring 3 tablespoons cooking oil to high heat. Add the garlic and stir while frying for about 30 seconds. Add the pepper pieces and pineapple and stir into the hot oil. Cook for about 2 minutes. Restir the sweet and sour sauce and add it to the pan. Add the previously fried pork pieces and heat thoroughly. Serve while hot.

BLUE RIBBON WINNER, TEXAS STATE FAIR

COQ AU VIN A LA BOURGUIGNONNE
Yield: 18–20 servings

    4 Tablespoons butter
    2 Tablespoons olive oil
    ¼ pound slab bacon (cut into ¼-inch cubes)
   16 peeled small white onions, 1-inch diameter
   16 small whole mushrooms
    1 green onion or shallot, finely chopped
    2 2½-pound frying chickens, cut into serving pieces
      Flour
      Salt and pepper
    ¼ cup brandy
    ½ cup chicken stock
    3 cups red wine (Burgundy or other dry red wine)
    3 cloves garlic, finely chopped
    3 Tablespoons parsley, chopped fine
    ½ teaspoon thyme
    2 bay leaves

In a large cast-iron skillet or Dutch oven, melt the butter and heat the olive oil. Add the bacon cubes and fry them until they are golden. Place the white onions into the hot fat and sauté them, rolling them around until they are colored nicely. Remove them from the skillet and reserve them in a bowl. Now add the mushrooms and chopped green onion and fry them, stirring with a wooden spoon until they are softened (usually 2–3 minutes). Remove them and reserve with the onions. If needed, add more olive oil to make a film of oil about ⅛ inch deep over the bottom of the pan. Roll the chicken pieces in flour, shaking off any excess, and fry them a few pieces at a time until they are golden brown on both sides. As each piece is colored, remove it and reserve in a separate bowl from the vegetables.

When all the chicken pieces are cooked, pour off all the fat from the pan and return the chicken to it. Pour the brandy over the chicken and heat it slightly. Ignite it with the flame from a match and let it burn until all the flames are gone.

Transfer the chicken pieces to an ovenproof casserole and pre-heat the oven to 350 degrees. Add 2 tablespoons of flour to the juices remaining in the skillet and stir over medium heat, scraping up any pieces that are stuck to the bottom. Add the chicken stock and wine and stir until smooth. Strain this liquid over the chicken pieces. Add the chopped garlic, parsley, thyme and bay leaves and bring the contents to a boil over high heat. Immediately cover the casserole tightly and place on the middle shelf of the oven.

After 30 minutes have passed, carefully add the onions and mushrooms to the casserole and moisten them well with the liquid. Replace the lid and cook for another 12 to 15 minutes. Keep warm until time to serve. At serving time, sprinkle some chopped parsley over the chicken.

BLUE RIBBON WINNER, TEXAS STATE FAIR

DONNA M. MORGAN — ALBUQUERQUE, NEW MEXICO

Donna Marie Morgan, encouraged by her neighbor's success in state fair competition, decided to enter the New Mexico State Fair in 1975. That first year, Donna entered eighteen categories, and won twelve ribbons. In recent years she has won blue ribbons in everything from canned mushrooms and fruit to pickles and jelly. Below is her blue ribbon winner Potatoes Con Queso from the 1982 New Mexico State Fair.

POTATOES CON QUESO
Yield: 4 servings

    5 medium potatoes, peeled and sliced very thin
    5 Tablespoons butter
    2 Tablespoons flour
1½ teaspoons salt
1½ cups milk
  ¾ cup grated cheddar cheese
    1 small jar diced pimientos
    1 can diced green chile

Make the white sauce with the above ingredients as follows:

Melt the butter, add flour, and stir to a smooth consistency. Add the milk gradually. Add salt. Then stir in the cheese until melted and well blended; add pimientos and chile. Turn sauce and potatoes into a well-buttered casserole and bake at 350 degrees for approximately 1 hour or until potatoes are tender.

BLUE RIBBON WINNER, TEXAS STATE FAIR

WINNIE OSBORNE — SYRACUSE, NEW YORK

TAMALE PIE
Yield: 6 servings

  2 Tablespoons salad oil or olive oil
  2 cups finely chopped onions
  1 clove garlic, crushed
  1 3½ pound broiler-fryer, cut up
  1 can stewed tomatoes
  1 can tomato sauce
½ cup canned chicken broth (condensed, undiluted)

2 teaspoons salt
1½ to 2 Tablespoons chili powder
1 teaspoon oregano
1 can corn with peppers, undrained (Mexicorn)
1 cup pitted black olives
2 cups yellow cornmeal
½ cup grated cheddar cheese

Wash the chicken and pat dry. In hot oil, using a Dutch oven, sauté onion and garlic until the onion is tender. Add the chicken pieces, stewed tomatoes, tomato sauce, chicken broth and 1 teaspoon of salt. Bring to boil, stirring occasionally. Reduce heat and simmer (covered) for 30 minutes or until tender. Remove from heat and let stand uncovered until chicken is cool enough to handle. Remove chicken pieces from pot. Remove and discard the skin and bones, leaving only chicken in large pieces. Add the chili powder and oregano to liquid in Dutch oven. Boil uncovered until liquid is reduced to about 3 cups. Skim off excess fat if necessary. Stir in the chicken, corn and olives and set aside.

In a medium saucepan, combine cornmeal with 4 cups of water and 1 teaspoon of salt. Bring to boil, stirring constantly. Boil until thickened. Remove from heat and let stand for about 5 minutes.

Preheat oven to 375 degrees. Line bottom and sides of a 3-quart shallow baking dish with about half of the cornmeal mixture. Fill with the chicken mixture. Spoon the remainder of the cornmeal mixture around the edges of the pie. Sprinkle with cheese and bake uncovered about 30 minutes or until bubbling in the center of pie begins.

BLUE RIBBON WINNER, NEW YORK STATE FAIR

GERALDINE HOOVER — MT. WOLF, PENNSYLVANIA

Thirty-five years ago Geraldine Hoover decided that store-bought noodles just weren't good enough for her family. With the help of her husband's grandmother, Geraldine developed her recipe and her skills so well that her neighbors and even her husband's co-workers were soon clamoring to buy her homemade egg noodles. Even the local grocery stores in the

York area carry Geraldine's egg noodles on their shelves, which is a high honor in the heart of Pennsylvania Dutch country. So good are they, in fact, that for the past several years, these noodles have won all the blue ribbons at the York County Fair. We're sure that you'll agree with Geraldine's family that homemade is worth the effort.

PENNSYLVANIA DUTCH EGG NOODLES
Yield: About 3 pounds

12 large eggs
 1 teaspoon salt
    Few drops yellow food coloring (optional)
 9 cups unsifted, all-purpose flour

Break the eggs into a bowl. Add the salt and food coloring (if desired). Beat to make sure the eggs are mixed well. Into a larger bowl, put about 7 cups of the flour. Add the eggs and mix by hand with a large wooden spoon. When mixed well, work in more flour with your hands. Knead the dough as you would bread dough. The dough should be dry when all the flour is worked in. Divide the dough into manageable pieces and roll thin on a lightly floured surface. Lay rolled dough on cloths until partly dried.

Turn the dough occasionally so it dries on both sides. When dry enough, roll two sheets of noodle dough together to form a cylinder. With a butcher knife, cut strips of the desired noodle width along the length of the cylinder. Shake apart and leave to dry on cloth, turning three or four times as drying. Noodles can be used immediately or saved for later use. To store, allow noodles to dry about five days. Pack into paper bags and store in a dry place. (Plastic bags will draw moisture and mold.) Noodles can be stored this way for several months.

BLUE RIBBON WINNER, YORK INTER–STATE FAIR

MILDRED POLODNA — HOWELLS, NEBRASKA

Mildred and Milo Polodna farm soybeans and corn on a 240-acre farm in Howells, Nebraska. They also raise approximately two hundred fifty hogs a year and have about forty head of whiteface stock cows for calving.

Recent years have been difficult in agriculture, but the Polodnas have still managed to put three children through college. Their oldest son, Gary, is a graduate of the University of Nebraska and the Harvard Business School. Their second oldest, Roland, is majoring in agriculture at the University of Nebraska and their youngest, Mary, is filling out college applications.

Mary is one of the reasons for her mother's blue ribbon. She has been a 4–H member and her mother always attended her competitions. This year Mary competed in the State Style Review at the fair and Mildred drove the hundred-mile trip to Lincoln to be with her. The trip was certainly worth the effort since Mildred succeeded in winning a blue ribbon for her Filet Veggy Casserole on her first try.

FILET VEGGY CASSEROLE
Yield: 6 servings

- 1 package (16 oz.) frozen whiting fish
- 2 Tablespoons lemon juice
- Salt and pepper to taste
- 2 Tablespoons flour
- ¼ cup butter, melted
- 1 package (20 oz.) frozen Cape Cod–style vegetables (French-cut green beans, corn, broccoli and red peppers)
- 1 package (10 oz.) frozen green beans
- 1 can (10½ oz.) cheddar cheese soup
- 2 teaspoons Dijon mustard
- ¼ cup milk
- 1 teaspoon dill weed

Cut the fish into bite-size pieces and sprinkle with lemon juice, salt and pepper. Coat the fish with flour and sauté in butter until lightly brown. In a 9×13-inch pan, mix together the green beans and Cape Cod–style vegetables and spread evenly in a pan. Mix together the soup and mustard and spread evenly over the vegetables. Place the pieces of fish on top of the vegetables and sprinkle with dill weed. Bake in 350-degree oven for 30–35 minutes.

BLUE RIBBON WINNER, NEBRASKA STATE FAIR

PIERINA SLAVIERO — WAUWATOSA, WISCONSIN

Fifty-three years ago a young girl of twenty-one left her home in Revo, Italy, a town in the Tyrolean Alps, to immigrate to this country. She was looking for a better life but, unfortunately, arrived in July 1929, just in time for the Great Depression. That September she married Adolph Slaviero whom she had known for only six weeks. In spite of the short courtship and the difficult times, the Slavieros enjoyed a happy and loving marriage for thirty-two years.

Pierina Slaviero is seventy-five years of age today. She is the mother of three, a grandmother of four and, at this young age, already a great-grandmother of three. She does all the cooking and cleaning, tends two garden plots and competes at the Wisconsin State Fair.

Although she spent her early years in Pennsylvania she later moved to Chicago and now lives with her daughter in Wauwatosa, Wisconsin. Pierina is a newcomer to state fair competition; she first entered in 1979. Nonetheless, she has already accumulated six ribbons and we are hoping that she wins many more.

HOMEMADE NOODLES
Yield: About 1 pound

3½ cups white flour, approximately
2 large eggs
½ cup water
½ teaspoon salt

In a large bowl beat the eggs, salt and water well. Add the flour slowly until a ball is formed. Mix in the rest of the flour by hand

and knead until the dough is smooth. Cover the dough with a bowl and let the dough rest for about 10 minutes before rolling it out.

To make the noodles: divide the dough into two balls. Place one ball on a floured board or pastry cloth and flatten it with your hand into an oblong about 1 inch thick. Dust the top lightly with flour. Using a heavy rolling pin, start at one end of the oblong and roll it out lengthwise away from you. Turn the dough often, rolling it first on one side, then on the other, flouring the board and rolling pin occasionally, until 1/16 inch thick. Roll up the dough tightly into a long roll, and with a sharp knife cut into crosswise slices about 1/4 inch thick. Separate and unroll the slices. Spread the noodles on a clean tablecloth, tossing them gently with fingers to unfold them. Let the noodles dry completely. Follow the same procedure with remaining dough.

BLUE RIBBON WINNER, WISCONSIN STATE FAIR

FRANK HALL — PALMER LAKE, COLORADO

BROCCOLI SOUFFLE
Yield: 4 to 6 servings

- 4 Tablespoons butter
- 4 Tablespoons flour
- 1 cup milk
- 1/4 teaspoon mustard
- Dash cayenne pepper
- Salt and pepper to taste
- 1 cup shredded sharp cheese
- 3 eggs, separated
- 1 cup cooked, chopped broccoli, well drained
- 1/4 teaspoon cream of tartar

Melt the butter. Add the flour, stirring constantly until smooth but not browned. Gradually add the and milk to make a thick white sauce. Season with mustard, cayenne, salt and pepper. Remove from heat and stir in the shredded cheese. Beat the egg yolks well. Drain the broccoli and add along with egg yolks to the cheese mixture. Beat egg whites and cream of tartar until stiff. Fold into the cheese mixture. Pour into ungreased 1½-quart soufflé dish. For "high hat" soufflé, using the edge of a teaspoon, make a groove 1 inch from the edge. Set the dish in a pan of water 1 inch deep. Bake at 350 degrees for approximately 50–60 minutes or until puffed and golden brown. Serve immediately.

BLUE RIBBON WINNER, COLORADO STATE FAIR

GREEN CHILI
Yield: 6 servings

       3 pounds pork shoulder with bone
      ¼ cup oil
       2 garlic cloves
       1 teaspoon salt
       1 Tablespoon black pepper
       1 Tablespoon cumin
       1 pint water
       4 cups diced, seeded green chilies
      ¼ cup diced, seeded jalapeno peppers
       2 cups skinned, chopped fresh tomatoes (or substitute canned)

Prepare the meat by cutting away from the bone. Process half of the meat through a meat grinder on coarse or in a food processor. Cut the remaining half in 1-inch cubes. Heat the oil in a heavy skillet and brown the garlic. Remove garlic and add all the meat, including the bone, and brown evenly. Add the salt, pepper and cumin. Stir well. Add water and simmer until the meat is tender. Remove bones and discard. Add the chilies, peppers and tomatoes and simmer on low heat until thick. Freezes well.

BLUE RIBBON WINNER, COLORADO STATE FAIR

MRS. CECILIA (CECE) SYPAL — BRAINARD, NEBRASKA

When you are the mother of seven children you learn to cook "out of necessity," according to CeCe Sypal. Married for over thirty-six years to Valerian Sypal, she has kept busy raising six sons and a daughter, working on their two-hundred-acre dairy farm, assisting the altar society at the Dwight Assumption Church and being a 4–H leader. Somehow CeCe finds the time to continue pursuing photography, a hobby she began as a sixteen-year-old. Her children have had their lives carefully documented in the hundreds of photos and movies CeCe has taken over the years. And, as if that is not enough to keep a person busy, CeCe has also raised six hundred hybrid irises and in 1970 started to compete at the Nebraska State Fair. Her success there has given her close to eight hundred ribbons, and made her quite a celebrity in the Dwight–Brainard area. She has been interviewed by the local newspapers and on TV and is much in demand to give cooking demonstrations to the area women's clubs. The Shrimp Pizza below and her Rhubarb Pie (page 197) will allow your family to sample the pleasures that the Sypal family has enjoyed for thirty-six years.

SHRIMP PIZZA
Yield: 2 Pizzas

CRUST (2 Pies)
- 1 package yeast
- ¼ cup warm water
- 1 teaspoon sugar
- 1 teaspoon salt
- 2 Tablespoons salad oil
- 1 Tablespoon Parmesan cheese (optional)
- 1 cup warm water
- 4 cups flour

Dissolve the yeast in ¼ cup of warm water. Mix the sugar, salt, oil and cheese in 1 cup of warm water. Combine this with the yeast mixture and add 2½ cups of flour. Beat well. Add approximately

2 more cups of flour, and mix until the dough is light and not sticky. Place in a greased bowl and let rise until almost double. Divide in half and roll into 13-inch circles. Grease 2 pizza pans and roll out dough to fit the pans. Pinch edges to form a rim.

TOPPING
¼ cup Parmesan cheese
1 can (6 oz.) tomato paste
½ teaspoon oregano
½ teaspoon dry basil leaves
½ cup black olives, chopped
   Dash of garlic salt
1 can (5 oz.) shrimp, drained
6 ounces mozzarella cheese, shredded

Sprinkle the prepared crust with ¼ cup of Parmesan cheese, spread the tomato paste on top and sprinkle on seasonings and olives. Distribute the shrimp and shredded mozzarella cheese evenly and again sprinkle with Parmesan. Bake in 400-degree oven for approximately 20–25 minutes. Additional topping suggestions: sliced mushrooms, green and red pepper slices.

BLUE RIBBON WINNER, NEBRASKA STATE FAIR

JUNE ROBBINS — GREAT FALLS, MONTANA

June Robbins helped pay her way through Brigham Young University by decorating cakes, a craft she learned as a young girl working in a bakery. Although she is a schoolteacher by profession, June presently devotes her life to raising five children, Justin, Rebecca, Tina, Kathy and Timmy. But her cake-decorating skills still come in handy. In addition to winning blue ribbons at the state fair, June has also established a substantial cake-decorating business in her home.

June has had the good fortune to attend many state fairs across the country. Her White Cake recipe has won a blue ribbon at both the Idaho and Montana State Fairs. However, her favorite blue ribbon victory came for a cake recipe that has also won in both states. That recipe came from her husband's grandmother, Mrs. P. L. Carver of Pocatello, Idaho. According to June, "It was a special moment to surprise Grandma Carver with that blue ribbon, especially since she had used it to bake me my own wedding cake years before!"

June teaches baking at the local YWCA and has also passed her talents on to her children. The three oldest competed for the first time at this year's Montana State Fair and the oldest, Justin, beat his mother out by taking a red ribbon in the cinnamon roll category.

June's husband, Bob, doesn't compete himself but probably gives her good advice on how to invest her profits. He's the chief financial officer for the First Interstate Bank in Great Falls.

Below is June's blue ribbon recipe for Tortillas. You'll also find her White Cake on page 152 and her Spice Cake on page 154.

ROBBINS' NEST FLOUR TORTILLAS
Yield: 16 large tortillas

This recipe has been adapted from notes a missionary friend brought back after living in Mexico.

4 cups flour
1 heaping Tablespoon baking powder
1 teaspoon salt
1 to 1¼ cups warm water

Cut together all of the ingredients with a pastry blender, adding the water gradually, until well blended. Turn the dough (which should feel like slightly dry biscuit dough) onto a floured surface and knead well; sprinkle sparingly with flour to ease any stickiness. Let the dough sit under a bowl for 5 minutes. Pinch off quarter-sized balls for each tortilla. Roll out on a lightly floured surface until very thin and about 6 to 8 inches in diameter. Fry in a very small amount of oil or best of all in an ungreased, well-seasoned frying pan. Nonstick surfaces are also excellent. When bubbles rise on the uncooked surface, turn immediately. When done, place in a warm oven in a tighly covered baking dish while the rest are being prepared. Best when used immediately.

BLUE RIBBON WINNER, MONTANA STATE FAIR

WYONNE CORNELIOUS — MILWAUKEE, WISCONSIN

Wyonne Cornelious's interest in nutrition and diet has led her to a career in vegetarian cooking. After studying nutrition at Milwaukee Area Technical College, Wyonne began doing research on food values and diets and writing monthly articles for the Outpost *newspaper. She has also become an instructor at her alma mater.*

Wyonne's roommate encouraged her to enter the 1982 Wisconsin State Fair and she won the blue ribbon on her first try. To understand just how good her entry was, you should know that Wyonne didn't realize there would be no facilities to heat her entrée. It was judged ice cold against stiff competition and still won the blue ribbon.

We have included here Wyonne's special hints which should prove helpful for those interested in health food preparation.

"Unless you know how to prepare dried peas and beans, they can be bland and cause intestinal distress. The challenge in preparing them is in combining them with the correct amount of oil, spices and heat." Her favorite bean herbs are savory and juniper berries for "adding flavor, promoting digestibility and eliminating gas." She also feels you should "soak beans overnight and discard the water to help eliminate gas and also shorten cooking time.

"Juniper berries have a spicy bittersweet flavor commonly used in marinades, sauerkraut, cabbage and bean dishes. If used in beans, wrap in cheesecloth or place in a tea ball and remove after cooking.

"Savory comes in two varieties, summer and winter. They both have a piquancy that makes them possible salt substitutes. Winter savory is stronger and more bristly and woody tham summer savory. Either savory will enhance the flavor of all vegetable and bean dishes."

Here is Wyonne's personal recipe for preparing the black-eyed peas to be used in her prize-winning Medley.

TO PREPARE PEAS
2 cups dry black-eyed peas
4 cups water or vegetable broth
2 large cloves garlic, minced
½ stick (2 oz.) butter or margarine
2 Tablespoons vegetable broth powder, (optional; available at health food stores)
2 Tablespoons whole wheat, oat or millet flour

¼ cup cold water
1 Tablespoon onion powder
1 Tablespoon vegetable seasoning
2 teaspoons savory
2 teaspoons juniper berries (in tea ball or wrapped in cheesecloth)
1 teaspoon salt
   Dash cayenne pepper

Soak the beans overnight in 2 quarts of water. Discard water and rinse the beans. In a large heavy pot, combine the beans, water or vegetable broth and all the other ingredients, except for the flour and ¼ cup water. Bring to a boil, cover and cook over low flame for 1½ hours. Fifteen minutes before the cooking time is up, dissolve the flour in ¼ cup of cold water and stir into the misture. This will thicken the broth, add flavor and ast as a binder in the final casserole.

BLACK-EYED PEA AND CORN MEDLEY
Yield: 4 generous servings

2 Tablespoons olive oil
3 cloves garlic, minced
4 small salad onions (stems chopped, bulbs quartered)
1 cup celery, finely chopped
2 cups corn (fresh or frozen)
1 teaspoon sea salt
2 teaspoons vegetable seasoning
1 cup sweet peas
1 Tablespoon onion powder
¼ teaspoon thyme
¼ teaspoon basil
⅛ teaspoon cayenne pepper
1 Tablespoon vegetable broth powder (optional)
2 cups cooked black-eyed peas with broth (see above)
1 Tablespoon whole-wheat flour
2 small or medium tomatoes, cut into 16 parts

In a large heavy skillet, heat 2 tablespoons of olive oil over high heat. Sauté the garlic and onion until tender. Add the celery, stirring for 2 minutes. Add the corn, sprinkle with ½ teaspoon of salt and 1 teaspoon of vegetable seasoning. Sauté for 30 seconds. Add the sweet peas and sprinkle with remaining salt, vegetable seasoning, onion powder, thyme, basil, cayenne pepper and vegetable broth powder. Stir for an additional 30 seconds. Turn heat off. Stir in the cooked black-eyed peas with broth. Pour into a casserole dish. Bake at 350 degrees for 20 minutes. After 15 minutes add chopped tomatoes and continue cooking for the last 5 minutes. If additional thickening is necessary, mix together 1 tablespoon whole-wheat flour and 2 tablespoons cold water and add to pot.

BLUE RIBBON WINNER, WISCONSIN STATE FAIR

EVELYN GATES — BEATRICE, NEBRASKA

"Pies are really my specialty," says Evelyn Gates, and she prepares a lot of them by "guess" like her mother used to do. So it came as a big surprise to Evelyn when she won the blue ribbon for her Pizza recipe instead of her pie. Evelyn and her husband, Harlan, live in Beatrice, Nebraska. Harlan is a retired truck driver and Evelyn is active in the 4–H and is one of Avon's top agents. Evelyn enjoys competing at the Nebraska State Fair where she is a frequent blue ribbon winner. She has also won local pie contests and several years ago she won a trophy in a cake baking contest sponsored by the March of Dimes.

SAUSAGE PIZZA
Yield: 1 pizza

CRUST
1 teaspoon active dry yeast
¾ cup plus 2 Tablespoons warm water
3 cups flour

Dissolve the yeast in water, add the flour and mix. Knead the dough, place in a greased bowl, cover with a greased top and let stand for 1 hour. Pat the dough out in a pizza pan to fit.

TOPPING
- ¾ pound Italian sausage
- ¾ cup pizza sauce
- ¾ cup tomato sauce
- ¼ cup green pepper, chopped
- ¼ cup onion, chopped
- ¼ cup mushrooms, cut up
- 1½ cups mozzarella cheese
- ½ cup grated Parmesan cheese
  Green pepper rings and ripe olives for garnish

Remove the sausage from its casing and simmer in a pan for 5 minutes with the chopped green pepper and onions. Drain. Place the sausages on the crust, then add toppings. Finish with cheeses and bake at 400 degrees for 20 minutes.

BLUE RIBBON WINNER, NEBRASKA STATE FAIR

CAROLYN E. JENDREK — BALTIMORE, MARYLAND

The following recipes are part of the Convenience Dinner blue ribbon winner at the Maryland State Fair. For futher information on this entry, please turn to pages 7–8.

TURKEY CHOW MEIN
Yield: 5 quarts

- 2 quarts turkey broth
- 2 quarts turkey meat, cooked

1 quart chopped celery
2 cups sliced onion
2 cups bean sprouts
2 small cans water chestnuts, sliced

Distribute all of the above into 5 1-quart canning jars. Seal and process in pressure canner for 90 minutes at 10 pounds pressure. To thicken use cornstarch, water and soy sauce as necessary. Serve over Chinese noodles or rice.

SEAFOOD AND WILD RICE
Yield: 2 quarts

4 cups wild and long grain rice, cooked, browned in butter
¼ cup chopped onion
¼ cup chopped celery
1 Tablespoon chopped parsley
½ teaspoon rosemary
1 cup shrimp, cooked
1 cup crab meat
2 cups chicken stock

Distribute all the ingredients into two 1-quart canning jars. Seal and process 90 minutes at 10 pounds pressure.

SNOW PEAS
Wash, pack vertically in canning jars. Seal and process 40 minutes at 10 pounds pressure.

BLUE RIBBON WINNER, MARYLAND STATE FAIR

3

BREADS, ROLLS AND BISCUITS

ROBERT L. CROWE — JACKSONVILLE, ILLINOIS

Another multitalented state fair contestant is Robert Crowe of Jacksonville, Illinois. Somehow in recent years Robert has found time away from his job as superintendent of schools to win the Amateur Athletic Union swimming championship, to be crowned the Morgan County Cookout King, and to publish three children's books.

Thanks to Mr. Crowe we offer you the following magnificent blue ribbon winner from the 1982 Illinois State Fair.

MAGNIFICENT TRIPLE TREAT BREAD
Yield: 2 loaves

- 2¼ cups lukewarm (110 degrees) water
- 3 packages active dry yeast
- 6 Tablespoons honey
- 6 Tablespoons vegetable oil
- 1½ teaspoon salt
- 5½ cups all-purpose flour
- 1 cup whole wheat flour
- 1 cup rye flour
- 1 Tablespoon cocoa
- 1 teaspoon caraway seeds

Combine ¾ cup of the water with 1 package of yeast and then add the following ingredients: 2 tablespoons of honey, 2 tablespoons of oil, ½ teaspoon salt and 1½ cups of all-purpose flour, in a food processor. Process with metal blade for 15 seconds. Pour dough into a separate bowl and cover.

Make two more batches using the above directions. Let all three batches of basic dough rest 20–30 minutes.

For each of the following, process until dough forms a ball, then knead on a floured surface for 2 minutes. In processor bowl, combine one batch of the basic dough with 1 cup all-purpose flour. (Process, remove, knead.) Combine the next batch in processor bowl with 1 cup whole wheat flour. (Process, remove, knead.) Combine the third batch with 1 teaspoon caraway seeds, 1 tablespoon cocoa and 1 cup rye flour. (Process, remove, knead.)

Divide each batch into 2 portions. Roll each piece into a 15-inch rope. On a greased baking sheet, braid together a rye, white and whole wheat rope. Repeat for the remaining dough. Cover, and let rise 1 hour. Bake at 350 degrees for 30 minutes. Cool. Brush with butter.

BLUE RIBBON WINNER, ILLINOIS STATE FAIR

MONA HENSON — DOUGLAS, WYOMING

It's always nice to see new contestants win the Grand Prize in a baking contest. Mona Henson of Douglas did just that in the 1981 Wyoming State Fair. Then she turned around and repeated her success in 1982. Mona's whole wheat bread is a terrific blue ribbon favorite.

WHOLE WHEAT BREAD
Yield: 2 large loaves

6 Tablespoons brown sugar
4 Tablespoons shortening
2 Tablespoons salt

1 cup powdered milk granules
2 packages yeast
½ cup warm water
3½ cups hot water
2½ cups whole wheat flour
12 to 12½ cups white flour

Stir the brown sugar, shortening, salt and dry milk in a large mixing bowl. Dissolve the yeast in ½ cup warm water; set aside. Add 3½ cups of hot water to the ingredients in the bowl. Stir until dissolved and add the whole wheat flour. Beat in thoroughly. Stir in the dissolved yeast. Add white flour, 2 cups at a time, beating thoroughly. Turn out on a floured board and knead for 15 minutes. Oil dough, let rise until doubled (about one hour), punch down. Let rise one hour again, punch down. Let rise one hour. Bake at 350 degrees for one hour. Oil the top.

BLUE RIBBON WINNER, WYOMING STATE FAIR

FAITH MIKITA — MONMOUTH, ILLINOIS

Faith Mikita of Monmouth, Illinois, is a Grand Champion in every regard.

She holds the title for being the first person ever to win the Grand Championship in the "Bake Off" during their first year of competition at the Illinois State Fair. She did this in 1979 with her delicious German Dark Rye Bread. In 1982 she repeated her performance by winning Grand Champion Bread, Best Bread of Show and Best of Class for breads at the Illinois State Fair. The Raisin-Orange Bread that carries this pedigree, along with that special Rye bread and Faith's Raisin loaves, are provided below for your enjoyment.

Faith Mikita now teaches a course, "The Joy of Breadmaking," at Carl Sandburg Junior College.

Her achievement is particularly noteworthy because Mrs. Mikita has overcome many serious handicaps along the way. She is legally blind in one eye and has recently had a difficult operation on her legs. The latter unfortunately kept her out of competition at the 1981 state fair.

Difficulties and all, Faith Mikita was back in competition in 1982 and has provided us with three of her great recipes.

RAISIN–ORANGE BREAD

Yield: 2 loaves

A fat, moist loaf replete with raisins, this bread is iced with a frosting of chopped walnuts beaten into a blend of confectioners sugar, butter and orange juice. There are bits of orange peel in the yellow eggy dough which contrast nicely with the dark raisins. In the oven it rises two or three inches above the pan to give the bread an open and airy texture.

Toasts beautifully, and freezes well if wrapped tightly in plastic wrap or foil.

```
5  to 5½ cups all-purpose flour, approximately
2  packages dry yeast
1  cup milk and ¼ cup water, or
1¼ cups water and ½ cup nonfat dry milk
1  orange rind, grated
1  teaspoon ginger
½  cup butter
½  cup sugar
1½ teaspoons salt
2  eggs, room temperature
1½ cups raisins
```

Grease two medium (8½×4½-inch) baking tins, or use Teflon. In a large mixer bowl, measure 2 cups of flour and sprinkle the yeast over it. Blend with a wooden spoon. In a saucepan, measure milk, water, orange rind, ginger, butter, sugar and salt. Put over low heat until it reaches 120 degrees, stirring constantly. Pour the mixture into the flour and yeast, add the eggs and beat with an electric mixer at low speed until the flour is moistened. Beat for 3 minutes at high speed, or for the same length of time with a wooden spoon. Scrape down the bowl and stir in raisins. Gradually add more flour to form a soft mass that cleans the sides of the bowl. Work in the flour by hand when the dough gets too stiff for the spoon. Turn the soft dough out onto a lightly floured work surface — a counter top or bread board — and knead with a strong push-turn-fold motion until the dough is smooth and elastic. If the dough is sticky or too moist (slack), add ½ cup flour and work it into the dough. Knead for 6 minutes.

Return the dough ball to the bowl, pat with buttered fingers, and cover tightly with plastic wrap. Set the bowl in a warm place (80–85 degrees) until the dough has doubled in size. You can test if it has risen by poking a finger into it; the dent will remain. This first rising takes 1¼ hours. Punch down the dough in the bowl, turn it out on a floured surface and knead briefly (1 minute), and let rest under a towel or piece of wax paper for about 15 minutes. Divide the dough into two parts, and press each part into a flat oval. Fold in half, pinch the seam tightly closed and pat into the shape of a loaf. Place in the pans and, with a sharp knife or razor blade, make three diagonal slashes ¼ inch deep across the top of each loaf. Cover the pans with wax paper and put in a warm place until dough has doubled in volume. The second rising takes approximately 1 hour. Meanwhile, prepare the topping:

GLAZE
1   cup confectioners sugar
2   teaspoons butter, room temperature
½   cup walnuts, finely chopped
2   to 4 Tablespoons orange juice

Blend the confectioners sugar with the butter, walnuts and orange juice to spreading consistency.

Preheat oven to 375 degrees. (If using glass pans, reduce temperature to 350 degrees.) Place the loaves in the hot oven until well browned. When tapping the bottom crust yields a hard hollow sound, they are done. Remove bread from the oven. While the loaves are warm, spread the glaze on the top crusts. However, allow the loaves to cool before serving.

BLUE RIBBON WINNER, BEST OF SHOW, ILLINOIS STATE FAIR

RAISIN–LOVERS' SURPRISE LOAVES

Yield: 2 loaves

4½ cups unbleached or bread flour, stirred
2 cups unsifted whole wheat flour, stirred
2 packages active dry yeast
1 Tablespoon salt
2 teaspoons baking powder
2 cups buttermilk
⅓ cup honey
3 Tablespoons butter or margarine
1 cup golden raisins soaked in 2 tablespoons lemon juice, at least ½ hour
2 Tablespoons soft butter or margarine
2 Tablespoons honey
½ teaspoon cinnamon
   Melted butter or margarine

Combine 4 cups of unbleached or bread flour and the whole wheat flour. In a large bowl, thoroughly mix 2½ cups of the flour mixture with baking powder, salt, and undissolved yeast. Combine the buttermilk, honey, and margarine in a saucepan. Heat to 120–130 degrees; margarine need not be melted. Add to the dry ingredients. Beat for 1 minute; scrape the bowl; beat for 3 minutes at medium speed. Add 1 cup of the flour mixture, or enough of the flour mixture to make a thick batter. Beat at high speed for 2 minutes. Stir in well-drained raisins and enough of the flour mixture to make a soft dough. Turn the dough out onto a lightly floured surface. Cover the dough with a bowl; let rest for 10 minutes. Knead until smooth and elastic. Cover and let rest for 15 minutes. Meanwhile, combine the 2 tablespoons of honey, 2 tablespoons of butter and ½ teaspoon cinnamon. Punch the dough down and divide it in half. Roll half of the dough into a 12×8-inch rectangle. Brush with half of the butter, honey, cinnamon mixture. Roll tightly from the 8-inch side as for jelly roll. Seal the edges firmly and fold underneath. Place the loaf, seam side down, in a greased 8½×4½×2½-inch loaf pan. Repeat with the remaining dough. Cover; let rise until doubled. Bake at 350 degrees for about 30–35 minutes. Cool on wire racks. Brush with melted margarine.

BLUE RIBBON WINNER, ILLINOIS STATE FAIR

GERMAN DARK RYE BREAD
Yield: 2 loaves

The simplest sandwich becomes something special when you make it with this delicious dark bread. It's a masterful blend of cocoa powder, molasses, caraway seeds and rye flour.

    3 cups sifted unbleached or bread flour
    2 packages active dry yeast
    ¼ cup cocoa powder
    1 Tablespoon caraway seeds
    2 cups water
    ⅓ cup molasses
    2 Tablespoons butter or margarine or salad oil
    1 Tablespoon sugar
    1 Tablespoon salt
    3 to 3½ cups rye flour

In a large mixer bowl, combine the unbleached or bread flour, yeast, cocoa powder and caraway seeds until well blended. In a saucepan, combine the water, molasses, salad oil (or butter or margarine), sugar and salt; heat until just warm, stirring occasionally. Add to the dry mixture in the mixer bowl. Beat at low speed with an electric mixer for 30 seconds, scraping the sides of the bowl constantly. Beat for 3 minutes at high speed. By hand, stir in enough rye flour to make a soft dough. Turn onto a floured surface; knead until smooth, about 5 minutes. Cover; let rest 20 minutes. Punch down and divide the dough in half. Shape each half into a round loaf; place on a greased baking sheet or baking sheet sprinkled with cornmeal; or in two greased 8-inch pie plates. Brush the surface of the loaves with a little cooking oil. Let rise until doubled, about 30 to 45 minutes. Slash the tops of the loaves with sharp knife. Bake in a 350-degree oven for 25 to 30 minutes, or until breads are done. Remove from pan to wire racks to cool. Brush with melted butter.

BLUE RIBBON WINNER, ILLINOIS STATE FAIR

MARY LYNN RUPP — MILWAUKEE, WISCONSIN
MARY LYNN CERETTO — FRANKLIN, WISCONSIN

Mary Lynn Ceretto gets a lot of practice cooking and baking for five children in Franklin, Wisconsin. She also gets a lot of competition from her sister-in-law, Mary Lynn Rupp. They not only share the same first name but a common interest in bread baking.

Mary Lynn Rupp (née Ceretto) specializes in breads, and won one of her blue ribbons for her Italian Christmas Bread in the newly created ethnic bread category at the Wisconsin State Fair. She also won the blue ribbon for her Stollen. Her sister-in-law, Mary Lynn Ceretto (née Wastak) has provided us with a very special blue ribbon recipe for Sour Dough Bread.

If you get confused remembering which Mary Lynn is which, just think what it was like before Mary Lynn Rupp was married. In those days, there were two Mary Lynn Cerettos baking bread in the heart of America's Dairyland.

MARY LYNN CERETTO — FRANKLIN, WISCONSIN

SOUR DOUGH BREAD
Yield: 2 loaves

 ½ cup milk
 1 cup water

1½ Tablespoons vegetable oil
1 package yeast
¼ cup warm water
1½ Tablespoons sugar
2½ teaspoons salt
4¾ cups sifted flour
2 Tablespoons starter dough (recipe follows)
1 egg white

Combine the milk, water and oil; bring to a boil. Remove from heat and let cool to lukewarm (95–100 degrees). Dissolve the yeast in warm water. Add with the sugar and salt to the cooled milk mixture. Place the flour in a large bowl. Make a well in the center and pour the milk mixture into it. Add the starter dough and stir until well blended. Do not knead. The dough will be soft. Place the dough in a greased bowl, cover and let rise in a warm place until doubled in bulk (about one hour). Turn out onto a lightly floured board and divide into two even portions. Roll each into an oblong (or other desired shape). Place on aluminum foil–covered baking sheet. Let rise uncovered for one hour. Bake at 425 degrees for 15 minutes. Reduce oven temperature to 350 degrees and bake for 15–20 minutes longer. Brush the top and sides with 1 egg white beaten with 1 tablespoon cold water. Bake 5 minutes longer. Cool in a draft (as an open window) for a crisp crust.

SOUR DOUGH STARTER
¼ cup milk
½ cup water
2 teaspoons vegetable oil
1 package yeast
¼ cup warm water (110–115 degrees)
2 teaspoons sugar
1½ teaspoons salt
2⅓ cups sifted flour

Combine the milk, water and oil; bring to a boil. Remove from heat and cool to lukewarm. Dissolve the yeast in warm water.

Add, with sugar and salt, to the cooled milk mixture. Stir the liquid into flour just enough to blend thoroughly. Cover; let stand in warm place for 12–18 hours to sour. Store leftover starter dough in refrigerator. Makes enough starter for about 12 loaves.

BLUE RIBBON WINNER, WISCONSIN STATE FAIR

MARY LYNN RUPP — MILWAUKEE, WISCONSIN

ITALIAN CHRISTMAS BREAD (PANETTONE)
Yield: 3 loaves

    1½ cups scalded milk
     ½ cup sugar
     2 Tablespoons salt
     6 Tablespoons butter
     1 Tablespoon anise flavoring
     2 packages dry yeast
     ½ cup warm water
     4 eggs, beaten
    1½ Tablespoons anise seeds
    3½ to 6½ cups flour
    1¼ cups red and golden candied cherries, cut up
     ¾ cup seedless golden raisins
     1 cup slivered almonds

Scald the milk. Add the sugar, salt, butter and anise flavoring. Dissolve the yeast in water. Add the scalded milk mixture. Add beaten eggs and anise seeds. Add 3½ cups of flour and beat, gradually adding enough of the remaining flour to make it kneadable. Knead 8–15 minutes. Place in a greased bowl. Cover; let rise until doubled in bulk. Punch down and gently knead out air bubbles. Let rest for 10 minutes. Divide the dough and cherries, raisins and almonds into three sections. Knead fruit into each section. Form into three round balls. Grease thoroughly three 2-pound coffee cans and place dough in each can. Cover; let rise until doubled, about 30 minutes. Bake at 350 degrees for 25–35 minutes. Remove from cans and cool. Frost with confectioners sugar frosting (below). Decorate with citron or candied cherries, if desired.

CONFECTIONERS SUGAR FROSTING
2 cups confectioners sugar
6 Tablespoons butter
1 Tablespoon vanilla
6 to 8 Tablespoons hot milk

Cut the butter into the sugar. Add the vanilla. Beating with an electric mixer, add the hot milk gradually until desired consistency is reached.

BLUE RIBBON WINNER, WISCONSIN STATE FAIR

STOLLEN
Yield: 3 loaves

1½ cups scalded milk
½ cup sugar
2 Tablespoons salt
6 Tablespoons butter
1 Tablespoon vanilla
2 packages dry yeast
½ cup warm water
3 eggs, beaten
1¼ cups cut-up citron
¾ cup raisins
1 cup almonds
3 to 6½ cups white flour

Scald the milk. Add the sugar, salt, butter and vanilla. Cool until lukewarm. Dissolve the yeast in warm water. Add the scalded milk mixture and beaten eggs. Add 3 cups of flour and beat, gradually adding more flour until the dough is kneadable. Place on a floured bread board and knead for 8–15 minutes, adding more flour as necessary. Place the dough in a greased bowl. Cover, let rise until doubled in bulk, 1–1½ hours. Punch down and knead out air bubbles. Let rest 10 minutes. Cut the dough in three sections. Divide the citron, raisins and almonds into three even piles. Knead one section of dough at a time with the citron mix. Shape into a flat oval. Fold the top over the bottom of the dough and place on greased sheets. Let rise until doubled. Bake at 400 degrees for 5 minutes, reduce to 350 degrees for 25–35 minutes longer. Let cool and frost with confectioners sugar frosting (below). Decorate with bits of citron.

CONFECTIONERS SUGAR FROSTING
2 cups powdered sugar
6 Tablespoons butter
1 Tablespoon vanilla
6 to 8 Tablespoons hot milk

Cut the butter into the sugar. Add the vanilla. Beating with an electric mixer, add the hot milk gradually until desired consistency is reached.

BLUE RIBBON WINNER, WISCONSIN STATE FAIR

THE PHILLIPS FAMILY — CENTERVILLE, IOWA

Mildred Phillips, one of the most consistent winners at the Iowa State Fair, has collected more than five thousand ribbons over the years. This ranks her as the top prize recipient among all the contestants we interviewed.

Mrs. Phillips's cooking skills have earned her special awards from companies like the Meredith Corporation, Pillsbury, the Archway Cookie Company, Better Homes and Gardens and General Mills. She is truly a grand champion in the culinary category.

Mildred's daughter, Olive Jean Tarbell, has followed in her mother's footsteps. In addition to being a frequent blue ribbon winner at the Iowa State Fair, she has appeared in television commercials for two leading New York advertising agencies. And to prove that talent can run in a family, Olive passed her skills on to a third generation, her daughter Robin.

Robin Tarbell follows in the Phillips–Tarbell tradition of fine cooks. So, it was only natural that she took up cooking at an early age. She entered her first state fair competition in 1976, while still in high school. This year she won fifty-seven ribbons including seventeen blues.

You will find a selection of Phillips–Tarbell recipes throughout this book.

OLIVE JEAN TARBELL — CENTERVILLE, IOWA

ORANGE ROLLS
Yield: 2 loaves

2	cups milk, scalded
1	cup sugar
1	stick margarine
1½	teaspoons salt
1	cup mashed potatoes
3	eggs
2	packages dry yeast
½	cup warm water
3	to 4 cups flour
	Orange marmalade

To the scalded milk, add the sugar, margarine, salt and mashed potatoes. Beat the eggs, warm water and yeast. Add to the lukewarm milk mixture. Add about 3 cups of flour and beat until well mixed. Add additional flour as needed to make soft dough. Put in a greased bowl and set it in a warm place about one hour until double in size. Punch it down and let it rise again. On a lightly floured surface roll half the dough into a 16×8-inch rectangle.

Spread with orange marmalade. Roll lengthwise, as for jelly roll. Seal the edge; cut into 1-inch slices. Place, cut sides down, in greased 9×9×2-inch pan. Cover. Repeat with the remaining dough. Let rise until double (30–40 minutes). Bake in moderate oven (350 degrees) about 20–25 minutes. Remove from pan. Can be frosted with orange icing.

BLUE RIBBON WINNER, IOWA STATE FAIR

THE "NANTZ GIRLS"

IMOGENE JOHNSON — CHARLES CITY, VIRGINIA
BONNIE MCALLISTER — COLONIAL HEIGHTS, VIRGINIA
JOY STARKEY — CHARLES CITY, VIRGINIA

Bonnie McAllister, Imogene Johnson and Joy Starkey are known as the "Nantz Girls" down southern Virginia way. The three sisters are consistent winners at the state fair in Richmond. In fact, they win so often that the Richmond Times–Dispatch *once reported that somebody was overheard commenting that "if it hadn't been for the Nantz girls, there wouldn't have been any winners at all."*

Bonnie, the youngest, was the first of the Nantz sisters to enter the state fair baking competition, in 1965. Imogene and Joy "caught the bug" from her and the trio have now become a tradition in a state where traditions are taken seriously.

But fame has not gone to their heads. Imogene told us that she is pleased that the competition is getting keener. But it saddens her when she sees someone looking at their entry and not seeing a ribbon. She herself once won a white ribbon in a category where no red or blue ribbon was awarded. She's glad that the judges maintain such high standards and hopes it will continue.

We hope the Nantz Girls continue competing too. It's their top skills that have helped establish state fair cooking contests as the standard of excellence for America's best cooks.

Below is Bonnie's Pocket Bread. You'll find some other sure winners from the Nantz Girls on the following pages — German Chocolate Cake (page 138), Buttermilk Coconut Pie (page 191), Champion Sponge Cake (page 139), Dream Bars (page 225) and 1–2–3–4 Cake (page 137).

BONNIE MCALLISTER — COLONIAL HEIGHTS, VIRGINIA

POCKET BREADS
Yield: 6 pockets

  1 package dry yeast
1⅓ cups warm water (105–115 degrees)
  1 teaspoon salt
  ¼ teaspoon sugar
  1 Tablespoon vegetable oil or olive oil
  3 to 3½ cups all-purpose flour
     Cornmeal

Dissolve the yeast in warm water in a large bowl. Stir in the salt, sugar, oil and 1½ cups of flour. Beat until smooth. Stir in enough of the remaining flour to make the dough easy to handle. Turn the dough onto a lightly floured surface and knead until smooth and elastic, about 10 minutes. Place in a greased bowl, turning the dough to grease the top. Cover. Let rise in a warm place until double, about one hour. Punch down the dough. Divide into six equal parts and shape into balls. Let rise 30 minutes. Sprinkle three ungreased cookie sheets with cornmeal. Roll each ball into a circle ⅛ inch thick. Place two circles in opposite corners of each cookie sheet. Let rise 30 minutes. Heat oven to 450 degrees. Bake until loaves are puffed and light brown, about 10 minutes. (Mrs. McAllister brushes her loaves with milk before baking to give them a shine and golden color.)

BLUE RIBBON WINNER, VIRGINIA STATE FAIR

DORA FLEMING — GREAT FALLS, MONTANA
JONATHAN SMITH — POWELL, WYOMING
CHARLENE WARREN — ALBUQUERQUE, NEW MEXICO

Dora Fleming's family competes from border to border. Up on the Canadian border Dora has been participating at the Montana State Fair since 1931. Over the years she has won about five hundred blue ribbons plus many more in other colors.

Dora's sister Lucille Murray and son, Warren Smith, have also competed at the Montana State Fair.

Warren has now moved south to Powell, Wyoming, and Dora expects he will soon be joining the competition at the Wyoming State Fair. So, too, will his son Jonathon, who is also a blue ribbon winner at the Montana State Fair. Jonathon's unusual blue ribbon recipe for "Rocks" can be found on page 248.

A distant cousin of Dora's, Mae Mismer was a regular competitor and a frequent winner at the Missouri State Fair. And down in New Mexico, protecting our southern border, you'll find Dora's oldest daughter, Charlene Warren, winning blue ribbons at the New Mexico State Fair. Charlene's prize-winning recipe for Easy Strawberry Jam can be found on page 303.

Dora is a true all-American winner. She has been active in 4–H and her children attended the National Citizenship Encampment in Washington, D.C. Two were state winners and attended the National 4–H Congress in Chicago.

Dora, who loves to travel, has participated in the Friendship Force and has been to Korea, Japan, England and Scotland. Recently she has been accepted as a member of the Daughters of the American Revolution, a true honor for this Montana matriarch.

We are pleased that Dora and her family have agreed to share their favorite recipes with our readers. Now they will become coast-to-coast favorites in addition to being border-to-border winners. Here are Dora's special wheat bread recipes.

DORA FLEMING — GREAT FALLS, MONTANA

WHOLE WHEAT DATE BARS

½ cup margarine
1 cup sugar
1½ cups whole wheat flour
1 teaspoon soda
½ teaspoon salt
1¾ cup quick oatmeal
Date filling (below)

Cream the margarine with the sugar, then add the rest of the ingredients. Mix well. Put half the mixture in a greased 9×13-inch pan. Spread with date filling, top with remaining mixture. Bake 25–30 minutes at 350 degrees.

DATE FILLING
Mix 1 pound of dates, cut up, with 1 cup water and 1 scant cup of sugar. Cook to jam consistency.

BLUE RIBBON WINNER, MONTANA STATE FAIR

NORWEGIAN WHEAT BREAD
Yield: 2 loaves

2½ cups unsifted rye flour
3 cups unsifted all-purpose flour
2 Tablespoons honey
1 Tablespoon salt
½ cup wheat germ
2 packages dry yeast
2¼ cups milk
¼ cup butter or margarine

Combine the flours. Remove 1½ cups and to it add the salt, wheat germ, and dry yeast. Combine the milk, butter and honey in a saucepan and heat until the liquid is warm and the butter melted. Gradually add the hot milk mixture to the dry ingredients. Beat for 2 minutes. Add 2 more cups of flour mixture and beat for 2 minutes more. Stir in the additional flour to make a soft dough. Turn onto a lightly floured board and knead until smooth and elastic — 8–10 minutes. Place in a greased bowl, turning the dough to grease the top. Cover and let rise in a warm place, free from draft, until doubled. Punch down; turn out onto a lightly floured board. Divide in half and let rest until gluten relaxes (about one hour). Shape into two round loaves and slightly flatten the top. Make six cuts from the center to the edge of each loaf after they have been placed in greased pie pans to maintain the shape of the loaf. Let rise until double in bulk. Bake in 400-degree oven for 30–35 minutes. Remove from pans and cool on rack. For soft crust, brush with melted butter.

BLUE RIBBON WINNER, MONTANA STATE FAIR

WHOLE WHEAT BANANA BREAD
Yield: 1 loaf

    ½ cup butter
    ½ cup honey
    1 egg
    1 cup stone-ground or home-ground whole wheat flour
    ½ cup unsifted, unbleached white flour
    1 teaspoon soda
    ¾ teaspoon salt
    1½ cups mashed bananas
    ¼ cup yogurt or buttermilk

Preheat oven to 350 degrees. Cream together the butter and honey. Beat in the egg. Mix or sift together all the dry ingredients. Combine the bananas with the yogurt or buttermilk. Add the dry ingredients alternately with the banana mixture to the butter mixture, stirring just enough to combine well. Turn into an oiled 9×5 loaf pan. Bake 50–60 minutes or until done. Cool in pan for 10 minutes. Remove from pan and finish cooling on a rack.

BLUE RIBBON WINNER, MONTANA STATE FAIR

CATHY JUSTICE — BECKLEY, WEST VIRGINIA

Cathy Justice loves the West Virginia State Fair . . . she has attended almost every year of her life. Her husband, Jim, manages a 4000-acre farm in Gap Mills, West Virginia and regularly enters his corn in the grain competition. Cathy normally enters her quarter horse in the equestrian contest.

But in 1980 a pregnancy kept Cathy from riding in the competition. Since she still wanted to be a part of the fair, she decided to enter the baking competition for the first time. Cathy's Old-Fashioned Corn Bread recipe took top honors on its first try and has since won an additional blue ribbon at the 1982 West Virginia State Fair.

OLD–FASHIONED CORN BREAD
Yield: 9 2½-inch squares

- 1 cup all-purpose flour
- 1 cup yellow cornmeal
- 1 cup buttermilk
- ¼ cup sugar
- 1 egg, beaten
- 3 Tablespoons cooking oil
- 1 teaspoon baking powder
- ½ teaspoon baking soda
- ½ teaspoon salt

Oil a 7¼×7¼×2-inch pan. Set aside. Combine all the dry ingredients. Add the beaten egg, oil and buttermilk. Stir only enough to mix well. Bake in preheated 425-degree oven for 25–30 minutes or until golden brown. Cut into squares and serve hot.

BLUE RIBBON WINNER, WEST VIRGINIA STATE FAIR

CHRISTINE KOSMERL — GREAT FALLS, MONTANA

It's been an eventful year for sixteen-year-old Christine Kosmerl. She played her flute in the school band that entertained President Reagan when he visited Great Falls and she also won a blue ribbon for her banana bread at the state fair. A contestant since she was eleven, Christine has won fourteen ribbons including a Sweepstakes award.

Her younger brother, David, also enters the fair in the children's division, and he and Christine belong to the Great Falls square dance club. Both Christine and David love cooking and plan to continue entering their specialties in the fair.

BANANA BREAD
Yield: 2 loaves

1⅓	cups sugar
⅔	cup butter
4	eggs
4	Tablespoons milk
4	teaspoons baking powder
½	teaspoon soda
3½	cups flour
1	teaspoon salt
2	cups very ripe bananas, mashed
1	cup walnuts or pecans

Cream the sugar and butter. Add the eggs and milk. Add the sifted dry ingredients alternately with the mashed bananas. Add the nuts. Bake in two 5½×9½-inch loaf pans for 50–60 minutes at 350 degrees.

BLUE RIBBON WINNER, MONTANA STATE FAIR

MARMALADE–OATMEAL BREAD
Yield: 2 loaves

1	cup quick oats
2	cups boiling water
2	packages dry yeast
⅓	cup warm water
½	cup orange marmalade
¼	cup honey
2	Tablespoons butter or margarine, softened
2½	teaspoons salt
6	cups flour

In a large bowl, cover the oats with boiling water and let stand until lukewarm (about 30 minutes). Dissolve the yeast in warm water. Add the marmalade and honey to the lukewarm oats and mix well. Stir in the softened butter, salt and yeast. Add the flour, 2 cups at a time, mixing well after the first two additions and kneading in the last 2 cups by hand on a floured surface. Place the dough in a greased bowl, turn, cover and let rise for about 2 hours or until doubled in bulk. Punch down. Shape into two loaves and place in two greased 1-pound loaf pans. Let rise until doubled. Bake on the lowest oven rack in a preheated 325-degree oven for about 50 minutes or until golden brown and loaves sound hollow when tapped. Cool on racks. This bread is excellent toasted and freezes well.

BLUE RIBBON WINNER, NEW YORK STATE FAIR

PUMPERNICKEL LOAVES

Yield: 2 loaves

    7   cups white four
    3   cups rye flour
    2   Tablespoons salt
    4   large shredded-wheat biscuits
   ¾   cup yellow cornmeal
    3   packages dry yeast
  3½   cups water
   ¼   cup dark molasses
    2   squares (1 oz. each) unsweetened chocolate
    1   Tablespoon butter or margarine
    2   cups mashed potatoes (room temperature)
    2   teaspoons caraway seeds

Combine the white and rye flours. In a large bowl thoroughly mix 2 cups of the flour mixture, salt, shredded wheat, cornmeal and yeast. Combine the water, molasses, chocolate and butter in a saucepan and heat on low until the liquids are very warm (120–130 degrees). Gradually add to the dry ingredients and beat for 2 minutes at medium speed. Add the potatoes and 1 cup of the flour mixture. Beat at high speed for 2 minutes. Stir in the caraway seeds and enough of the remaining flour mixture to make a stiff dough. Turn out onto a lightly floured surface. Cover and let rest for about 15 minutes. Knead until smooth and elastic, about 15 minutes. Let rise in a greased bowl, covered, until doubled in bulk (about one hour). Punch down. Divide the dough into two portions and form into two smooth, round balls. Flatten each into a mound. Place on a greased baking sheet; cover and let rise about one hour until doubled in bulk. Bake at 375 degrees for about 35 minutes or until loaves sound hollow when tapped. Remove to wire racks to cool.

BLUE RIBBON WINNER, NEW YORK STATE FAIR

BRIOCHES
Yield: 12 brioches

    2 cups all-purpose flour
    ½ teaspoon salt
    1 Tablespoon sugar
    1 package active dry yeast
    ¼ cup lukewarm water
    2 eggs, beaten
    ¼ cup melted butter
       French egg wash (below)

Sift the flour, salt and sugar into a bowl. Mix the yeast with the
warm water and let stand for 5 minutes. Stir the yeast mixture,
butter, and eggs into the flour with a wooden spoon. Stir the
dough until it leaves the sides of the bowl clean, then turn the
dough onto a lightly floured surface and knead for 5 minutes. Let
rise in an oiled plastic bag at room temperature for 1½ hours, or
until doubled in bulk. Turn the risen dough out onto a lightly
floured surface and knead again until smooth. Let the dough rise
again (in oiled plastic bag) for about one hour. Knead the dough
again and shape into a long sausage. Divide this into 12 equal
pieces. Brush 3-inch patty pans with oil. Small muffin tins can be
used. Shape ¾ of each piece of dough into a ball and place it in
the prepared pan. With a floured finger, press a deep indentation
into each ball. Make knobs out of the remaining ¼ pieces of
dough, then insert the knobs into the indentations in the dough already in the pan. Press the knob down gently to join the two
doughs. This makes the top knot. Brush each brioche carefully
with French Egg Wash (below), making sure the wash does not
get into the crack around the top knot. Bake in a preheated 425-

degree oven for 10 minutes until golden brown. Remove from pans immediately. Let cool or serve warm. To remove top knot, grasp and wiggle, pulling upward gently. Fill with jelly for snacks or melted chocolate for dessert and replace top knots.

FRENCH EGG WASH
1 egg yolk
1 teaspoon water
1 Tablespoon milk

Beat all the ingredients together.

BLUE RIBBON WINNER, NEW YORK STATE FAIR

MARY KUTHY — SPRINGFIELD, ILLINOIS

Mary Kuthy is another newcomer to state fair competition. This is only her second year. She is also a newcomer to Illinois; her husband was appointed State Dental Director only three years ago.

Mary grew up in Monticello, Maine, just two miles from the Canadian border. She became a nurse in Bangor and went on to Dartmouth to become a physician's assistant, which is her profession today. Mary admits that she sorely misses Maine and hopes to return some day. In the meantime, one of her main interests is winning blue ribbons at the Illinois State Fair. This Russian Black Bread recipe is one of her favorites.

RUSSIAN BLACK BREAD
Yield: 2 loaves

⅓ cup cornmeal
¾ cup boiling water
¾ cup cold water
2 packages dry yeast
¼ cup warm water
2 teaspoons sugar

2 ounces unsweetened chocolate, melted
¾ cup molasses
2 Tablespoons butter
1 Tablespoon salt
2 teaspoons caraway seeds
1 cup cold mashed potatoes
1 to 1½ cups whole wheat flour
3 to 4 cups rye flour
1 cup white flour
1 egg, beaten

Add the cornmeal to boiling water. Stir until thick and smooth. Add cold water gradually; let cool. In a large bowl mix the yeast with ¼ cup warm water and sugar, stir and let set until bubbly. Melt chocolate and butter. Cool. To the yeast add the cornmeal, chocolate, molasses, butter, salt, caraway seeds and potatoes. Beat well. Add 1 cup of whole wheat flour and beat 2 minutes. Add 3 cups of rye flour and mix — if mushy add another ½ cup of whole wheat or rye flour. Turn onto a floured board and knead with white flour (the dough will be sticky). Put the dough in a buttered bowl, set covered, in a warm place, about one hour until doubled in bulk. Punch down, turn onto a board, and knead a few times. Cut in half and shape into two round balls. Place on a greased baking sheet sprinkled with cornmeal. Let rise about one hour until doubled. Glaze with the beaten egg. Bake 10 minutes at 400 degrees then turn down oven to 350 degrees for 25 minutes. Cool. Slice thin. This is great with soups, cheese and wine.

BLUE RIBBON WINNER, ILLINOIS STATE FAIR

SWEET ROLLS
Yield: 2 loaves

BASIC RICH DOUGH
  1 cup scalded milk (cooled)
  2 packages dry yeast
  1 cup more of scalded milk
  1 cup hot mashed potatoes
  8 cups flour (approximately)
  1 cup (2 sticks) butter, softened
  1 cup sugar
1½ teaspoons salt
  4 large eggs

Soften the yeast in 1 cup of lukewarm milk. Combine the other cup of milk, mashed potatoes and 1 cup of the flour. Mix until thoroughly blended. When yeast is thoroughly dissolved add the yeast and milk mixture to the bowl and blend in well. Cover and let rest a few minutes. Cream the butter and sugar, add the salt and eggs and beat well. Add to the yeast mixture and mix. Gradually add most of the remaining flour to make a firm dough. Knead well and place in a bowl. Brush with melted butter, cover and let rise about one hour in a warm place. When the dough has doubled in bulk, punch down and roll out on a floured board. Make into desired shapes, let rise and bake.

FILLING
  ½ cup butter
  ¾ cup brown sugar
  1 cup preserves (pineapple, strawberry, plum, etc.)
  2 Tablespoons cinnamon
  1 cup raisins

1 cup broken pecans
1½ ounces of rum, liquor, etc.

Melt the butter in a pan. Add sugar, preserves, cinnamon, raisins, pecans and stir well until the mixture is thoroughly heated and the sugar is well dissolved. Remove from heat and add liquor flavoring. Take half of the basic rich dough and roll into a long rectangle about ½ inch thick or less. Spread with filling mixture over entire surface, leaving about 1 inch of top along the long axis uncovered. Roll up in jelly roll fashion. Cut into rings about 1 inch thick. Butter each roll by dipping it into a pan of melted butter and place into a buttered pan. Let rise about one hour until light. Bake in a 375-degree oven for 20 minutes. Turn out of pans to cool. Glaze rolls well.

ALTERNATE FILLING
1 cup slivered almonds
1 stick butter
1 cup sugar
2 egg yolks, beaten

Combine the almonds, butter, and sugar. Brush the dough with 2 beaten egg yolks and spread the filling. Roll up and slice or form into a ring and bake in a 375-degree oven for 20 minutes.

BLUE RIBBON WINNER, TEXAS STATE FAIR

HUSH PUPPIES
Yield: 6 to 8

¼ cup flour
2 teaspoons baking powder
½ teaspoon salt
¾ cup cornmeal
1 egg
½ cup milk

1 green onion, finely minced
1 pimiento, finely minced
3 Tablespoons parsley, finely minced
½ teaspoon garlic powder
  Cayenne pepper

Mix all the dry ingredients together in a bowl, add the egg, milk and seasonings. Stir just until moistened. Drop from a spoon into hot cooking oil. These may also be squeezed from a pastry bag, fitted with a star tube, directly into the hot fat. These form pretzel shapes and are light and crisp. The flavor is improved if the oil has previously had shrimp or fish fried in it.

BLUE RIBBON WINNER, TEXAS STATE FAIR

CAROL STINE — FINCHVILLE, KENTUCKY

It takes a very special talent to make a suit for your husband, and Carol Stine has that talent. She has a blue ribbon from the Kentucky State Fair to prove it. Carol's daughter Laurie has the same talent. She made a jump suit and won a blue ribbon for it at this year's fair.

Bread baking is a specialty of Carol's. She makes six loaves every other week and carries a timer in her pocket to be sure she doesn't miss a step. Homemade bread takes more time and may not save money, Carol admits, but it sure "spoils your family."

We think these Stine family recipes are something special.

EGG BREAD
Yield: 3 loaves

2 packages dry yeast
½ cup warm water
½ cup melted butter or margarine
2 cups warm water
1 teaspoon salt

½ cup sugar
4 eggs, beaten
6 cups all-purpose flour
2 cups bread flour

Add the yeast to ½ cup of warm water and let stand for 10 minutes. In a large bowl, beat together by hand the butter, 2 cups of warm water, salt, sugar and eggs. To this add the yeast mixture and flour. Knead the dough until it becomes smooth, elastic and satiny. Grease a large bowl, put the dough in and then turn it over to grease the top. Cover with a damp towel and place out of drafts. Permit to rise about 1½ hours, punch down, and let rise until double, about one hour. Now separate into three balls and let rest on floured board about 10 minutes. Shape into loaves and place in three greased bread pans. Cover again and let loaves rise to the top of the pans. Bake at 375 degrees for 35–40 minutes.
Remove bread from pans immediately and let cool on racks.

BLUE RIBBON WINNER, KENTUCKY STATE FAIR

BRAIDED CINNAMON SWIRL ORANGE BREAD

2 packages active dry yeast
1 cup scalded milk
¼ cup shortening
1 egg, slightly beaten
1 Tablespoon grated orange peel (optional)
¼ cup warm water
½ cup sugar
1½ teaspoons salt
¾ cup orange juice
6½ to 7 cups all-purpose flour
    (1 cup of bread flour can be used in this)
½ cup sugar
1 Tablespoon cinnamon

Combine the yeast and warm water and let rest for 10 minutes. Sift flour. Stir 2 cups of flour into scalded milk, sugar, salt, orange juice, shortening and orange peel (if desired); beat until smooth. Stir in the yeast and 1 slightly beaten egg; beat well. Add enough remaining flour to make a soft dough. Knead on a floured surface until smooth (10 minutes). Place in a greased bowl. Cover and let rise until double (one hour). Punch down; divide in six equal portions. Cover; let rest 10 minutes. Roll each into a rectangle, ½ inch thick. Combine ½ cup of sugar and 1 tablespoon of cinnamon. Spread each rectangle with the sugar mixture. Sprinkle each with 1 teaspoon of water; smooth with a spatula. Roll into 6 long ropes and seal the edge; braid three together for each loaf, and place sealed edge down in greased loaf pans. Cover; let rise till double (one hour). Bake at 350 degrees for 30 minutes. Cool. Frost with icing made of 1 cup confectioners sugar and 4 teaspoons orange juice, if desired.

BLUE RIBBON WINNER, KENTUCKY STATE FAIR

CASSANDRA MYERS — FLORENCE, MISSISSIPPI

The 4–H Club offers tremendous encouragement to the junior bakers of America. Cassandra Myers is a fourteen-year-old 4–H member and has been a regular competitor at the Mississippi State Fair for the past four years. Her mother, Martha, was also a 4–H member and a state fair competitor before her.

In the past four years Cassandra has collected a total of 142 ribbons including twenty-five at this year's fair.

CORN MUFFINS
Yield: 12 muffins

    2 eggs
1¼ cups buttermilk
1½ cups yellow cornmeal

¾ cup flour
1 teaspoon salt
2½ teaspoons baking powder

Beat the eggs and milk. Sift the remaining ingredients together; add the egg mixture and beat well. Spoon into hot greased muffin tins. Bake in hot oven (450 degrees) until brown — about 15 minutes.

BLUE RIBBON WINNER, MISSISSIPI STATE FAIR

BETTIE GLASSEY — WHITEMAN AFB, MISSOURI

Competition was fierce in the biscuit category at the Missouri State Fair. When Bettie Glassey arrived with her entry, she was surprised by the number of entries in that competition. In fact, she really didn't expect to win at all.

When she arrived back later she was thrilled to see the blue ribbon on her biscuits.

BISCUITS
Yield: 12–16 biscuits

2 cups sifted flour
4 teaspoons baking powder
½ teaspoon salt (optional)
½ teaspoon cream of tartar
2 teaspoons sugar
½ cup shortening
⅔ cup milk (powdered, reconstituted may be used)

Sift together the flour, baking powder, salt, cream of tartar, and sugar; cut in half the shortening until mixture resembles corn-meal. Cut in the remaining shortening until the mixture resembles coarse crumbs. Add the milk all at once; stir only until the dough follows the fork around the bowl. Turn out on a lightly floured surface; knead gently 30 seconds. Pat or roll ½ inch thick; cut with a biscuit cutter. Bake on an ungreased cookie sheet in hot oven (450 degrees) for 10–12 minutes.

BLUE RIBBON WINNER, MISSOURI STATE FAIR

ANN YARBOROUGH FOSNACHT — COLUMBIA, SOUTH CAROLINA

Ann Fosnacht considers herself a jack of all trades and a master of none. But tasting this receipe will convince you that Ann has certainly mastered the art of making muffins. This blue ribbon winner won the South Carolina Sweepstakes award in 1982, and her recipe for these muffins will convince you that baking from scratch is well worth the effort.

ENGLISH MUFFINS
Yield: About 24 muffins

    2 cups all-purpose flour
    2 Tablespoons honey
    2 teaspoons salt
    2 teaspoons powdered sugar
    1 package active dry yeast
 1¾ cups milk
   ¼ cup water
    1 Tablespoon margarine
    1 egg
    4 cups all-purpose flour (approximately)
   ½ cup cornmeal (approximately)

In a large mixer bowl stir together 2 cups of flour, the honey, salt, powdered sugar and dry yeast; set aside. In a saucepan, heat the milk, water and margarine until very warm (120–130 degrees). Add gradually to the yeast-flour mixture and beat at medium speed for 2 minutes. Add the egg and 1 cup of flour. Beat at high speed for 2 minutes. Stir in just enough remaining flour to make a soft dough. Knead on a lightly floured surface until smooth and elastic, adding more remaining flour if dough is sticky. Cover with plastic wrap and let rise in warm, draft-free place until double, about one hour. Punch down. Cover and let rise again until double, about 45 minutes. Punch down. On a lightly floured surface roll out ½ inch thick. With 3¼-inch round cutter (or clean tuna can opened at both ends) cut out muffins. Sprinkle cookie sheets lightly with cornmeal. Place muffins about 1 inch apart and sprinkle with additional cornmeal. Cover; let rise in a warm, draft-free place until double, about 45 minutes. Heat lightly greased griddle or frying pan to about 260 degrees. With a wide metal spatula carefully remove the muffins (do not compress or puncture the muffins or they will collapse) to the griddle. Bake over very low heat 8–10 minutes on each side or until light brown. (Muffins should sound hollow when tapped.) Cool on racks. To serve, split with fork tines or cut with a sharp knife.

BLUE RIBBON WINNER, SOUTH CAROLINA STATE FAIR

THE MORSE FAMILY — GREAT FALLS, MONTANA

The Morse family is so active at state fair time that Mrs. Morse had to add a second oven in order to accommodate the entire family's entries. Stan and Marjory Morse and their daughters, Kim and Kandice, have won many blue ribbons at the Montana State Fair over the past ten years.

Thanks to the Morses you can enjoy some extra-special blue ribbon favorites from the big sky country. Stan offers you his Dill Seed Bread here, and you'll find Marjory's, Kim's and Kandice's recipes in the pie and cookie sections.

DILL SEED BREAD
Yield: 4 small loaves

2 packages yeast
½ cup warm water
2 teaspoons sugar
½ teaspoon ginger
2 cups creamed cottage cheese
2 Tablespoons vegetable oil
4 Tablespoon sugar
2 Tablespoons finely chopped onion
4 Tablespoons dill seed
½ teaspoon soda
2 eggs
5 cups flour
2 teaspoons salt

Mix the first four ingredients; let sit. Mix the cottage cheese, sugar, oil, onion, dill seed, soda and eggs. Add the yeast mixture and beat well. Add the flour. Let rise until double in bulk. Punch down. Divide into four small loaves and let dough rise again. Bake in 350-degree oven for 30 minutes. Spread butter over the tops and sprinkle with a dash of salt.

BLUE RIBBON WINNER, MONTANA STATE FAIR

RUBY DRAFTS — LEXINGTON, SOUTH CAROLINA

Ruby Drafts has been entering the South Carolina State Fair for almost fifty years. It's the beginning of a tradition in the Drafts family.

Her biscuits were the Sweepstakes Winner every year for the past seven years, except in 1980. That year Ruby's daughter Frances took first place.

SODA BISCUITS
Yield: Approximately 24 biscuits depending on size of cutter

- 2 cups self-rising flour
- ½ teaspoon soda
- 4 Tablespoons shortening
- ⅔ cup buttermilk

Blend all the dry ingredients and shortening with a pastry blender. Stir in the buttermilk with a fork just until mixed well. Turn out onto a lightly floured board. Knead until the dough is smooth. Roll out and cut with a biscuit cutter. Place on an ungreased baking sheet and bake at 425 degrees for about 12 minutes.

BLUE RIBBON WINNER, SOUTH CAROLINA STATE FAIR

MAUREEN HARROD — LOUISVILLE, KENTUCKY

Maureen Harrod always enjoyed attending the Kentucky State Fair, but she's a relative newcomer to the cooking contest. She first entered in 1976 and was pleased to win a blue ribbon on her first try.

Maureen takes pride in her family-oriented life-style. Her three children, Tracy, Judy and Kenny, are already following in her footsteps by winning their own ribbons at the state fair.

Even if you're a newcomer to home-baking, we think you'll enjoy preparing her recipes.

BLUEBERRY MUFFINS
Yield: 12 muffins

- 1¾ cups sifted flour
- 2 Tablespoons sugar

2½ teaspoons baking powder
¾ teaspoon salt
1 egg, well beaten
¾ cup milk
¼ cup sugar
⅓ cup salad oil or melted shortening
1 cup fresh or frozen (well drained) blueberries

Sift the first four ingredients into a mixing bowl; make a well in the center. Combine the egg, milk, sugar and salad oil. Add all at once to the dry ingredients. Stir quickly only until the dry ingredients are moistened. Fold in the blueberries. Fill greased muffin pans or paper cups ⅔ full. Bake at 400 degrees for 25 minutes.

BLUE RIBBON WINNER, KENTUCKY STATE FAIR

PATRICIA OLDHAM — ALBUQUERQUE, NEW MEXICO

Patricia Oldham sets very high standards for her recipes. When she finds a recipe she likes, she adapts it to meet those high standards. Then she enters the finished product in the New Mexico State Fair.

The recipe then undergoes continued modification until it satisfies both her and the state fair judges.

Patricia's Oatmeal Bread was adapted from a Pillsbury Bake-Off recipe . . . not a bad start. But now it has also met the Oldham test after years of modification. Patricia is now satisfied with this bread, and will withdraw it from competition now that it has won a blue ribbon and also the "Best Loaf" at the 1980 and 1982 New Mexico State Fair. If you have never had a bread that can make the claim that it was so good it was retired from competition, try a slice of Patricia's best.

WHOLE GRAIN OATMEAL BREAD
Yield: 2 loaves

3 to 3¾ cups unbleached flour
⅔ cup dry milk powder

1 Tablespoon salt
2 packages active dry yeast
6 Tablespoons honey
2 Tablespoons molasses
2¾ cups minus 2 Tablespoons warm water (120–130 degrees)
¼ cup cooking oil
1 cup rolled oats
4 cups whole wheat flour

In a large mixer bowl, combine 2 cups of unbleached flour, dry milk powder, salt and yeast. Add honey, molasses, water and cooking oil. Beat at medium speed for 2 minutes. Add the rolled oats, whole wheat flour and enough unbleached flour to make a stiff dough. Knead on a lightly floured surface until smooth and elastic, about 5 minutes. Or knead with the dough hook of the mixer for 3 minutes. Place in a greased bowl, turning to grease the top. Allow to rise 20–30 minutes. Punch down, divide and form into two loaves. Place in two 8×4-inch or 9×5-inch pans. Allow to rise until double, about 40 minutes. Bake in 375-degree oven 30–35 minutes. Remove from pans. Cool.

Variations: Add 1 teaspoon cinnamon, ½ teaspoon nutmeg and 1 cup raisins for Oatmeal Raisin Bread. Or substitute 1 cup cracked wheat for rolled oats for Cracked Wheat Bread.

BLUE RIBBON WINNER, NEW MEXICO STATE FAIR

SHARON SHELDEN — DOUGLAS, WYOMING

On a cold winter night, when your cowboys ride in from the range after punching "little dogies," why not treat them to a warm loaf of Sharon Shelden's Nut Bread. Sharon calls herself a true Wyoming cowgirl who grew up on a ranch in Glenrock, Wyoming. She originally began entering state fair competition as a child and continues to compete today in both the Culinary and Arts and Crafts categories.

Sharon and her husband, Buck, now work on a ranch on the outskirts of Douglas, Wyoming.

NUT BREAD
Yield: 1 loaf

> 1½ cups sifted flour
> 1 teaspoon baking powder
> ½ teaspoon salt
> ¾ cup sugar
> ½ cup shortening
> ½ cup chopped nuts
> 2 eggs
> ½ cup milk

Mix the dry ingredients. Cut in the shortening. Mix in the nuts. Set aside. Beat eggs and milk into the dry ingredients. Mix until just blended. Pour batter into 9½×4½×2¾-inch greased pan. Bake at 375 degrees for one hour.

BLUE RIBBON WINNER, WYOMING STATE FAIR

FERN HARMON — GRANGER, IOWA

The Harmons own a 230-acre farm in Granger, Iowa, and keep busy raising corn, soybeans, beef cattle and chickens. Their daughters have grown up and have chosen to live in nearby Adel and Des Moines. It may be difficult "keeping them down on the farm," but you can bet they return often for Fern Harmon's good home cooking.

Below you will find Fern's Granola Bread and Honey Whole Wheat Bread. On page 98 is a mouth-watering recipe for Raised Doughnuts and on page 221 is Fern's Honey–Lemon Specials, which won Best Cookie at the Iowa State Fair.

GRANOLA BREAD
Yield: 1 loaf

- 1 cup warm water
- 1 package active dry yeast
- 1 teaspoon salt
- 1 Tablespoon honey or molasses
- 2 Tablespoons oil
- 2 to 2½ cups unsifted flour
- 1¼ cups granola

In a large bowl, soften the yeast in warm water. Stir in the salt, honey, oil and 1½ cups of flour: beat well. Stir in the granola and remaining flour to form a stiff dough. Knead on a floured surface until smooth, about 8 minutes. Cover and let rise in a warm place until double in size, about one hour. Punch down and shape into a loaf. Place in a greased 9×5-inch loaf pan. Cover and let rise until double in size, about 45 minutes. Bake at 350 degrees for 40 minutes or until golden brown. Remove from pan and cool.

BLUE RIBBON WINNER, IOWA STATE FAIR

HONEY WHOLE WHEAT BREAD
Yield: 2 loaves

- 1 cup water
- 1 package active dry yeast
- 1 cup milk, hot
- 1 Tablespoon salt
- ¼ cup shortening
- ¼ cup honey
- 2¾ cups whole wheat flour
- 2¾ cups white flour

Soften the yeast in warm water in a large bowl. In another bowl, combine the hot milk, salt, shortening and honey. Stir until dissolved. When cool to lukewarm, add to the yeast mixture. Add the white flour and beat. Stir in the whole wheat flour to make a moderately stiff dough. Turn out on a lightly floured surface. Knead till smooth (8–10 minutes). Shape into a ball and place in a lightly greased bowl. Cover; let double (1–2 hours). Punch down. Divide into two parts. Let rest for 10 minutes. Shape loaves. Place in greased bread pans. Let rise until double. Bake at 350 degrees for 45–50 minutes.

BLUE RIBBON WINNER, IOWA STATE FAIR

RAISED DOUGHNUTS
Yield: 4 dozen doughnuts

 2 packages active dry yeast
 ⅔ cup warm milk
 2 cups boiling water
 ½ cup shortening
 ⅔ cup sugar
 4 eggs
 2 teaspoons salt
 9 to 10 cups sifted flour

In a large mixing bowl add the yeast to warm milk. Add the shortening, sugar and salt to boiling water and stir until dissolved. When cool, add to the yeast and milk. Stir in eggs and half the flour. Beat until smooth. Add the remaining flour. Knead on a lightly floured surface. Place in a greased bowl, turning once to grease surface. Cover and let rise until double in bulk, about 2 hours. Punch down. Roll out dough ½ inch thick. Cut and let rest 15 minutes. Fry in 375-degree deep fat. Sugar or glaze.

BLUE RIBBON WINNER, IOWA STATE FAIR

ZORA ANDERSON — MORRIS, ALABAMA

Zora Anderson waited sixty-eight years to enter the cooking competition at the Alabama State Fair. "It was quite exciting," she explains. "It's the only time I ever won anything in my life." She has also had a lot of practice getting ready for the fair. She began making biscuits when she was nine and has baked them almost every day since she was married in 1932.

Zora has two children, five grandchildren and five great-grandchildren. She lives in a small rural area near Birmingham, Alabama, and is active in the Baptist Church.

BAKING SODA BISCUITS
Yield: 10–12 biscuits

¼ teaspoon baking soda
½ teaspoon salt
2 teaspoons baking powder
2 cups plain flour
⅔ cup shortening
½ cup milk
½ cup water

Sift the dry ingredients together. Add the shortening and work together with a fork. Add the milk and water. Stir until firm enough to knead. Turn onto a floured cloth and knead for 1–1½ minutes. Roll out the dough and cut. Place on an ungreased pan or cookie sheet and bake at 450 degrees until brown on top, approximately 10 minutes.

BLUE RIBBON WINNER, ALABAMA STATE FAIR

MARIE AND ANN HATTRUP — MORO, OREGON

Marie and Kenneth Hathrup grow wheat on 3200 tillable acres in Moro, Oregon. It's a tough business, Marie admits, because it's so difficult to get good yields and good prices in the same year. And, even when you do, you never know when to sell. The Hathrups brought in a good crop in 1982 but, unfortunately, wheat prices have been low for the past few years.

Kenneth brought a special honor to the family this year. He was named Oregon Conservation Farmer of the Year by the Oregon Wheat League.

Marie enjoys participating at the Oregon State Fair but can't every year because Salem is 150 miles from Moro. When she does, she gives the other contestants a run for their money. She has twice been named Queen of the Kitchen and also won Queen of Home Economics. In off years she judges at several county fairs and also gives cooking demonstrations, especially for breads.

The Hathrups' oldest daughter works in Portland and has also won many awards for baking. They have two children attending Oregon State University and a younger daughter in the eighth grade.

Daughter Ann attended the state fair with her mother last year and won the Home Economics Award and also picked up the most points in canning. She was her class valedictorian and is now a freshman in pre-med.

Below are Marie and Ann's blue ribbon recipes from the Oregon State Fair.

ANN HATTRUP — MORO, OREGON

BUTTER BISCUITS
Yield: Approximately 10 biscuits

      2 cups unbleached flour
      4 teaspoons baking powder
      3 Tablespoons sugar
     ½ teaspoon salt
     ½ teaspoon cream of tartar
     ½ cup butter
     ¾ cup milk

Sift the dry ingredients into a bowl. Using a pastry blender, cut in the butter to the size of peas — do not overwork dough or cut in butter too fine. Mix in milk. Gather the dough into a ball and roll or pat to a ½-inch thickness. Do not knead. Cut with a 3-inch cutter. Place on an ungreased pan close together and bake at 450 degrees for 10 minutes or until nicely brown.

MARIE HATHRUP — MORO, OREGON

PERFECT LIGHT WHEAT BREAD
Yield: 2 loaves

    2 cups scalded milk
    3 Tablespoons sugar
    ¼ cup butter
    1 Tablespoon salt
    ¼ cup molasses
    2 packages active dry yeast
    ½ cup warm water
 1½ cups whole wheat flour
    6 cups unbleached white flour

Combine the scalded milk, sugar, butter and salt. Stir to dissolve, add molasses and cool to lukewarm. Dissolve the yeast in warm water and add to the milk mixture. Stir in whole wheat flour and half of the unbleached flour. Beat until smooth. Add the remaining flour and knead until smooth on a lightly floured surface — approximately 5 minutes. Place in a greased bowl, turn once to grease the top. Cover; let rise about one hour until double in warm place (80 degrees). Knead down the dough and let it rest for 15 minutes. Divide in half, shape into loaves and place in greased 9½×5¼×2¾-inch loaf pans. Cover; let rise until double. Bake at 375 degrees for about 45–50 minutes on next-to-bottom rack. Turn out immediately on cooling racks.

Bob and Norma Thompson raise native hay on their 240-acre ranch in Laramie, Wyoming. It has been a hectic year for the family, and we are pleased that they found the time to share their lives and recipes with us.

Their son Darrell suffered an unfortunate accident but is now undergoing rehabilitation and has returned to school to learn a new field. On the brighter side was the wedding of their only daughter, Cathy . . . Norma, great baker that she is, added to the occasion by making the wedding cake.

Below is Norma's blue ribbon Cinnamon Roll recipe. You'll find her White Cake on page 136. Both are top favorites at the Thompson ranch house.

CINNAMON ROLLS

Yield: This is for a large batch. It will make enough for 4 dozen cinnamon rolls and 2 tea rings

```
6   cups scalded milk
4   packages active dry yeast
3   teaspoons sugar
1½  cups butter or margarine
1½  cups sugar
3   teaspoons salt
9   cups flour, approximate
3   eggs
¾   teaspoon vanilla
    Cinnamon
    Sugar
```

Heat milk to scalding. Put a ½ cup of milk into small bowl and add 3 teaspoons sugar and cool to just warm, then add yeast and let set. Add the butter, ½ cup of sugar, and salt to the rest of the milk and cool to warm. Pour both milk mixtures into a large mixer bowl, and add about half the flour. Beat 3 minutes, then add eggs and beat again. Put dough hook on and add enough flour to make a soft dough. Knead 5 minutes. Remove from mixer and put in a greased bowl, turning once to grease top.

Let rise until double. Divide into six pieces. Roll out each until about ½ to ¾ inch thick. Spread with butter and sprinkle with cinnamon and sugar. Roll up and cut into 1-inch rolls. Put in pans. Let rise until about double. Bake in 375-degree oven for 20–30 minutes. The dough can also be used for Tea Rings. Sprinkle with brown sugar and chopped nuts along with cinnamon, butter and sugar. Bake in 350-degree oven for about 40 minutes.

BLUE RIBBON WINNER, WYOMING STATE FAIR

JUDY KINNEY — KNOXVILLE, IOWA

The Kinneys of Knoxville, Iowa, were intrigued with designs for homes that they had seen in Mother Earth News. *Unfortunately, the cost of those homes were a little out of reach, so they did the next best thing: they designed their own.*

They have been living in their unique quarters for four years now and enjoying the many benefits that it provides. Perhaps the most important benefit is fuel efficiency. The house is heated by a wood stove and they survived last year's difficult Iowa winter on only three cords of wood.

Judy and Robert are medical technologists at Mercy Hospital Medical Center in Des Moines. In their spare time they enjoy organic gardening and competing at the county and state fair.

Judy's Garden Bread recipe originally took only a fourth place but has since won a blue ribbon after undergoing a number of modifications. According to Judy the secret to the recipe is the use of liquefied zucchini, which you can easily prepare in a blender.

GARDEN BREAD
Yield: 2 loaves

   3 eggs
1½ cups sugar
 ⅓ cup oil

⅔ cup peeled zucchini, liquefied in blender
2 cups peeled zucchini, grated
3 teaspoons cinnamon
1 teaspoon soda
1 teaspoon baking powder
3 cups flour
1½ teaspoons real vanilla

Beat the eggs until foamy, add sugar slowly and beat. Add the oil, vanilla, zucchini and stir well. Add the dry ingredients and beat slowly, pour into two greased and floured 9×5-inch loaf pans. Bake in 325-degree oven for 50 minutes.

BLUE RIBBON WINNER, IOWA STATE FAIR

NANCY WARREN — LINCOLN, NEBRASKA

Nancy Warren had never competed in a state fair. This year her two daughters were competing as campfire girls so she decided, "What the heck, I'll give it a try myself."

Her specialties are sewing and dough-art Christmas tree ornaments. Her efforts in these categories earned her three blue ribbons. But, in fact, it earned her much more because she and a friend, Pat Stolley, went on to earn almost $800 by selling their dough-art ornaments.

Nancy also won a blue ribbon for her Sour Cream Cinnamon Roll recipe against tough competition. One of the reasons is the special flavor that the sour cream gives, but the topping also adds a lot and is Nancy's own unique touch.

Nancy and her husband, Dave, live in Lincoln where he is a bank examiner for the state of Nebraska.

SOUR CREAM CINNAMON ROLLS

2 cups sour cream
4 Tablespoons shortening
6 Tablespoons sugar

1 teaspoon baking soda
1 teaspoon salt
2 large eggs
2 packages active dry yeast
4 cups flour

TOPPING

3 Tablespoons cinnamon
1 Tablespoon butter, softened
¼ cup brown sugar
¼ cup white sugar

Bring the sour cream to a boil in a large saucepan. Remove from heat and stir in the shortening, sugar, soda and salt. Blend well. Cool until lukewarm. Add the unbeaten eggs and yeast. Mix in the flour with a spoon and turn onto a lightly floured board. Knead lightly a few minutes to form a ball. Cover with a damp cloth and let stand for 5 minutes. Roll ½ inch thick into a rectangular shape. Blend the topping mixture and spread over the dough. Roll up the dough and cut into 1-inch slices. Place on a baking sheet and let stand for about 2 hours. Bake at 350 degrees for about 20 minutes. Cool and sprinkle with powdered sugar.

BLUE RIBBON WINNER, NEBRASKA STATE FAIR

RUBY MACRAE — GLENROCK, WYOMING
DAVID MACRAE — GLENROCK, WYOMING

Cooking with honey is a specialty of Ruby MacRae . . . it's also a specialty of her son David. This mother-and-son team are frequent winners in the "Cooking with Honey" category at the Wyoming State Fair. Occasionally they even find themselves competing against each other.

Ruby couldn't compete last year because she took her daughter to college, but the MacRaes did compete the year before and expect to be back in action at this year's fair. In fact, in 1981 David won the championship of the "Cooking with Honey" junior division.

Here are David's Honey Cinnamon Rolls and you will find his candy winners on page 263. Ruby's fine Honey Chocolate Cake is on page 148.

HONEY CINNAMON ROLLS
Yield: Approximately 3 dozen rolls

    ½ cup warm water
    2 packages active dry yeast
    ½ cup milk, scalded and cooled
    ½ cup honey
    1½ teaspoons salt
    2 eggs
    ½ cup shortening
    5½ cups unsifted flour

FILLING
    6 Tablespoons softened butter
    1 cup sugar
    4 teaspoons cinnamon

Dissolve the yeast in water. Add the cooled milk, honey, salt, eggs, shortening and half of the flour to the yeast. Mix until smooth. Add the remaining flour. Knead until smooth. Place in a greased bowl, cover and let rise until double. Divide the dough in half. Punch down and roll the dough into an oblong shape. Spread the filling and, beginning at the wide side, roll up and seal the edges by pinching them together. Slice into 1-inch pieces. Place on a greased baking sheet. Bake at 350 degrees for 15 minutes.

BLUE RIBBON WINNER, WYOMING STATE FAIR

DARLYS ORTH — AMES, IOWA

This pan roll recipe comes from Nashua, Iowa, which is famous because it is the home of the Little Brown Church in the Vale and because it is the birthplace of Darlys Orth, blue ribbon winner at the 1982 Iowa State Fair.

Darlys now lives in Ames, Iowa, where she and her husband, Ron, are raising two children, Dave (seventeen) and Julie (fifteen). This is her first entry in the state fair competition, but she has previously been active as a 4–H leader. In addition to her 4–H activities, Darlys is a substitute in the Ames Public School Cafeteria System and is her church wedding reception chairwoman.

PAN ROLLS
Yield: Approximately 3½–4 dozen rolls

1 cup warm water
1 Tablespoon sugar
4 teaspoons active dry yeast
1 cup hot water
½ cup sugar
¼ cup shortening
2 eggs, beaten
1 teaspoon salt
8 cups flour

Place the 1 cup of warm water, 1 tablespoon of sugar and the yeast into a large bowl. Stir until the yeast is dissolved. Add the hot water, sugar, shortening, eggs, and salt. Mix well and then add as much flour as you can with a mixer. Turn out onto a floured surface. Knead in enough remaining flour to make a moderately stiff dough that is smooth and elastic. Shape into a ball. Place in a greased bowl; turn once. Cover; let rise in a warm place, about one hour, until double. Punch down; shape into desired rolls. Place in a greased pan and let rise until double. Bake at 350 degrees for 12–15 minutes.

BLUE RIBBON WINNER, IOWA STATE FAIR

Bobbie's goal is perfection, especially when it comes to one of her favorite pastimes, baking bread. Her first try at competition was at the Wasatch County Fair in Utah, where she managed to squeak out a fifth place. That just wasn't good enough, so Bobbie's competitive spirit took over. The following year she did much better and by 1975 she had graduated to the cooking competition at the Utah State Fair.

The Sweet Roll Dough recipe that Bobbie has provided has won a blue ribbon every time it was entered. It has also helped her accumulate enough points to be a three time Sweepstakes winner at the fair. As Bobbie points out, it is an extremely versatile recipe. It requires no kneading and can be used for a variety of bakings including dinner rolls, scones, Swedish tea rings, sweet rolls and even pizza.

Bobbie and her husband, Kerry, are raising six children in Sandy, Utah, on the outskirts of Salt Lake City. The pride with which she spoke of her children once again demonstrates the strong family orientation of the state fair winner.

SWEET ROLL DOUGH
Yield: Approximately 3 dozen rolls

    1   package active dry yeast
    ½   cup warm water
    1½ cups scalded milk
    ½   cup butter
    ½   cup sugar
    2   teaspoons salt
    6   cups flour
    2   eggs

Dissolve the yeast in warm water. Combine the milk, butter, sugar, salt and 3 cups of flour. Beat with an electric mixer for 2 to 4 minutes, until smooth and slippery. Beat in eggs one at a time, blending thoroughly. Add the yeast mixture and beat well. Add an additional 3 cups of flour and beat well. The dough will be sticky and will not require kneading.Place the dough in a greased bowl, cover with greased wax paper and lid. Place in the refrigerator for a minimum of 3–4 hours or up to 3 days. Roll out on a floured surface. Make desired shapes and let rise for 1½ hours. Bake in 375-degree oven for approximately 15 minutes. This dough can be used for dinner rolls, sweet rolls, tea rings, pizza and with addition of raisins, scones.

BLUE RIBBON WINNER, UTAH STATE FAIR

LOUANNE BEBB — GLENBURN, MAINE

If you decide to go hunting in Maine, contact Bill Bebb in Bradford. Bill is a professional guide who built his own log cabin on a 126-acre piece of land and converted it into a hunting camp. Bill's specialties are moose, deer and bear.

But the real treat in staying at the camp are the good foods that Bill's wife, Louanne, prepares in the kitchen. You can expect a blue ribbon bread topped with blue ribbon jams. She'll even prepare you a boxed lunch to take on the hunt. Inside you'll usually find her blue ribbon Toll House Cookies (page 249). Louanne enjoys competing at the Bangor State Fair, where she has already collected twenty blue ribbons in only three years of competition.

OLD–FASHIONED OATMEAL BREAD
Yield: 2 loaves

        2   packages active dry yeast
        ½   cup warm water
        2   Tablespoons sugar
        1   cup oatmeal (old-fashioned rolled oats)
        1   teaspoon salt
        ⅓   cup shortening
        ½   cup molasses
        2   eggs, beaten
        5½ to 6 cups sifted all purpose flour
        1½ cups boiling water

Dissolve the yeast in ½ cup of warm water to which 2 tablespoons of sugar have been added. In a mixing bowl combine the rolled oats, salt, shortening, molasses and boiling water. Stir until the shortening melts and the mixture is lukewarm; then add the eggs and the dissolved yeast. Stir to mix well. Stir in flour. Some flours are heavier than others and the size of the eggs used will make a difference in the amount of flour needed to make a dough. Knead the dough on a lightly floured board until smooth. Put into a large greased bowl, cover with waxed paper and a towel and refrigerate for 2 hours. (Yes, it will rise to the top of the bowl in the refrigerator). After 2 hours remove the dough from the refrigerator, and punch down. Knead the dough on a lightly floured board. Shape into 2 loaves. Put into greased bread pans. Let rise about one hour to double in bulk. Bake in a moderate oven (350 degrees) for 45–60 minutres. Remove from the pan and cool on racks.

BLUE RIBBON WINNER, BANGOR STATE FAIR

4

CAKES AND DESSERTS

CAKES

DORIS UNDERWOOD — LOUISVILLE, KENTUCKY
ELIZABETH HALL — LOUISVILLE, KENTUCKY
CATHY YOUNG — LOUISVILLE, KENTUCKY

*If you're on your way to the Kentucky State Fair we must warn you to be-
ware of the Outer Loop gang. These are some pretty tough hombres, and
they are out to keep you from winning a blue ribbon.*

*This notorious gang gets its name from the fact that they all live in
brick houses on Louisville's Outer Loop. The gang is headed up by Doris
Underwood, who can be a mean baker when she wants to be. Riding shot-
gun you can usually find Aunt Elizabeth Hall, another tough customer in
the culinary category.*

*The third member of this gang is Cathy Young, Doris's daughter. At
first you might think Cathy is sweet because she occasionally competes in
the Honey Department at the fair. But we warn you, approach with care:
Cathy is armed with some terrific baking skills.*

*All three brick hideouts on the Outer Loop were built by one of the
founders of this gang, grandpa Gus Hall. They were originally occupied
by strangers but have since returned to the members of the Hall family.*

*Thanks to Doris, Elizabeth and Cathy we have some very arresting reci-
pes to offer you. Below you will find both Elizabeth's Candied Fruit Cake
and her Golden Glow Cupcakes. Look for Cathy's Old-Fashioned Sugar
Cookies on page 224 and Doris's famous Strawberry-Rhubarb Pie on page
192.*

ELIZABETH HALL'S CANDIED FRUIT CAKE
Yield: 2 fruit cakes

- 1½ pounds pitted dates
- 1 pound candied cherries (whole)
- 1 pound candied pineapple
- 2 cups sifted all-purpose flour
- 2 teaspoons double acting baking powder
- ½ teaspoon salt
- 4 eggs
- 1 cup granulated sugar
- 2 pounds pecan halves
- Glaze (recipe below)

Cut dates and pineapple in coarse pieces and leave cherries whole. Keep a few pieces of cherries, pineapples and nuts to decorate the top. Combine the flour, salt and baking powder by sifting together. Mix the fruit and dry ingredients together, separating pieces so all are coated. Beat the eggs with an electric mixer until frothy; gradually adding sugar, beat until blended. Mix fruit and egg mixture with nuts. Grease two 9-inch tube pans or two 9×5×3-inch loaf pans and line with brown paper. Pack the dough into the pans, pressing down to fill empty spaces. Preheat oven to 275 degrees and bake. Bake tube pans 1¼ hours and loaf pans 1½ hours. When done, the top of the cake should look dry.

Glaze the top and decorate with reserved fruit and nuts, then brush glaze over them.

GLAZE
- ½ cup white corn syrup
- ¼ cup water

Let come to a boil and cool. Using a pastry brush, brush on cake.

GOLDEN GLOW CUPCAKES
Yield: 12 cupcakes

2 cups cake flour
3 teaspoons baking powder
1 teaspoon salt
1¼ cups sugar
½ cup shortening
1 cup milk
2 eggs
1 teaspoon vanilla

Sift together the flour, baking powder, salt and sugar. Add the shortening and ¾ cup of the milk and beat for 2 minutes. Add the remaining ¼ cup of milk, the eggs and vanilla and beat for 2 minutes. Pour the batter into greased muffin tins or paper cups, filling two-thirds up. Bake at 350 degrees for 30 minutes.

PAT HEATH — NEW KENT, VIRGINIA

Pat and Chuck Heath decided to give up the city life in order to get back to basics. They purchased a piece of land in rural Virginia and built their own "Lincoln Log" cabin home.

Everything they did was done the good old-fashioned way, by hand. Pillows in all shapes and colors, handhooked rugs, jars of jams, jellies, preserves and vegetables. Chuck even made fine quality custom furniture and cabinets.

Back to basics meant lots of good home cooking, which naturally led to the county and, eventually, the state fair cooking competition. Pat began to perfect her skills at the New Kent County Fair. She started on a small scale about three years ago but quickly became a leading competitor. In 1982 she took home seventy-eight ribbons and won the Sweepstakes award by collecting more points than any other contestant.

With that formidable showing behind her, Pat began preparing for the Virginia State Fair in September. Once again her skills paid off and the Heaths returned to their log cabin home with three red, two white and seven blue ribbons.

GOLDEN CRUNCH COFFEECAKE
Yield: 16 servings

    3 cups all-purpose flour, sifted
    3 teaspoons baking powder
  ½ teaspoon salt
  ½ cup butter
1½ cups sugar
    4 eggs
    1 teaspoon vanilla
    1 cup milk
    1 cup brown sugar, firmly packed
    2 Tablespoons butter
    2 Tablespoons flour
    1 teaspoon ground cinnamon
    1 cup chopped walnuts

Sift together 3 cups of flour, baking powder and salt. Cream together ½ cup of butter and the sugar until light and fluffy. Add eggs, one at a time, beating well after each addition. Beat in vanilla. Add dry ingredients alternately with milk, beating well after each addition. Spread half the batter in a greased 13×9×2-inch baking pan. Combine the brown sugar, 2 tablespoons of butter, 2 tablespoons of flour, cinnamon and walnuts. Mix well. Sprinkle half of the crumbs over the batter. Spread with remaining batter. Top with remaining crumbs. Bake in 350-degree oven for 45 minutes or until done. Cut in squares and serve warm.

BLUE RIBBON WINNER, VIRGINIA STATE FAIR

RICK ROY — MAHOMET, ILLINOIS

Rick Roy first became interested in cooking when he joined a 4–H baking club at the age of twelve. Over the years, as his interest grew, he began competing in local county fairs and festivals. This naturally led to his participation in the Illinois State Fair where he has been a frequent blue ribbon winner.

Rick's Toasted Butter Pecan Cake won a blue ribbon on "Bake-A-Cake-Day" at the 1980 Illinois State Fair. It then went on to compete in the Grand Champion Bake-off. No man has ever won that competition, but Rick may have come closest: he came in second by only two points.

Rick is now retired as a contestant but remains active as a judge at county fair competitions. In addition, he and his wife, Sherry, farm 1500 acres of land outside Mahomet, Illinois. Following are some "down on the farm" favorites from Rick's Royal Acres Grain Farm.

TOASTED BUTTER PECAN CAKE

   3 Tablespoons butter or margarine
1⅓ cups chopped pecans
   ¾ cup butter or margarine
1⅓ cups white sugar
1½ teaspoons vanilla
   2 eggs
   2 cups all-purpose flour, sifted
   2 teaspoons baking powder
   ¼ teaspoon salt
   ⅔ cup milk

Dot 3 tablespoons of butter over chopped pecans in a shallow pan. Toast in moderate oven (350 degrees) for 15 minutes, stirring occasionally. Cream ¾ cup of butter and add sugar gradually, creaming until light. Add vanilla. Add eggs one at a time, beating well after each addition. Sift together the dry ingredients and add to the creamed mixture alternately with milk, beating after each addition. Fold in 1 cup of toasted pecans (reserve ⅓ cup for frosting). Bake in two greased and lightly floured

8×1½-inch round pans in moderate 350-degree oven for 30–35 minutes until done. Cool in pans for 10 minutes. Remove and cool completely. Use the following recipe for frosting:

BUTTER PECAN FROSTING
　4　Tablespoons butter or margarine, softened
　3　cups sifted confectioners sugar
2½　to 3 Tablespoons light cream
　1　teaspoon vanilla
　⅓　cup toasted pecans

Mix first four ingredients until smooth. Frost cake and garnish with pecans. Double recipe if heavier frosting is desired.

BLUE RIBBON WINNER, ILLINOIS STATE FAIR

ITALIAN COCONUT CREAM CAKE

　2　cups granulated sugar
　5　eggs, separated
　½　cup butter
　½　cup solid vegetable shortening
　2　cups all-purpose flour
　1　teaspoon baking soda
　1　cup buttermilk
　2　cups coconut
　1　teaspoon vanilla
　½　cup choppped pecans

Cream together the sugar, egg yolks, butter and shortening. Add flour, baking soda, buttermilk, coconut, vanilla and pecans. Mix well. Beat the egg whites until stiff and fold into the above mixture. Pour the batter into three round 8-inch cake pans which have been greased and floured. Bake in 350-degree oven until done, approximately 30–35 minutes. Remove from pans and cool completely. Frost this rich and moist cake using the following recipe:

FROSTING

8 ounces cream cheese
6 Tablespoons butter
2 cups sifted confectioners sugar
1 teaspoon vanilla

Mix ingredients until smooth.

BLUE RIBBON WINNER, ILLINOIS STATE FAIR

CHARLES SMITH — CITRUS HEIGHTS, CALIFORNIA

If you need courage to enter a state fair contest, think of Charles Smith of Citrus Heights, California. He has been totally disabled with rheumatoid arthritis for the past eighteen years.

Four years ago, as therapy, he took up cooking as a hobby. Two years later, in 1981, he gained enough confidence to enter three cakes in the California State Fair baking contest. All three won blue ribbons. In 1982 he entered his Cocoa Fudge Cake and won an additional blue ribbon. This recipe also took third place in the Best of Class competition.

People like Charles Smith are an inspiration to all of us. We are pleased that he has allowed us to share his recipe with you.

COCOA FUDGE CAKE

2 cups cake flour
1½ cups sugar
⅔ cup cocoa
1½ teaspoons baking soda
1 teaspoon salt
1½ cups buttermilk
½ cup shortening
2 eggs
1 teaspoon vanilla

Preheat oven to 350 degrees. Grease and flour a 9×13-inch pan, two round 8-inch pans, or one Bundt pan. Beat all ingredients on low speed of a mixer, for 30 seconds, scraping the bowl constantly. Beat on high speed for 3 minutes. Bake 30–40 minutes until a toothpick comes out clean. Cool 10 minutes and turn out. Frost as desired.

BLUE RIBBON WINNER, CALIFORNIA STATE FAIR

ALYCE J. BULLIS — BALDWINSVILLE, NEW YORK

Wouldn't you love to try the cheesecake that won the New York State Fair? Thanks to Alyce Bullis you can now have that opportunity. We know you will enjoy it because it represents the true homemade tradition that state fair recipes offer. As Alyce herself pointed out, this blue ribbon winner is one that she prepares "mainly for her family and friends." That's what makes it so special!

CHEESECAKE

CRUST
 2 cups graham crackers
 ½ cup melted butter
 ¼ cup chopped pecans

Mix ingredients together, and pat into the bottom and sides of a 9-inch spring form pan. Bake at 350 degrees for 15 minutes. Cool thoroughly.

FILLING
 3 8-oz. packages cream cheese
1½ cups sugar
 4 eggs
 1 pint sour cream
 ½ pint heavy cream
 2 Tablespoons lemon juice
 ½ teaspoon vanilla

Blend the sugar and cream cheese. Add the eggs one at a time, beating well after each addition. Add the remaining ingredients and mix well. Pour into the cooled crust. Bake at 350 degrees for one hour. Turn off oven and let sit with oven door closed for one hour. Open oven door and let sit in oven for 30 minutes longer. Remove from tin and cool thoroughly.

GLAZE
⅔ cup apricot or peach jam
2 Tablespoons Amaretto liqueur
  Fresh peach slices

Mix together. Arrange fresh peach slices on top of the cooled cheesecake. Pour jam and liqueur mixture over all.

BLUE RIBBON WINNER, NEW YORK STATE FAIR

RHEA TERRY — ODESSA, TEXAS

Rhea Terry decided to enter a family favorite in the New Mexico State Fair and won the blue ribbon on her first try. Rhea, a Texas native, finds this a great holiday treat for non-fruit cake lovers, and we think you'll like its southwestern twist. This year Rhea and her family have moved back to Texas, and Rhea plans to enter the Texas State Fair.

LEMON FRUIT CAKE

1 pound pecans
1 bottle (2 oz.) lemon extract
2 cups sugar
4 cups flour
2 cups butter or margarine
8 eggs
2 teaspoons baking powder
1 pound candied pineapple
1 pound candied cherries

Soak pecans, covered tightly, overnight in the lemon extract. Cream the butter and sugar together. Add eggs. Sift the baking powder and flour together. Halve the cherries, quarter the pineapple slices but leave the pecans in large pieces. Use a small amount of flour mixture to lightly coat the fruits and nuts. Slowly beat the remaining flour into the butter and egg mixture. Fold in the fruits and nuts. Pour the batter into a greased and floured tube pan and bake slowly at 225–250 degrees for 2 hours plus, until cake tests done. Use red and green fruit for a festive touch. Soak lightly in brandy and wrap well with cheesecloth. Overwrap cheesecloth with foil.

BLUE RIBBON WINNER, NEW MEXICO STATE FAIR

CINDY PATTERSON — COVINGTON, VIRGINIA

Cindy Patterson of Covington, Virginia, traveled to the West Virginia State Fair to win a blue ribbon in the cake contest. It was no easy feat. One of the other contestants was Beulah Arthur of Clintonville, West Virginia . . . Cindy's grandmother.

Cindy, twelve years of age, is in the seventh grade at Boiling Springs elementary school. She is a cheerleader and a 4–H member, which may be where she learned to compete so well against her grandmother.

BLACK WALNUT SPICE CAKE

    ½ cup soft shortening
    ¾ cup brown sugar
    ¾ cup white sugar
    2 eggs
    2 cups sifted Softasilk, or 1¾ cup sifted all-purpose flour
    1 teaspoon baking soda
    ⅓ teaspoon allspice
    ½ teaspoon salt
    1 cup buttermilk
    ⅔ cup black walnuts

Grease and flour two 8-inch round cake pans. Cream the shortening and brown and white sugars together until fluffy. Thoroughly beat in the eggs. Set aside. Sift together the flour, baking soda, allspice and salt. Alternately stir buttermilk and the flour mixture into the creamed butter and sugar mixture. Last, fold in the black walnuts. Pour into prepared pans and bake at 350 degrees for 35 to 40 minutes or until cake tests done.

ICING
½ stick margarine
½ cup brown sugar
¼ cup milk
1 teaspoon vanilla
½ cup confectioners sugar (approximately)

Bring the margarine and brown sugar to a boil. Remove from heat and add the milk and vanilla. Then beat in enough confectioners sugar to make icing stiff enough to spread.

BLUE RIBBON WINNER, WEST VIRGINIA STATE FAIR

KAY ATKINSON — MILWAUKEE, WISCONSIN

In 1973 Kay Atkinson saw an ad in the local newspaper announcing the upcoming Wisconsin State Fair. Just for fun she decided to mail in the coupon and enter the cooking competition. That first year she won a fourth-place ribbon and has become a regular contestant ever since. Mrs. Atkinson has taken first-place honors for a number of her recipes over the years. We think you'll enjoy her Carrot Cake recipe, which won a blue ribbon at the 1982 Wisconsin State Fair.

CARROT CAKE

2 cups sugar
1 cup oil

    4 eggs, unbeaten
    3 cups grated raw carrots
    ¾ cup nuts
    2 cups flour
    2 teaspoons baking soda
    2 teaspoons cinnamon
    ½ teaspoon salt

Cream the sugar and oil until light and fluffy, then add the eggs. Cream again. Fold in the carrots and nuts. Blend with the creamed mixture. Grease and flour a 11×15-inch sheet pan or three 8- or 9-inch round pans. Bake at 350 degrees about 40 minutes, or until a toothpick inserted in the center comes out clean.

    FROSTING
    1 package (8 oz.) cream cheese
    1 pound confectioners sugar
    ¼ cup butter
    1 teaspoon vanilla

Beat until smooth. Add nuts if desired.

BLUE RIBBON WINNER, WISCONSIN STATE FAIR

LISA LONG — DECATUR, TEXAS

In addition to maintaining a straight A average in the eighth grade, thirteen-year-old Lisa manages to find time for a wide range of activities. She's an active 4–H member, plays junior high basketball and blows a mean sax for the All-District band.

Lisa first entered state fair competition at the age of four and has been participating successfully ever since. A list of the awards she has won at the state fair and in 4–H competition would almost require a book itself. Of special note is the fact that she took first place in a state 4–H photography project. Her picture of her brother Wayland riding his cutting horse is now on display at the National 4–H Center in Chicago. Next year it will tour the country with the Kodak display.

Lucky for us Lisa also expresses her talents in the kitchen. She is, no doubt, inspired by her aunt, Sue Mercer, who is a home economist.

Lisa has won many ribbons in the cooking contest at the Texas State Fair. We have selected two that we think you will enjoy.

THREE–LAYER BROWNIE DELIGHTS OR BROWNIE SQUARES
Yield: About 3 dozen squares

BAR
½ cup margarine
1 ounce unsweetened chocolate
1 cup sugar
1 cup flour
2 cups chopped pecans
1 teaspoon baking powder
1 teaspoon vanilla
2 eggs

FILLING
6 ounces cream cheese
½ cup sugar
2 Tablespoons flour
¼ cup margarine, softened
1 egg
1 teaspoon vanilla
¼ cup chopped pecans
1 package (6 oz.) chocolate chips

FROSTING
¼ cup margarine
1 ounce unsweetened chocolate
¼ cup milk
2 ounces cream cheese
3 cups powdered sugar
1 teaspoon vanilla
2 cups miniature marshmallows

Preheat oven to 350 degrees. Grease and flour a 13×9-inch pan. In a large saucepan, melt ½ cup margarine, and 1 ounce chocolate. Add the remaining bar ingredients and mix well. Spread in the prepared pan. Cream the filling ingredients except the chocolate chips. Spread over the chocolate mixture. Sprinkle with chocolate chips. Bake 25–35 minutes, or until a toothpick inserted into the center comes out clean. Sprinkle with marshallows and bake 2 minutes longer. Melt the margarine, chocolate, milk and cream cheese. Stir in powdered sugar and vanilla until smooth. Immediately pour over marshmallows and swirl together. Cut into squares.

BLUE RIBBON WINNER, TEXAS STATE FAIR

TEXAS PECAN CAKE

½ cup butter
½ cup vegetable shortening
2 cups sugar
5 eggs, separated
2 cups all-purpose flour, sifted
1 cup buttermilk
1 teaspoon baking soda
1 teaspoon vanilla
½ to 1 cup chopped pecans

Cream the butter, shortening and sugar. Add the egg yolks one at a time, beating after each addition. Combine the baking soda and flour. Add alternately with buttermilk, beginning and ending with dry ingredients. Add vanilla and pecans. Fold in stiffly beaten egg whites. Pour batter into two 8-inch pans, greased and floured. Bake at 325 degrees for 25–30 minutes.

FILLING AND ICING FOR TOP
1 package (8 oz.) cream cheese
1 stick butter

1 teaspoon vanilla
1 pound powdered sugar
½ to 1 cup chopped pecans

Cream softened cream cheese and butter. Add vanilla. Beat in powdered sugar a little at a time. Add pecans. Spread between layers and on top of cake.

ICING FOR SIDES OF CAKE
1 Tablespoon cornstarch
½ cup white sugar
½ cup brown sugar
1 cup evaporated milk
3 egg yokes, slightly beaten
½ cup butter
1 teaspoon vanilla
½ cup finely ground pecans

Combine the cornstarch and sugars in a saucepan. Stir in milk. Blend in egg yolks. Stir in butter and vanilla. Cook over medium heat, stirring constantly until thickened. Remove from heat and add pecans. Let cool slightly before spreading.

BLUE RIBBON WINNER, TEXAS STATE FAIR

BRENDA FINCHER — APEX, NORTH CAROLINA

If you want a great pound cake you have to go to the Carolinas, where pound cakes are a state tradition. And if you want to try the best of the best, sink your teeth into Brenda Fincher's blue ribbon winner at the North Carolina State Fair.

Brenda has been visiting the state fair for years but has only recently decided to enter the cooking competition. Winning a blue ribbon on one of her first tries proves, once again, that newcomers have an equal chance of taking top honors.

MILLION DOLLAR POUND CAKE

    3 cups sugar
    2 cups butter, softened
    6 eggs, room temperature
    4 cups all-purpose flour
    ¾ cup milk
    1 teaspoon almond extract
    1 teaspoon vanilla extract

Combine the sugar and butter, and cream together until light and fluffy. Add eggs, one at a time, beating well after each addition. Alternately add flour and milk to the creamed mixture, beating well after each addition. Stir in flavorings. Pour batter into a well-greased and floured 10-inch tube pan. Bake at 300 degrees for one hour and 40 minutes or until cake tests done.

BLUE RIBBON WINNER, NORTH CAROLINA STATE FAIR

LAEL ARRASMITH — AMES, IOWA

It has been about twenty-five years since Emma Arrasmith first taught her granddaughter Lael how to make an angel food cake. Lael learned well. In 1982 she used her grandmother's recipe to take first place in the angel food cake category at the Iowa State Fair.

Lael spends the long cold winter in Iowa sifting through seed catalogues and caring for her many house plants, including a 100-year-old Christmas cactus. Fortunately for us she has maintained her interest in baking and has allowed us to share the recipe that has been in her family for at least three generations.

GRANDMA ARRASMITH'S ANGEL FOOD CAKE

- 1½ cups sugar
- 1 cup cake flour or,
- 1 cup plus 2 Tablespoons all-purpose flour
- 1½ cups egg whites, room temperature (12 eggs)
- ¾ teaspoon salt
- 1½ teaspoon cream of tartar
- 1¼ teaspoons vanilla
- ½ teaspoon almond extract

Sift the two flours together with ½ cup of the sugar six times. In another bowl, beat the egg whites until frothy, then add the salt, cream of tartar and vanilla and almond extracts. Continue beating until the egg whites stay in the bowl when inverted. Fold the remaining cup of sugar into the egg whites 2 tablespoons at a time. Fold 100 times. Fold the flour mixture into the egg whites 2 tablespoons at a time. Pour batter into an ungreased tube pan and bake at 350 degrees for 60 minutes.

BLUE RIBBON WINNER, IOWA STATE FAIR

THE FOLSE FAMILY — DALLAS, TEXAS

BIG ORANGE CHIFFON CAKE

- 5 egg yolks, unbeaten
- 8 egg whites (reserve 3 yolks for frosting)
- 2¼ cups sifted cake flour
- 1 Tablespoon double-acting baking powder
- 1½ cups granulated sugar
- 1 teaspoon salt
- ½ cup salad oil

    3 Tablespoons grated orange rind
    ¾ cup orange juice
    ½ teaspoon cream of tartar

Let eggs come to room temperature and preheat oven to 325 degrees. Into a large bowl sift together the flour, sugar, baking powder and salt. Follow with the next ingredients in this precise order: make a well in the flour and pour in salad oil, add egg yolks, orange rind and orange juice. Using an electric mixer at medium speed, beat until smooth. Pour egg whites into another large bowl and add cream of tartar. Beat with mixer at high speed until whites become very stiff and hold peaks. Do not underbeat. They should be stiffer than for meringue. Be certain beaters and bowl are clean and free of grease. Slowly pour the egg yolk batter over the whites and fold into the mixture gently, until just blended. Turn the batter into an ungreased 10-inch tube or angel cake pan. Insert and withdraw a table knife all around the batter to lift out any air bubbles. Bake at 325 degrees for 55 minutes then increase temperature to 350 degrees and bake for another 10–15 minutes or until cake tests done. Remove, invert pan and cool completely before removing from pan. Frost with Orange Butter Cream Frosting.

    FROSTING
    1 cup (2 sticks) butter, softened
    ⅛ teaspoon salt
    7 cups sifted confectioners sugar
    3 unbeaten egg yolks (saved from whites in above recipe)
    1 Tablespoon grated orange rind
    2 Tablespoons milk
    2 Tablespoons Grand Marnier liqueur

Beat all ingredients together until a smooth frosting is formed. Add more milk if needed to make a smooth texture. Spread on cake.

BLUE RIBBON WINNER, TEXAS STATE FAIR

CHOCOLATE ANGEL CAKE

15 egg whites (2 cups)
2 cups sugar
1¼ cups cake flour, sifted
¼ cup powdered sugar, sifted
¼ cup cocoa
½ teaspoon salt
1½ teaspoons cream of tartar
1 teaspoon vanilla extract

Sift the cake flour 4 times then measure 1¼ cups of it. Sift the powdered sugar 4 times, then measure ¼ cup of it and mix into the flour. Sift cocoa 4 times, then measure ¼ cup of it and mix into the flour. Sift all together once and place on wax paper.

Place all the egg whites into a large copper egg bowl. The eggs MUST be at room temperature, and greater success will be achieved if the eggs are fresh from the hen house and have not been in cold storage. Add ½ teaspoon of salt to the egg whites and beat until they are just frothy or foamy. At this point, add the 1½ teaspoons of cream of tartar. Using a large wire whisk, beat the egg whites until soft peaks form. Be certain to stop before they become stiff or "dry." Now comes a very important process — that of gently and gradually folding the sugar into the eggs. Continuing to use the wire whisk to fold with, start adding 1 to 2 tablespoons of the sugar at a time by sprinkling it over the surface of the egg whites. EXTREMELY carefully and slowly lift the whites over the sugar with the whisk and gently turn them down to the bottom of the bowl. About 12 to 14 strokes such as this are required to mix and dissolve each addition of sugar. Carefully continue adding the sugar until 2 cups are incorporated into the egg whites. Do not hurry this process! It may require 15 minutes or more. When all the sugar is used, then sprinkle the vanilla over the surface of the mixture and fold into the whites the same way, using the whisk.

Now pour the flour mixture into the sifter and gradually sift small amounts onto the egg white mixture. Fold this into the batter with the whisk in the same manner the sugar was added. Again, do not hurry this procedure. Continue until all the flour is combined into the batter.

Carefully pour the batter into an ungreased 10-inch tube pan. Using a spatula, gently insert it into the batter several times and withdraw it gently. This removes any large air bubbles that may be captured in the batter.

Place in a pre-heated 275-degree oven and slowly bake for one hour and 20 minutes or until the cake tests done. A wire cake tester is inserted into the cake and when it comes out clean, it is an indication that it is done.

Remove from oven and invert the pan over a soft drink bottle and let it cool thoroughly before removing from pan.

Clean off any crumbs and ice with Coffee Cream Frosting (below) or your favorite icing or slice and top with fresh fruit or berries and whipped cream. Also, this may be served with chilled brandied fruit.

COFFEE CREAM FROSTING
  1 cup butter, softened
  ½ teaspoon salt
  5 cups powdered sugar, sifted
  7 to 8 Tablespoons milk
  1 teaspoon vanilla
  3 Tablespoons powdered instant coffee

Place the butter in a mixing bowl and cream it until it is light, using a rotary mixer. Add the salt and gradually add the powdered sugar as you continue mixing. Add the milk as the mixture thickens so as to keep the icing spreadable. Add the vanilla and coffee and continue to beat until all the sugar is well absorbed. Spread over the cake. Some of the icing may be placed in a pastry bag and piped over the cake in decorative patterns.

BLUE RIBBON WINNER, BEST OF SHOW, TEXAS STATE FAIR

CHOCOLATE MINT TORTE

  2 envelopes unflavored gelatin
  ½ cup water
  1¼ cups brown sugar
  ⅔ cup crème de menthe
  1 package (12 oz.) chocolate chips
  8 eggs, separated
  ½ teaspoon salt
  2 cups heavy cream (for whipping)
     Pie crust dough (sufficient for 4 9-inch circles)
     Sliced almonds

In a saucepan mix the gelatin, water, ½ cup of brown sugar, and crème de menthe. Place it over low heat and stir until all is dissolved and well mixed. Add the chocolate chips and stir until they melt. Remove from heat and stir in the egg yolks, one at a time, beating after each addition. Cool.

Place the egg whites in a mixing bowl, add the salt and beat until stiff peaks form. Gradually beat in the remaining ¾ cup of brown sugar until the meringue is very stiff. Next, carefully fold the beaten egg whites into the chocolate mixture. Whip the 2 cups of cream until stiff and fold it into the mixture. Refrigerate until it starts to set.

In the meantime make some pie crust dough from your favorite recipe and, on a floured board, roll it extremely thin. Cut it into four 9-inch circles. Preheat the oven to 425 degrees. Place the circles between two cookie sheets and bake for 10 minutes. Remove the top cookie sheet and continue cooking until the pastry rounds are done to a light brown. Remove from oven and cool. Handle carefully as they will be crisp, delicate and flaky!

Assembling the Torte. On a large round platter or cake serving plate place a little dab of the chocolate mint filling near the center. Place one of the pastry rounds on this very neatly. This acts as a glue and prevents the torte from slipping. Spoon a layer of the filling all over the pastry and sprinkle the surface with sliced almonds. Next place another pastry round on top and cover with filling, sprinkle with almonds. Continue until the four pastry rounds are used — finishing with a layer of the filling. Chill until firm.

You will have some of the filling left over. Spoon it into stemmed glasses or custard cups, refrigerate, and serve at another time as a mousse.

TOPPING
2 cups whipping cream
1 cup sugar
1 Tablespoon vanilla
German sweet chocolate

Whip the cream until thickened and gradually add the sugar. Flavor with vanilla and continue beating until stiff. "Ice" the entire torte with whipped cream. Some of the whipped cream can be placed in a pastry bag and piped onto the completed torte as decoration. Shave some German Sweet Chocolate with a potato peeler and sprinkle over the top as a final decoration. Chill for several hours and serve cold.

BLUE RIBBON WINNER, BEST OF SHOW, TEXAS STATE FAIR

DOROTHEA COVERDALE — HARRINGTON, DELAWARE

Horse racing is the favorite pastime of Dorothea and Lindale Coverdale. They raise horses in Delaware and race them at the Harrington Racetrack and at Dover Downs. Fortunately, while Lindale's horses are running for the roses, Dorothea's bakings are vying for blue ribbons. Below is the Applesauce Cake recipe that won top honors at the Delaware State Fair.

APPLESAUCE CAKE
Yield: 16 servings

- 15 ounces seedless raisins
- 8 ounces black walnuts, chopped fine
- 2 cups sugar
- Pinch of salt
- 1 Tablespoon cinnamon
- 1 teaspoon nutmeg
- ¾ cup butter
- 2½ cups all-purpose flour
- 2 teaspoons baking soda
- 2 cups applesauce, chunky or smooth

Cover raisins with 1 inch of water and simmer until soft. Drain and let cool. Coat chopped nuts with flour and set aside. Cream the butter and sugar together, at medium speed on the mixer. Heat the applesauce very warm, and add baking soda. Add this mixture to the creamed sugar and butter, then add flour and salt, stirring well until mixed. Add raisins and nuts. Pour in a greased and floured tube pan. Bake in 350-degree oven 50–60 minutes, or until a toothpick inserted comes out clean. Remove from oven, let set 10 minutes covered with a tea towel, then turn out on plate covered with powered sugar.

BLUE RIBBON WINNER, DELAWARE STATE FAIR

CISSY WYATT — SYLACAUGA, ALABAMA

Cissy Wyatt is truly a beautiful woman. She donates her cash prizes from the Alabama State Fair to her garden club for use in Sylacauga's beautification program. Cissy has won over five hundred ribbons in the past twenty years and Sylacauga has won many national and state awards for its cleanliness and beautification.

On the day we called, the Wyatts were celebrating Auburn's victory in the Tangerine Bowl. Cissy's husband, David, and their three sons, Steve, Hub and Mark, are all Auburn graduates.

The Wyatt marriage got off to quite an unusual start thirty-three years ago. Cissy and David were married on the nationally televised "Bride and Groom" show on November 10, 1949.

Cissy's Lane Cake will provide a beautiful addition to any celebration in your family.

LANE CAKE

    1 cup vegetable shortening
    2 cups sugar
    7 egg whites (reserve yolks for frosting)
    3 cups plain or all-purpose flour, sifted twice before measuring
    ½ teaspoon salt
    2 teaspoons baking powder
    1 cup milk
    2 teaspoons vanilla

Cream the shortening and sugar well. Add unbeaten egg whites all at once. Turn the mixer on low and mix just until smooth. Do not overbeat. Sift the flour, salt and baking powder together. Add all at once to the creamed mixture. Add all the milk, turn the mixer on low and combine. Stop the mixer and add the vanilla and beat until smooth. Bake in three 10-inch cake pans, greased and floured, in 325-degree oven for 12 minutes. Don't pour the layers too thick. You can always make a few cupcakes with leftover batter to serve with lemon or hot fudge sauce.

    FROSTING
       7 egg yolks
       ½ cup (1 stick) margarine, softened
       ½ cup (1 stick) butter, softened
    1½ cups sugar
       1 No. 2 can crushed pineapple, drained well

½ teaspoon salt, scant
1½ teaspoons vanilla
1 cup dark raisins
1 cup chopped pecans
1 cup coconut

In a double boiler, beat the egg yolks well. Add the sugar and beat until light and fluffy. Add the salt, margarine, butter and pineapple. Cook over medium heat until thick, stirring occasionally. Remove from hot water and add vanilla. When completely cold, add 1 cup dark raisins, 1 cup chopped pecans and 1 cup coconut. Mix and spread on cold cake layers.

BLUE RIBBON WINNER, ALABAMA STATE FAIR

EDITH ISIDORO — ALBUQUERQUE, NEW MEXICO

The New Mexico State Fair gives us a blue ribbon Banana Nut Cake. The blue ribbon was won by Edith Isidoro, a graduate student at the state university. The rigors of study have not stopped Edith from competing at the state fair. She has been a regular contestant since her junior high school days.

Edith credits her cooking talents to her mother, also an award winner and a home economist.

BANANA NUT CAKE

(This recipe has been adjusted for 5000 ft. elevation. For cooking at low altitudes increase flour by 3 tablespoons and temperature to 400 degrees.)

2½ cups cake flour, sifted
1⅓ cups sugar
1 teaspoon baking powder
1 teaspoon baking soda
1 teaspoon salt

⅔ cup shortening, softened
¾ cup buttermilk
1¼ cups mashed ripe bananas (about 3)
3 large eggs
⅔ cup pecans, finely chopped

Sift the first five ingredients together. Add the shortening, buttermilk and bananas and beat for 2 minutes. Add the eggs and beat an additional 2 minutes. Fold in the nuts. Bake in two round 9-inch pans, greased and floured, at 375 degrees for 25 minutes or until it tests done with a toothpick. Ice with any white icing. "For the fair I decorated the top with whole shelled pecans," says Edith Isidoro.

BLUE RIBBON WINNER, NEW MEXICO STATE FAIR

NORMA THOMPSON — LARAMIE, WYOMING

WHITE CAKE

(High altitude recipe. For cooking at low altitudes increase flour by 3 tablespoons and temperature to 400 degrees.)

3 cups cake flour, sifted
2 teaspoons baking powder
¾ teaspoon salt
1½ cups sugar
½ cup vegetable shortening
1 cup water
2 teaspoons clear vanilla
4 egg whites

Mix and sift dry ingredients into a mixing bowl. Add shortening and water. Beat 2 minutes with an electric mixer, slow to medium speed. Scrape the sides and bottom of the bowl several times. Add vanilla and egg whites. Beat 2 more minutes on same speed. Turn into two 8-inch round, greased and floured pans or one 8×12×2-inch pan. Bake at 375 degrees for 25–30 minutes. Cool 10 minutes and turn out on wire rack. Ice with Butter Cream Icing.

BUTTER CREAM ICING
- 1 pound (4 cups) powdered sugar, sifted
- ½ cup vegetable shortening
- ¼ cup warm water
- 1 teaspoon clear vanilla

Put all the ingredients in a mixing bowl and beat about 5 minutes. It may take more water. Spread evenly over cake.

BLUE RIBBON WINNER, WYOMING STATE FAIR

IMOGENE JOHNSON — CHARLES CITY, VIRGINIA

1–2–3–4 CAKE

- 1 cup butter
- 2 cups sugar
- 4 eggs
- 3 cups flour
- 1 teaspoon salt
- 3 teaspoons baking powder
- 1 cup milk
- 1 teaspoon vanilla

Separate the eggs and beat egg whites. Beat the butter and sugar until very light and creamy. Add well-beaten egg yolks. Sift flour twice with salt and baking powder. Add milk a little at a time with flour. Add vanilla. Fold in beaten egg whites. Bake in a moderate oven (350 degrees) for about 30 minutes.

BUTTER CHOCOLATE FROSTING

4 squares unsweetened chocolate
1 cup confectioners sugar
2 Tablespoons hot water
2 eggs
6 Tablespoons butter

Melt the chocolate in a double boiler. Remove from boiling water. Add the sugar and water and blend. Add the eggs, one at a time, beating well after each addition. Add the butter, one-third at a time, again beating well after each amount is added. More sugar may be added to make the spreading consistency right.

BLUE RIBBON WINNER, VIRGINIA STATE FAIR

GERMAN CHOCOLATE CAKE

1 package (4 oz.) Bakers German Chocolate
½ cup boiling water
1 cup butter or margarine
2 cups sugar
4 eggs, separated
1 teaspoon vanilla
2½ cups flour
½ teaspoon salt
1 teaspoon baking soda
1 cup buttermilk

Melt the chocolate in boiling water. Cool. Separate the eggs and beat egg whites; set aside. Cream the butter and sugar until fluffy. Add egg yolks, one at a time, and beat well after each. Add melted chocolate and vanilla. Mix well. Sift together flour, salt and soda. Add alternately with buttermilk to the chocolate mixture, beating after each addition until smooth. Fold in the beaten egg whites. Grease and flour three 8- or 9-inch layer pans. Pour batter into pans and bake at 350 degrees for 20 to 30 minutes until done. Cool and frost tops only.

COCONUT PECAN FROSTING
1 cup evaporated milk
1 cup sugar
3 egg yolks
½ cup butter or margarine
1 teaspoon vanilla
1⅓ cups coconut
1 cup chopped pecans

Combine the first five ingredients. Add the coconut and pecans. Cook and stir over medium heat until thickened, about 12 minutes. Beat or stir until thick enough to spread. Makes 2½ cups.

BLUE RIBBON WINNER, VIRGINIA STATE FAIR

JOY STARKEY — CHARLES CITY, VIRGINIA

CHAMPION SPONGE CAKE

1¼ cups flour, sifted
1 cup sugar
½ teaspoon baking powder
½ teaspoon salt
6 eggs, separated
1 teaspoon cream of tartar
½ cup sugar
¼ cup water
1 teaspoon vanilla

Sift together the flour, sugar, baking powder and salt. Beat egg whites at high speed until frothy. Add cream of tartar. Gradually add the ½ cup of sugar, beating until stiff but not until airy peaks form. Combine egg yolks, water, vanilla and dry ingredients. Beat at medium high speed until thick and lemon colored (about 4 minutes). Gradually fold yolk mixture into the egg whites. Pour the batter into an ungreased 10-inch tube pan. Bake in 350-degree oven for 45 minutes or until cake tests done. Invert the tube pan on a funnel to cool. When completely cooled, remove from pan.

Although an icing recipe is given with the cake, Joy says she never ices it for the fair or at home. It is good served with fresh fruit or whipped cream, she suggests. Mrs. Johnson, Joy's sister, has a trick for making a cake turn out perfectly flat for icing that she was a tad reluctant to share but finally did. She turns her cake out on a linen towel and presses the center to flatten it.

BLUE RIBBON WINNER, VIRGINIA STATE FAIR

ANNA J. STONE — CIRCLEVILLE, OHIO

On a one-acre plot in Circleville, Ohio, Anna Stone and her husband, Ray, raise vegetables, berries and several varieties of fruit trees. Summer is a busy and happy time for Anna.

Anna enjoys competing at the Pickaway County Fair, at Circleville's famous pumpkin show and, of course, at the wonderful Ohio State Fair.

She was the Grand Champion at the Ohio State Fair this year, having accumulated the highest total points in arts and crafts. She competes in needlepoint and quilting in addition to the baking and canning categories. We thank her for her very special blue ribbon recipes.

Below is Anna's Chocolate Cake, which measured up to the exacting standards of the judges at the Ohio State Fair. On page 223 you will find her old family recipe for Raisin Date Cookies, which Anna considers her very best recipe. You can also look for her Pickled Beets on page 270.

CHOCOLATE CAKE

This cake has won a blue ribbon for the last two years at the state fair. In 1981 it was first out of forty-five chocolate cakes. This same recipe has won five years in a row at the Ohio State Fair.

    ¾ cup butter
    2¼ cups sugar
    1½ teaspoons vanilla
     3 eggs
     3 cups cake flour, sifted
    1½ teaspoons baking soda
    1½ cups ice water
     3 ounces unsweetened chocolate, melted

Cream together the butter and sugar in a mixing bowl until light and fluffy. Add vanilla and beat well. Add the eggs and beat well. Add melted chocolate and blend. Sift together the dry ingredients. Add alternately with water, starting with the flour and ending with the flour (the magic touch that makes a fine textured cake) Pour into three 9-inch layer pans, greased and lined with waxed paper. Bake at 350 degrees for 25–30 minutes. Cool on a rack 10 minutes and remove from pans.

    CHOCOLATE FROSTING
    ½ cup hydrogenated shortening
    8 cups sifted confectioners sugar
    ¼ cup half and half
    2 egg whites
    1 Tablespoon vanilla
    4 ounces melted chocolate

Blend all ingredients, beat on high speed until fluffy.

BLUE RIBBON WINNER, OHIO STATE FAIR

Mom doesn't enter the North Carolina State Fair but she's an inspiration to her three children who do compete. Nancy Brinkley admits that fair time is a little too hectic for her to participate but she encourages her children Julia (age eleven), Andrea (nine) and Brian (seven) to continue testing their own skills.

Mrs. Brinkley believes that children naturally enjoy cooking if their parents will allow them into the kitchen. She does, and the Brinkley children have each walked off with a blue ribbon. Next year the competition for space in the Brinkley kitchen is going to get tougher. Nancy's fourth child, Michael (age four), is planning to enter for the first time.

Brian's Mandarin Orange Cake and Andrea's Pound Cake are shown below. Look for her Butterscotch Brownies and Julia's Date Bars on page 222.

BRIAN BRINKLEY — CARY, NORTH CAROLINA

MANDARIN ORANGE CAKE

 1 box yellow cake mix
 ½ cup (one stick) margarine, softened
 4 eggs
 1 small can mandarin oranges with juice

Combine all ingredients and beat for 3 minutes. Bake at 325 degrees for 25 minutes. Makes three 9-inch layers. After layers have cooled ice them.

 ICING
 1 9-ounce container Cool Whip
 1 medium-size can crushed pineapple with juice
 3 ounces instant vanilla pudding
 1 cup pecans (optional)

Mix all ingredients and spread on layers. Store in refrigerator.

BLUE RIBBON WINNER, NORTH CAROLINA STATE FAIR

ANDREA BRINKLEY — CARY, NORTH CAROLINA

OLD-FASHIONED POUND CAKE

  1 cup butter
1¾ cup sugar
  1 teaspoon vanilla
  4 large eggs
  2 cups all-purpose flour

Cream butter, sugar and flavoring until fluffy. Add eggs, one at a time, and beat; continue beating at high speed for 10 minutes. Fold in flour (do not beat). Pour into greased and floured tube cake pan. Bake in a 350-degree oven for 1 hour.

BLUE RIBBON WINNER, NORTH CAROLINA STATE FAIR

MARCIA WALLEN — LINCOLN, NEBRASKA

Here's a terrific pumpkin recipe from a pumpkin specialist in Lincoln, Nebraska. Marcia Wallen is a registered dietician and her husband Stan, a Ph.D., is an extension food scientist at the University of Nebraska. Those are pretty good qualifications for a family that likes to cook.

But what really qualifies them in the pumpkin category is the side business they enjoy. Every autumn the Wallens open up a pumpkin stand called "The Pumpkin Patch" and sell gourds, Indian corn and, of course, pumpkins grown on their five acre plot. As an offshoot of this business, Marcia has compiled a recipe booklet called Pumpkin Potpourri *containing about seventy-five blue ribbon winners from the Nebraska State Fair.*

The Wallens have two children, Becky, age seven, and B.J., who is two and a half. This is their first attempt in a food competition but they have

CAKES AND DESSERTS / 143

previously enjoyed attending the Nebraska State Fair as well as the state fairs in New Mexico and Iowa.

If you are passing through Lincoln in the fall, stop at "The Pumpkin Patch" for some fresh pumpkins and Marcia's own cooking hints. In the meantime your family will enjoy this Pumpkin Nut Bundt Cake, blue ribbon winner at the Nebraska State Fair.

PUMPKIN NUT BUNDT CAKE

    1 package yellow cake mix
    2 teaspoons cinnamon
    ½ teaspoon ginger
    ½ teaspoon nutmeg
    3 eggs
       Water
    1 cup cooked pumpkin
    1 cup finely chopped nuts
       Lemon glaze (recipe below)

Combine the cake mix and spices in a bowl. Add the pumpkin, eggs and water as directed on cake mix package, substituting pumpkin for ⅓ cup of the water. Mix as directed. Stir in nuts. Pour batter into greased and floured 10-inch tube pan, or Bundt, or fluted pan (9-cup capacity). Bake in 350-degree oven for 45–60 minutes or until done. Cool 10 minutes; remove from pan. Drizzle with Lemon Glaze.

LEMON GLAZE
    1 cup powdered sugar
    1 teaspoon lemon juice
    ½ teaspoon grated lemon rind
       Cream

Combine the first three ingredients. Add just enough cream to make the glaze slightly runny.

BLUE RIBBON WINNER, NEBRASKA STATE FAIR

RUTH CROMMELIN — STANTON, NEW JERSEY

Ruth Crommelin has been active in 4-H since she was a child. This year she was selected as Hunterdon County 4-H Leader of the Year.

Her husband, Philip, is a consultant in electrostatic precipitation and she is active in several local organizations as well as working part time as secretary of the church in Stanton. Ruth also tends a flock of twenty-five Dorset sheep on her seven-acre farm in Stanton, New Jersey. Her love of sheep goes back many years and she presently serves as Secretary–Treasurer of the New Jersey Dorset Sheep Association.

Ruth has won numerous awards for baking, canning and flower growing over the past fifteen years. One of those was a blue ribbon for her Tropical Dream Cake recipe at the Flemington Fair.

TROPICAL DREAM CAKE

        2   cups granulated sugar
        1   cup oil
        3   eggs
        1   can (8 oz.) crushed pineapple, undrained
     1½   teaspoons vanilla
        2   cups all-purpose flour
        1   cup whole wheat flour
        1   teaspoon salt
        1   teaspoon baking soda
        1   teaspoon baking powder
        1   teaspoon cinnamon
        2   cups finely diced bananas

Beat the sugar and oil in a large mixing bowl; add the eggs, one at a time, beating after each addition. Blend in the undrained pineapple and vanilla. Stir together the flours, salt, baking soda, baking powder and cinnamon; blend into pineapple mixture. Stir in bananas. Turn into a greased 10-inch fluted tube pan. Bake at 350 degrees for 60–70 minutes, until a wooden pick comes out clean. Cool in the pan for 10 minutes; then turn out on a wire rack to finish cooling.

GLAZE
1¾ cups confectioners sugar, sifted
2 to 3 Tablespoons orange juice

Combine confectioners sugar and enough orange juice to make a "drippable" mixture. When cake is cool, drizzle glaze on top and down sides.

BLUE RIBBON WINNER, FLEMINGTON (N.J.) FAIR

GERALDINE LEWIS — FELTON, PENNSYLVANIA

America's best cooks look forward to the stringent competition at state fair cooking contests. Many begin planning months in advance. Some overcome tremendous obstacles to participate.

Geraldine Lewis of Felton, Pennsylvania, had serious surgery just a few months before the York County Fair in August. But even that couldn't keep her from participating in the baking contest. As her son Mike indicated, "She's an active woman, there's not much that can stop her."

Below is the Devil's Food Cake that won the blue ribbon at the York Inter-State Fair (Pennsylvania).

DEVIL'S FOOD CAKE

1 cup unsifted, unsweetened cocoa
2 cups boiling water
2¾ cups sifted all-purpose flour (sift before measuring)
2 teaspoons baking soda
½ teaspoon salt
½ teaspoon baking powder
1 cup butter, softened
2½ cups granulated sugar
4 eggs
2½ teaspoons vanilla

In a medium bowl, combine the unsweetened cocoa with two cups of boiling water, mixing with a wire whisk until smooth. Cool completely. Sift the flour with soda, salt and baking powder. Grease and lightly flour three 9-inch layer cake pans. In a large bowl of an electric mixer at high speed, beat the butter with sugar, eggs and vanilla, scraping the bowl occasionally, until light and fluffy — about 5 minutes. At low speed, beat in the flour mixture (in fourths) alternately with the cocoa mixture (in thirds). Begin and end with the flour mixture and do not overbeat. Divide evenly into pans, smoothing tops with a spatula. Bake in preheated 350-degree oven for 25–30 minutes or until surface springs back. Cool in pans for 10 minutes. Carefully loosen sides with spatula. Remove from pans and cool on racks.

FROSTING

    1 package (6 oz.) semi-sweet chocolate pieces
    ½ cup light cream
    1 cup butter
    2½ cups unsifted confectioners sugar

In a medium saucepan, combine the chocolate pieces, butter and cream, stirring over medium heat until smooth. Remove from heat. With a wire wisk, blend in confectioners sugar. Turn into a bowl and place over ice water. Beat until frosting holds its shape.

FILLING

    1 cup heavy cream
    ¼ cup unsifted confectioners sugar
    1 teaspoon vanilla

Whip cream with sugar and vanilla.

To assemble: On plate, place the first layer top side down and spread with half of the cream filling. Place the second layer top side down and spread the remainder of the cream filling. Place the third layer top side up. Frost sides of cake first, using a metal spatula, covering the whipped cream. Use the remaining frosting for the top, swirling decoratively. Refrigerate at least 1 hour before serving.

BLUE RIBBON WINNER, YORK INTER–STATE FAIR

HONEY CHOCOLATE CAKE

    ⅔ cup butter
    1 cup honey
    2 eggs
    2 cups sifted flour
    ⅓ cup cocoa
    1 teaspoon salt
    1 teaspoon baking soda
    2 teaspoons baking powder
    ¾ cup buttermilk

Preheat oven to 350 degrees. Sift the cocoa, flour and other dry ingredients together. Cream the butter and honey, and add the eggs. Beat well. Add buttermilk and dry ingredients. Beat about 2 minutes. Pour into a greased and floured pan. Makes 2 round layers or one 9×13-inch rectangle. Bake layers about 35 minutes or oblong pan 40–45 minutes. Serve warm with vanilla ice cream or may be frosted.

BLUE RIBBON WINNER, WYOMING STATE FAIR

When she was getting ready for the Kentucky State Fair, Blanche Falk went through her recipe box and came up with this sour cream cake. She doesn't know where it came from, "It was just on a recipe card," and she had never tried it before. She's glad she used it because it won her first blue ribbon in three years of trying at the Kentucky State Fair.

Blanche and her husband, Paul, have raised five children in Louisville, Kathy, Paula, Theresa, Mary Pat and Richard. Paul works in maintenance at General Electric, which has a major appliance center in the city.

Although Blanche is pleased with her blue ribbon, she's still anxious to win one for her cheesecake recipe, which has already scored second and third place victories. The reason she first entered competition three years ago was because her children convinced her that her own cheesecake was better than the one that had won that year. While we wait for Blanche to take top prize in that category you can enjoy her blue ribbon Sour Cream Cake recipe.

SOUR CREAM CAKE

3 cups sifted all-purpose flour
3 cups sugar
¼ teaspoon baking soda
1 cup sour cream
1 cup butter
6 eggs, separated

Sift the flour and measure. Sift flour twice more with the baking soda added. Cream the butter and sugar thoroughly. Add the egg yolks one at a time, beating well after each addition. Add flour and baking soda mixture alternately with sour cream to the creamed mixture. Beat the egg whites stiff and fold in. Bake in a large-sized, greased and floured angel food cake pan in a 300-degree oven for 1½ hours. Cake should come out with a nice brown crust on top. Turn cake out of pan immediately.

BUTTER CREAM FROSTING
4 Tablespoons butter
2 cups powdered sugar
1 teaspoon vanilla
3 Tablespoons cream

Cream butter until soft; gradually add 1 cup powdered sugar. Beat in flavoring. After 1 cup sugar has been thoroughly worked in, begin to add cream with remaining sugar, a little at a time until frosting reaches spreading consistency. Spread frosting over cake.

BLUE RIBBON WINNER, KENTUCKY STATE FAIR

AMY AND RHONDA SUTPHIN — FLEMINGTON, NEW JERSEY

Amy (age seventeen) is graduating from Hillsborough High School this June and plans to attend Beaver College next fall. She has been an A student and has been active in student government and the 4–H Club. Her hobbies include cooking, sewing and dancing and she looks forward to becoming a physical therapist after college.

Rhonda Sutphin (age thirteen) is in the eighth grade and is active in student council, cheerleading and gymnastics. She too has been active in 4–H and is especially interested in sports and cooking.

Their mother, Ethel, teaches at a nursery school and their father, Carl, is a zoologist and a farm manager for the Merck Research Farms. They can be proud of their daughters. Both are true blue ribbon winners.

Below is Rhonda's Chocolate Velvet Cake recipe. Amy's Apricot–Raisin Bars can be found on page 239.

CHOCOLATE VELVET CAKE

2¼ cups unsifted flour
1 teaspoon baking soda
¼ teaspoon baking powder
1⅓ cups sugar
3 eggs
1 teaspoon vanilla
1 cup mayonnaise
4 squares unsweetened chocolate, melted
1⅓ cups water

Grease and flour a 13×9×2-inch baking pan. In a bowl, stir the first three ingredients; set aside. In a large bowl with mixer at high speed beat the next three ingredients for 3 minutes or until fluffy. Reduce speed to low, beat in mayonnaise and melted chocolate. At low speed add the flour mixture in four additions alternately with water, beating just until blended after each addition. Pour into pan. Bake in 350-degree oven for 45 minutes or until tester comes out clean. Cool completely in pan.

BLUE RIBBON WINNER, FLEMINGTON (N.J.) FAIR

PATRICIA BOBROWSKI — LOUISVILLE, KENTUCKY

Patricia Bobrowski's home economics background and her teaching experience in that field have led to a lot of experimental dinners and a lot of contented guests. Besides making clothes, refinishing furniture and other creative endeavors, Patricia develops unique recipes for companies such as the Fulton Seafood Industry and General Electric (microwave ovens). Her Raspberry Whipped Cream Cake was created just for the Kentucky State Fair and proved to be a blue ribbon success for this new competitor.

RASPBERRY WHIPPED CREAM CAKE

     4 eggs, separated
    1¼ cups sifted all-purpose flour
     ¼ teaspoon salt
     1 cup sugar
     2 Tablespoons fresh lemon juice
     2 teaspoons grated lemon peel

Sift the flour with salt. Beat the egg whites until foamy. Gradually beat in ½ cup of sugar, beating after each addition. Continue beating until soft peaks form. In a small bowl beat the egg yolks at high speed until thick and lemon colored. Gradually beat in the remaining sugar and beat until smooth. At low speed, blend in the flour mixture. Add lemon juice, 2 tablespoons of water and the lemon peel, beating until just combined. With a wire whisk or rubber scraper gently fold the egg yolk mixture into the egg-white mixture just until blended. Pour the batter into two ungreased 8-inch cake pans. Bake at 350 degrees for 25 minutes or until surface springs back when gently pressed with a fingertip. Invert the cake layer by hanging it between two other pans. Cool completely — about one hour. With a spatula, carefully loosen the cake from the pan; remove. Cut each layer in half to make four layers and frost.

FILLING
3 cups boiling water
2 packages raspberry-flavored gelatin
1 to 2 cups whipped cream
  Sliced almonds or coarsely chopped pistachio nuts

Stir the boiling water into the gelatin until dissolved. Cool to lukewarm and then refrigerate. When the mixture begins to thicken, in about one hour, beat until frothy and fold into whipped cream. Refrigerate until firm. Spread on the layers and reassemble the cake. Frost cake with whipped cream. Decorate with nuts.

BLUE RIBBON WINNER, KENTUCKY STATE FAIR

JUNE ROBBINS — GREAT FALLS, MONTANA

ROBBINS' NEST WHITE CAKE
Yield: 1 cake or 3 dozen cupcakes

6 eggs, separated
2 cups sugar
½ cup vegetable shortening
½ cup (1 stick) margarine
3½ teaspoons baking powder
½ teaspoon salt

1 teaspoon vanilla
½ teaspoon lemon or almond extract
3⅓ cups cake flour (sifting is not needed)
1 to 1¼ cup milk

Preheat oven to 350 degrees. Beat the egg whites until stiff and set aside. Cream together well the sugar, shortening and margarine. Gradually beat in the baking powder, salt, egg yolks and flavorings, until light and fluffy. Add by thirds alternately the flour and milk. Beat the batter on medium speed until very smooth and glossy. It will have a heavy, rope-like texture. If it is too stiff, do not hesitate to add slightly more milk, 1 tablespoon at a time. Gently fold in the beaten egg whites. Turn into greased and floured pans of choice. (Recipe makes three 8-inch rounds or one generous 13×9-inch cake). Bake 20–30 minutes until the center tests clean and the top has lightly browned look.

Note: This recipe has also received the blue ribbon when used for cupcakes. Bottom browns quickly, so check carefully after 15 minutes. Cupcakes take about 20 minutes at 350 degrees.

ROBBINS' NEST WHITE CAKE ICING
Yield: Ices 3 dozen cupcakes, or a 13×9-inch or a large layer cake
4 Tablespoons margarine (room temperature)
1 cup vegetable shortening
1 teaspoon salt
1 Tablespoon vanilla
1 teaspoon almond or lemon extract
2 pounds powdered sugar
½ cup milk

Beat together the first 5 ingredients above then gradually add 1 pound of powdered sugar and milk. Blend together until very creamy then add another pound of powdered sugar very slowly. When all combined, beat at high speed 3–5 minutes.

Note: You may make icing in advance and freeze for later use.

BLUE RIBBON WINNER, IDAHO STATE FAIR and MONTANA STATE FAIR

ROBBINS' NEST SPICE CAKE

　¾ cup margarine (room temperature)
　2 cups white sugar
　1 cup brown sugar
2¼ teaspoon baking soda
1½ teaspoon salt
1¼ teaspoon cinnamon
　¾ teaspoon nutmeg
　¼ teaspoon (heaping) allspice
　　Pinch of cloves
　3 eggs
　2 cups applesauce
3½ cups flour
　　Up to ¼ cup water, if needed

Preheat oven to 350 degrees. Grease and flour three 8-inch rounds, or a generous 13×9-inch pan. Sift together flour, soda and salt. Cream the margarine, spices and sugars. Blend in eggs, and beat well until the mixture is fluffy. Gradually add the apple-sauce and flour mixture by alternate thirds. Beat on medium speed for 3–5 minutes. Batter should be thick, but creamy. Add a small amount of water if the applesauce is dry.

Optional: beat in 1 cup of pecans or walnuts and/or raisins (plump raisins in a small amount of boiling water, let stand 10 minutes, add to batter).

Pour batter into pans of choice. Bake 30–45 minutes, until center tests clean and top is a glossy cinnamon-brown.

Note: Rather than icing this, although cream-cheese frosting is excellent, you may prefer to brush the warm cake (after removing it from the pan) with dark Karo syrup. Looks wonderful, tastes great! Garnish with coarsely chopped pecans or walnuts.

BLUE RIBBON WINNER, MONTANA STATE FAIR and IDAHO STATE FAIR

BETSY AND BREK KATH — GARNER, NORTH CAROLINA

The Kath family always enjoyed attending the North Carolina State Fair and finally decided they should participate. Doug Kath specializes in children's toys and enjoys entering the craft division. Betsy Kath and her daughter Brek can usually be found at the baked goods competition where they have won blue ribbons for their Honey Devil's Food Cake and Coffee Rings, among others.

Brek is one of the youngest prize winners we have come across. Although she is now nine years old, she won her first blue ribbon when she was only six years of age. She may soon have new competition. Her younger brother Silas entered the State Fair for the first time in 1982 and Betsy is expecting a new addition to the family in June.

BETSY KATH — GARNER, NORTH CAROLINA

YEAST DOUGH FOR LOAVES OR COFFEE RINGS

I make a large batch so that I don't need to bake so often. This recipe yields six loaves or rings. You may freeze the finished product. The recipe may be halved for a smaller yield.

- 1 cup warm water
- 1 Tablespoon sugar
- 3 packages dry yeast
- 1 cup (2 sticks) margarine, melted
- 2 eggs
- 4 cups warm water
- 1 Tablespoon salt
- ½ cup honey
- ½ cup molasses
- 15 cups unbleached flour (approximately)

In a small bowl, place sugar in water and pour the dry yeast on top. (don't mix in the yeast). Let stand in a warm place for about

10 minutes or until the yeast is foamy. In a very large mixing bowl, mix the margarine, eggs, salt, honey and molasses together while the yeast is standing. Then add the yeast to this mixture. Add flour and mix well. Let the dough rest for 10 minutes on a floured surface. While the dough is resting clean your large mixing bowl and grease it thoroughly. Knead the dough for 10 minutes until it is not sticky. You will need to add small amounts of flour while kneading (approximately 1 cup). Place the dough in the greased mixing bowl and grease top of dough to keep a crust from forming. Let it rise until double in bulk in a warm place (about one hour). Punch the dough down and let it rise again in the mixing bowl. Punch dough down a second time and divide it into six pieces. Let the pieces rest on a floured surface for 10 minutes. Grease loaf pans and pans for coffee rings while the dough rests.

Loaves: Roll one piece of dough into a rectangle approximately 9 by 12 inches and roll into a loaf. Place in a loaf pan so that the ends touch the end of the pan. The sides will fill out while rising.

Coffee Rings: Roll one piece of dough flat with a rolling pin into a rectangle approximately 6 by 18 inches, the thinner the better. Combine filling ingredients (below), and spread on rectangle, and roll up into a long roll (18 inches long). Place into a greased circular pan.

FILLING
¼ cup margarine (cut into small pieces)
½ cup brown sugar
  Cinnamon (sprinkled on)
¼ cup lemon juice (sprinkled on)
½ cup chopped pecans
½ cup raisins or currants

Let formed loaves or rings rise to double the bulk in a warm place (about one hour). Place loaves or rings into a cold oven and turn on to 375 degrees. After 15 minutes reduce heat to 350 degrees and continue to bake until done (approximately 25 more minutes for loaves, and about 15 minutes more for coffee rings). You may need to cover the dough with tin foil if it browns too quickly. Cool. Brush the tops with margarine to soften the crust. Cool loaves on rack. Cool rings in pan.

TOPPING
½ cup sugar
¼ cup milk
¼ cup margarine
¼ cup honey
½ cup crushed nuts (pecans)

Mix the ingredients in a small saucepan and bring to a boil, stirring often. Boil a couple of minutes and remove from heat. The mixture will thicken slightly as it cools. You may pour it over the coffee rings while it is hot or wait until it cools.

BLUE RIBBON WINNER, NORTH CAROLINA STATE FAIR

BREK KATH — GARNER, NORTH CAROLINA

HONEY DEVIL'S FOOD CAKE

2½ cups sifted cake flour
¾ cup sugar
1 teaspoon salt
1 teapoon soda
1 teapoon baking powder
⅔ cup shortening
1 cup milk
3 eggs
1 teaspoon red food coloring
3 ounces unsweetened chocolate, melted
1 cup honey

Sift the first five ingredients together. Place shortening in a large mixing bowl and add milk, eggs, food color, chocolate and honey. Blend in sifted flour mixture. Beat until fluffy. Bake in 8- or 9-inch greased pans at 350 degrees for about 30 minutes. Top with seven-minute Honey Frosting.

HONEY FROSTING
1½ cups granulated sugar
¼ cup honey
⅓ cup cold water
2 egg whites
    Dash of salt
1 teaspoon vanilla

Mix together all the ingredients except the vanilla, then boil in the top of a double boiler for 7 minutes until stiff peaks form. Beat constantly while boiling. Remove from heat and add the vanilla. Beat 2 more minutes. Frost immediately.

BLUE RIBBON WINNER, NORTH CAROLINA STATE FAIR

RUBY AMERINE BOEHMER — PASO ROBLES, CALIFORNIA
MARY KAY BRALLIER — CARMICHAEL, CALIFORNIA
JAMES BRALLIER — CARMICHAEL, CALIFORNIA

The 1926 Grand Championship winner at the Oklahoma State Fair was Ruby Amerine. Ruby left Tulsa, Oklahoma during the war and took a job in a defense plant in California. Although she returned to Tulsa for a while, she relocated to California permanently in 1947. Ruby's Grand Championship Fruit Cake recipe from the 1926 Oklahoma State Fair, which has since won the blue ribbon at the California State Fair, is provided below.

The heritage of state fair competition has been passed on to Ruby's daughter Mary Kay Brallier, who now competes very successfully at the California State Fair. Mary Kay is an English teacher and her husband, Chuck, is a civil engineer. The Bralliers have four children: Mary, a biokinesiologist, Susan, who is preparing for medical school, Lynda, a data processor, and James.

All are good cooks but it is James who gives his mother competition at the state fair. The Granola Cookie recipe on page 244 is a mother-son blue ribbon winner. The recipe has taken top honors for both Mary Kay and James. You'll also enjoy Mary Kay's Polka-Dot Macaroons on page 245 and her Tutti-Fruitti Jam on page 302.

RUBY AMERINE BOEHMER — PASO ROBLES, CALIFORNIA

RUBY'S FRUIT CAKE

FRUIT
8 ounces candied pineapple
½ cup candied cherries
½ cup candied citron
½ cup candied orange peel
1 cup light raisins
1 cup dark seeded raisins (seedless are too dry)
⅓ cup currants
½ cup pitted dates
⅔ cup chopped almonds
1 cup chopped walnuts
⅔ cup port wine or brandy

Place fruit in covered container, mix well with port or brandy. Cover and let set overnight.

CAKE
½ cup butter, softened
1 cup brown sugar
3 eggs
¼ teaspoon soda
¼ teaspoon allspice
½ teaspoon cinnamon

1½ cups flour
½ cup brandy

In a large mixing bowl place the butter, brown sugar, eggs, soda, allspice and cinnamon. Mix well. Beat in the flour. Add fruit mixture, stirring only to blend. Fruit cake should have just enough batter to hold fruit together. Pour into a heavy round tube pan. Bake in very slow oven (300–325 degrees) for approximately 3 hours. Cake will spring back when done. Sprinkle cake with brandy and wrap tightly with foil. Cake should remain undisturbed for 3 weeks to give brandy time to absorb completely.

Note: For improved flavor and darker color, flour may be browned in slow oven, stirring constantly with a spatula to brown evenly. Flour should be light tan in color.

BLUE RIBBON WINNER, CALIFORNIA STATE FAIR and OKLA-HOMA (1926) STATE FAIR

SEAN POHL — YORK, NEBRASKA
BEVERLY DUNHAM — YORK, NEBRASKA

Early August is known as "reject-time" in York, Nebraska. That's when the friends and co-workers line up to savor what Bev Dunham considers her baking failures. When she's finally satisfied with her baked goods, Bev and her two sisters load their entries into the station wagon and off they go to the Nebraska State Fair. Bev has never returned empty-handed, having won numerous blue ribbons including the Sweepstakes award in breads. The baking interest, however, has not been passed on to Beverly's three daughters. Daughter Janet is a plumber, one daughter chose meat-packing as a career, while the third is a talented doll maker.

Fortunately, sons can inherit baking skills. Two of Bev's four sons are blue ribbon bakers as is her ten-year-old grandson Sean, who recently won his first blue ribbon. We include both Bev's Caramel Cake and Sean's Streusel-Filled Coffee Cake. Both are blue ribbon winners at the Nebraska State Fair.

STREUSEL–FILLED COFFEE CAKE

CAKE
1½ cups flour
¾ cup sugar
2½ teaspoons baking powder
¾ teaspoon salt
¼ cup shortening
¾ cup milk
1 egg

FILLING
½ cup brown sugar (packed)
2 teaspoons cinnamon
½ cup chopped nuts
2 Tablespoons melted butter

Preheat oven to 375 degrees. Grease 9-inch round layer or 8-inch or 9-inch square pan. Blend all the cake ingredients and beat vigorously one-half minute. Spread half the batter in the prepared pan. Mix the filling ingredients together. Sprinkle half the mixture over batter in the pan. Top with the remaining batter, then the remaining brown sugar mixture. Bake for 25–30 minutes, or until cake tests done.

BLUE RIBBON WINNER, NEBRASKA STATE FAIR

CARAMEL CAKE

    1 cup sugar
    ½ cup boiling water
       Cold water
    ½ cup shortening, softened
   1⅓ cups sugar
    3 eggs
   2⅓ cups flour
   2½ teaspoons baking powder
    1 teaspoon salt

Caramelize sugar: Melt sugar in heavy pan over low heat, stirring constantly. Heat until melted to a golden brown syrup. Remove from heat. Slowly add ½ cup of boiling water to caramelized sugar. Stir constantly over low heat until lumps are dissolved. Pour into measuring cup. Set ¼ cup aside to be used in icing. To remaining ¼ cup add enough cold water to equal 1 cup of liquid. Cream together ½ cup of shortening and 1⅓ cups of sugar. Beat in 3 eggs. Sift together the flour, baking powder and salt. Stir into sugar and egg mixture, alternating with caramel mixture. Grease and flour two 9-inch layer pans or a 13×9-inch oblong. Pour the batter into the prepared pans. Bake in 350-degree oven for 30–35 minutes. If using an oblong pan, bake for 35–45 minutes. Cool.

CARAMEL ICING
    6 Tablespoons butter
    ¼ cup caramel mixture
    ¼ cup cream
    3 cups sifted confectioners sugar
    ⅓ teaspoon salt
    1 teaspoon vanilla

Heat butter, caramel and cream. Beat in sugar, salt and vanilla.

BLUE RIBBON WINNER, NEBRASKA STATE FAIR

LEISA JOHNSON — MACOMB, OKLAHOMA

Sixteen years of age, Leisa Johnson has made her parents proud.

This Macomb high school junior and 4–H member is a regular winner at the Oklahoma State Fair. She was the state winner in the Bar-B-Que chicken contest and champion in the "Wheat Hearts" bread baking contest for Powatomie County for four consecutive years. At the 1982 Oklahoma State Fair she came in fourth in the "Blue Ribbon Chef Contest," a tremendous achievement considering that there were 2900 entrants.

This Swedish Tea Ring recipe won the 1982 blue ribbon at the Oklahoma State Fair.

SWEDISH TEA RING
Yield: 2 tea rings

¼	cup lukewarm water
2	packages dry yeast
1	cup milk
½	cup sugar
2	teaspoons salt
¼	cup shortening
2	eggs, beaten
5	cups flour, sifted
1	cup brown sugar
2	teaspoons cinnamon
1½	cups chopped raisins
1	cup chopped nuts
	Butter or margarine
1	cup powdered sugar

Measure warm water into a large warm bowl. Sprinkle in yeast, and stir until dissolved. Warm the milk; stir in sugar, salt and shortening. Cool until lukewarm. Stir the lukewarm milk mixture into the softened yeast, then add the eggs and half the flour. Beat until smooth. Stir in enough more flour to make a soft dough. Turn the dough out on a lightly floured board. Knead until smooth and satiny, about 8 minutes. Place the dough in a greased bowl, turning to grease the top. Cover and let rise in a warm place (about 80 degrees) free from drafts, until mixture has doubled in size (about 1 to 1½ hours). Punch down; turn out on lightly a floured board and let rest for 20 minutes. Mix brown sugar and cinnamon, add raisins and nuts, mix well. Divide the dough in half. Roll out each half into a rectangle 14 by 7 inches, and about ¼ inch thick. Brush with melted better. Spread the raisin mixture over the dough. Roll up from the long side and seal the edges. Place on a greased baking sheet seam side down. Form into ring. Pinch ends together. With scissors cut through the ring almost to center in slices about 1 inch thick; turn each section on its side. Brush lightly with melted butter. Cover; let rise in a warm place, free from draft, until doubled, about 1 hour. Bake in moderate oven at 375 degrees for about 30 minutes. Glaze while hot, with thin icing made from powdered sugar and 2 to 3 teaspoons milk, water or fruit juice.

BLUE RIBBON WINNER, GRAND CHAMPION, OKLAHOMA STATE FAIR

DESERTS

SHARON ROACH — LINCOLN, ILLINOIS

The blue ribbon winner of the dairy food competition at the Illinois State Fair was Sharon Roach of Lincoln, Illinois. Sharon got a start in cooking competition when she was a member of the 4–H Club as a child. She renewed that interest about nine years ago when she began competing at the Illinois State Fair.

Sharon's delicious, easy-to-prepare Pistachio Dessert will be appreciated by your family.

TASTY PISTACHIO DESSERT

- 45 Ritz crackers, crushed
- ¾ cup butter, melted
- 1½ cups milk
- 2 packages (3¾ oz.) instant pistachio pudding
- 1 quart vanilla ice cream
- 9 ounce container Cool Whip
- 2 large Heath Bars, crushed

Mix the crushed crackers and melted butter together and pat into a 9×13-inch pan. Bake at 350 degrees for 10 minutes. Cool. Beat the pudding with the milk, add the ice cream and mix well. Pour onto the cool crust. Top with whipped cream. Sprinkle with crushed Heath Bars. Refrigerate 4–6 hours or overnight.

BLUE RIBBON WINNER, ILLINOIS STATE FAIR

CAROLYN E. JENDREK — BALTIMORE, MARYLAND

The following two recipes are part of the five-part Convenience Dinner blue ribbon winner from Maryland. For more information, and the rest of the winning recipes, see pages 7–8 in the soup section.

BLACK RASPBERRIES

Wash, pack in canning jars, cover with boiling water, seal. Process 15 minutes in boiling water bath.

BLACK RASPBERRY COBBLER

⅔ cup sugar (less if commercially canned fruit is used)
1 quart processed berries (see above, or commercially prepared)
6 Tablespoons butter
¾ cup sugar
¾ cup flour
2 teaspoons baking powder
¾ cup milk

Preheat oven to 350 degrees. Mix the sugar and berries together. Place a deep baking dish (approximately 8 inches square) containing butter in oven until butter is melted. Make a batter of the sugar, flour, baking powder and milk. Pour over the melted butter but do not stir. Pour the fruit over the batter and bake approximately one hour. Batter will rise to the top and become brown and crisp when done. Can be made with any fresh or canned fruit or berries.

BLUE RIBBON WINNER, MARYLAND STATE FAIR

CASSANDRA AND HEATHER CORRIDON — DOVER, DELAWARE

State fairs are family events. One of the truly nice family stories comes from the 1982 Delaware State Fair where Sandy Corridon and her four-and-a-half-year-old daughter, Heather, competed in the fair's traditional homemade ice cream making contest.

Sandy's interest in food contests goes all the way back to her childhood days as a 4–H member in Frederick, Maryland. In those years she was a Grand Champion winner in the 4–H cake division at the Frederick County Fair. She was also the apple pie baking champion selected to represent Frederick High School at the Shenandoah Apple Blossom Festival.

Sandy and her family moved to Delaware three years ago but this was the first time she entered a state fair contest. And well she did. With the

Governor of Delaware looking on, Sandy and Heather edged out more than twenty other contestants to win a blue ribbon for their coffee ice cream recipe.

COFFEE ICE CREAM

 2½ cups sugar
 ¼ cup cornstarch
 3 to 4 Tablespoons instant coffee
 ½ teaspoon salt
 8 cups light cream
 6 eggs, slightly beaten
 2 Tablespoons vanilla

In a large saucepan, combine sugar, cornstarch, instant coffee and salt. Stir in 4 cups of light cream. Cook and stir over low heat until thickened and bubbly. Stir ¼ cup of the hot mixture into the eggs. Continue adding the hot mixture to the eggs until you have added about 2 cups. Then return the combined egg and hot mixture to the remaining hot mixture in the saucepan. Cook and stir one more minute. Chill. Add the remaining cream and vanilla. Freeze in 4- to 5-quart ice cream freezer.

BLUE RIBBON WINNER, DELAWARE STATE FAIR

ROBERT AND RACHEL CARROW — CLAYTON, DELAWARE

Robert Carrow and his thirteen-year-old daughter, Rachel, were the Grand Champions for ice cream in the fruit category at the Delaware State Fair. Rachel decided to enter the competition as part of a 4–H food project. Her father provided moral support.

 It was the first time the Carrows had entered a state fair competition. When you try their Cantaloupe Ice Cream you'll see why they managed to win a blue ribbon on their first try.

CANTALOUPE ICE CREAM

    1   medium, very ripe cantaloupe
  2½   cups sugar
    6   eggs
    4   cups heavy whipping cream (1 quart)
    1   cup milk

Spoon the cantaloupe from the rind and beat in a small mixing bowl until the melon liquefies, but small pieces of cantaloupe remain. Blend in sugar. Pour mixture into an ice cream freezer container. Set aside. Beat 6 eggs well. Blend in all cream and milk. Add to the freezer container and stir. Freeze.

Note: This is a rich ice cream which may be cut with more milk, if desired.

BLUE RIBBON WINNER, DELAWARE STATE FAIR

5

PIES

FLORENCE AND FRAN NEAVOLL — SALEM, OREGON

Florence and Fran Neavoll share everything in life. They work together, they live together and they share fond memories of growing up together on a farm in Lebanon, Oregon.

Those were difficult years. There were ten Neavoll children and everything had to be done by hand. They churned their own butter, washed clothes on a scrubbing board and pumped water from a well. They learned to cook and bake on a wood stove, which also provided heat in the winter. That stove provided a great deal of warmth for the Neavoll family.

Florence and Fran now enjoy the conveniences of the city but they can never forget those warm, wonderful years on the farm. They share the cooking skills and love that they learned growing up in a large family in Oregon. And they share the pleasure of winning blue ribbons at the Oregon State Fair.

We had a difficult time choosing which Neavoll recipes to share with our readers so we decided to provide a selection of their favorites. Below is Florence's Apple Creme Pie. You'll find her Peanut-Caramel-Marshmallow Clusters ("Goo Goo Bars") on page 259. Fran's Sugar Cookies and Viennese Walnut Cookies are on pages 213–215.

APPLE CREME PIE

    1 unbaked 9-inch pastry shell (recipe below)
    3 cups sliced apples (Gravensteins or Granny Smith are best)

1 cup marshmallow creme
1 Tablespoon lemon peel
1 teaspoon lemon juice
1 Tablespoon water

TOPPING
2 Tablespoons (firmly pressed) light brown sugar
¼ cup flour
2 Tablespoons butter
¼ teaspoon cinnamon
   Dash of salt
¼ cup ground walnuts

Mix the apples with marshmallow creme, lemon peel, lemon juice and water until blended. Arrange in the pastry shell. Cover with topping mixture which has been mixed well with a fork or pastry blender. Place apple pastry cutout on top (I use an apple cookie cutter). Bake at 375 degrees for 35 minutes or until apples are done (be careful not to overbake apples). If the top gets too brown during baking, place a piece of aluminum foil over the top. While pie is warm, drizzle with following icing:

ICING
¼ cup powdered sugar
1 teaspoon water
¼ teaspoon vanilla

CRUST
(Make the night before or chill at least one hour after mixing. Let come to room temperature before rolling out.)
3 cups regular pre-sifted flour
¾ teaspoon salt
½ teaspoon baking powder
1 Tablespoon granulated sugar
1¼ cups vegetable shortening
1 egg, beaten
1 Tablespoon vinegar
5 Tablespoons ice water

Sift the dry ingredients together. Cut about half the shortening into the dry ingredients with pastry blender until the mixture forms fine particles, then cut in the remaining shortening until mixture forms balls the size of peas. In a separate bowl, beat the whole egg, and add vinegar and ice water. Add about 7 table-spoons of this liquid mixture to the dry ingredients (2 tablespoons at a time) and toss very lightly with a fork. Form 3 balls of dough. If some dough crumbles, add a small amount of liquid until the particles adhere. Wrap each ball of dough in plastic wrap and chill. This makes three 9-inch crusts. Excess may be frozen. After crust has reached room temperature from the chilling process, roll between two sheets of plastic wrap. This prevents excess flour from being worked into dough and makes for easier handling of dough without stretching. To do this, lightly place a small amount of cold water on a kitchen counter, place a good-size sheet of plastic wrap down on the counter (the water holds it in place). Place a ball of dough in the center of wrap. Place another good-size sheet of plastic wrap on top of the dough and, using a rolling pin, roll the dough to desired thickness. Remove the top wrap, pick up the bottom wrap, crust and all, and place, dough side down, in a glass pie plate. The dough will not slip or stretch. Peel off the wrap and trim dough to about 1 inch from the edge of the pie plate and flute edge. Place in refrigerator while proceeding with preparing apples. After apple mixture is ready, remove the crust from refrigerator and brush bottom and sides (but not the fluting) with an egg white, using a pastry brush. This provides a sealing effect and the bottom crust will not become soggy. Proceed with filling with apple mixture and crumb topping.

Note: Do not use all of the egg white — just cover the crust lightly

BLUE RIBBON WINNER, OREGON STATE FAIR

GRACE EISENBREY — LAUREL, DELAWARE

Grace Eisenbrey loves to cook. Thank goodness, because she had a lot of cooking to do raising five children in Laurel, Delaware.

Grace has been a frequent blue ribbon winner at the Delaware State Fair over the past twenty years. Her interest and talent has rubbed off on her children. One daughter, Deborah Lynn, is studying gourmet cooking in Vienna, Virginia.

Grace's pumpkin pie has been a Eisenbrey family favorite for many years. We think it will be a favorite of yours too.

PUMPKIN PIE

    2 eggs, slightly beaten
    1 can (16 oz.) solid pack pumpkin
    ¾ cup sugar
    ½ teaspoon salt
    1 teaspoon ground cinnamon
    ½ teaspoon ground ginger
    1 can (13 fl. oz.) evaporated milk
    1 9-inch pie shell (recipe below)

Preheat oven to 425 degrees. Combine the filling ingredients in the order given. Pour into a pie shell. Bake 15 minutes. Reduce oven temperature to 350 degrees, and bake an additional 45 minutes or until knife inserted into center of pie comes out clean. Cool, garnish, if desired, with whipped topping.

    PIE CRUST
    1 cup sifted all-purpose flour
    ½ teaspoon salt
    ⅜ cup shortening
    ⅛ cup water

Sift the flour before measuring, spoon lightly into a measuring cup and level without shaking or packing down. Combine the flour and salt in a mixing bowl. With a pastry blender or two knives, cut in shortening until uniform. Mixture should be fairly coarse. Sprinkle with water a little at a time; toss with a fork.

Work the dough into a firm ball with your hands. Press the dough into a flat circle on a lightly floured surface and gently ease it into a pie plate. Trim edges and add filling.

BLUE RIBBON WINNER, DELAWARE STATE FAIR

PHYLLIS PRALL — MITCHELLVILLE, IOWA

It's a great compliment when your family likes your cooking so much that they encourage you to enter a state fair contest. That's what happened to Phyllis Prall of Mitchellville, Iowa.

Her first entry, a Microwave Nut Bar, won "Best Cookie in the State" in a contest sponsored by the Archway Cookie Company at the 1981 Iowa State Fair. You'll find that recipe on page 216.

In 1982, flush with her victory of the previous year, Phyllis decided to extend her talent to the pie baking contest. When she arrived at the fair with her entries she was shocked to see that there were "tons of other pies" in the contest. But the competition just wasn't enough and Phyllis managed to walk off with two additional blue ribbons for her Caramel Pecan and Almond Cream pies, the recipes for which are provided below.

CARAMEL PECAN PIE

    1 can (14 oz.) sweetened condensed milk
    ½ cup chopped pecans
    ½ cup packed brown sugar
      Pinch of salt
    1 Toasty Oat Crust (recipe below)

Combine the milk, sugar and salt in the top of double boiler. Cook over rapidly boiling water, stirring often until thickened (about 10 minutes). Remove from heat and stir in half the nuts. Pour into the pie shell and sprinkle with the remaining nuts. Cool and top with real whipped cream.

TOASTY OAT CRUST
    1 cup quick oats
    ⅓ cup chopped nuts
    ⅓ cup packed brown sugar
    ½ teaspoon cinnamon
    ¾ Tablespoon melted butter

Combine all the ingredients, mixing well. Press into bottom and sides of a very lightly oiled 9-inch pie plate. Bake at 375 degrees for 8–10 minutes.

BLUE RIBBON WINNER, IOWA STATE FAIR

ALMOND CREAM PIE

    4   cups milk
    1⅛ cup sugar
    3   Tablespoons cornstarch
    4   eggs, beaten
    2   Tablespoons unflavored gelatin
    2   Tablespoons hot water
    2   cups whipping cream
    1   teaspoon almond extract
    2   9-inch baked pie shells

In a double boiler, scald 3 cups of milk and then add sugar. Dissolve cornstarch in the remaining 1 cup milk, and add eggs. Pour a little of the hot milk mixture into the egg mixture, then blend both together in the double boiler. Stir until thick. Dissolve the gelatin in hot water and then mix into cooked filling. Refrigerate overnight. Whip filling until smooth. Whip cream until stiff and fold into filling with almond extract. Pour into pie shells. Refrigerate for 4 hours.

SINGLE PASTRY CRUST
    1½ cups sifted flour
    ½   teaspoon salt

½ cup shortening
4 to 5 Tablespoons cold water

Sift the flour and salt together. Cut in the shortening with a pastry blender until pieces are the size of small peas. Sprinkle 1 tablespoon of water over part of the mixture. Gently toss with a fork. Repeat until all is moistened. Form into a ball. Roll into a circle on lightly floured surface to ⅛ inch thick. Fit into 9-inch pie plate and flute the edge. Prick with fork and bake at 450 degrees for 10–12 minutes or until golden brown.

BLUE RIBBON WINNER, IOWA STATE FAIR

SHARON CROSBY — LOUISVILLE, KENTUCKY

Sharon Crosby had never entered the state fair competition because she didn't think her cooking was good enough. She can't recall what prompted her to enter in 1980 but she was right about her cooking: it wasn't good enough, and she didn't win a thing. Her two daughters did win, however, and they walked away with a total of six ribbons.

Sharon was so discouraged by her first attempt that she decided not to enter in 1981. Her daughters Elizabeth and Karen did, and won again.

In 1982 Sharon gave it another try. Daughter Karen had decided not to enter the fair, but Elizabeth did, with three items that didn't win a thing. This was to be Mom's year. Sharon took a fourth and a second place with two cookie recipes and won her first blue ribbon for this dark, rich Chocolate Pie that her family has prized for years.

CHOCOLATE PIE

9-inch baked shell (recipe below)
1½ cups sugar
⅓ cup cornstarch
½ teaspoon salt
3 cups milk

4 egg yolks, slightly beaten
1 Tablespoon vanilla
2 ounces unsweetened chocolate, melted
   Meringue topping (recipe below)

Stir together the sugar, cornstarch and salt in a deep saucepan. Blend the milk and egg yolks in a bowl; gradually stir into the sugar mixture. Stir constantly to prevent lumping. Cook over medium heat, stirring constantly, until the mixture thickens and boils. Boil and stir for 1 minute. Remove from heat. Stir in the melted chocolate and vanilla flavoring. Press plastic wrap over the top of the filling to keep skin from forming. Put in refrigerator for at least 2 hours until chilled. When ready to serve or complete, make a meringue or serve with sweetened whipped cream on top.

PIE SHELL
1½ cups all-purpose flour
½ teaspoon salt
½ cup butter or margarine (or ¼ cup each)
1 medium egg, slightly beaten
1 Tablespoon lemon juice or vinegar
⅛ cup ice water (or a little more)

Sift the flour and salt together into a large bowl. Cut in the butter just until the pieces are the size of small peas. Combine the egg, lemon juice or vinegar, and water. Stir into the flour mixture just to hold the dough together, blending with a fork. Chill the pastry for about 2 hours (or overnight). This is necessary because the addition of egg makes crust difficult to work with unless it is fully chilled at this point for easier rolling. Roll out chilled pastry on a lightly floured surface. Fit into a 9-inch pie pan. Prick several times with a floured fork to prevent swelling. Bake at 475 degrees for 8–10 minutes. Cool thoroughly before filling.

Pour the chilled chocolate filling into baked shell. Pile meringue on top, shaping with back of spoon to make peaks. Brown in 300-degree oven until lightly browned (about 10 minutes). Serve immediately. Leftover pie should be refrigerated.

MERINGUE TOPPING
4 egg whites, room temperature
¼ teaspoon cream of tartar
½ cup sugar

Whip the egg whites until foamy. Gradually blend in sugar and cream of tartar until stiff peaks form.

BLUE RIBBON WINNER, KENTUCKY STATE FAIR

MARILYN BERNHARDT — SPRINGFIELD, ILLINOIS

"If I can do it, anyone can," says Marilyn Bernhardt. "I didn't even realize I could cook well until I entered the Illinois State Fair six years ago." From that first moment in the spotlight, she decided that success was what she wanted and decided to go for it. This forty-two-year-old mother of five, and a grandmother to boot, started getting serious. Besides competing successfully at the state fair, she has also embarked on an acting and modeling career. She played five different characters in The Chicago Story *and has also completed filming* All the Sad Young Men *for NBC. But, despite her newfound career, Marilyn says she'll never give up her special domain, the kitchen. Look out, Illinois, she's already started on next year's fair entry.*

PEAR PIE WITH STREUSEL TOPPING
AND ALMOND CRUST
Yield: 6 servings

ALMOND PASTRY SHELL
1 cup sifted all-purpose flour
½ teaspoon salt
⅓ cup shortening
¾ cup finely chopped toasted almonds
2 Tablespoons ice water

Sift the flour and salt into a medium-size bowl. Cut in the shortening a with pastry blender or two knives, until mixture is like coarse cornmeal. Stir in the almonds. Sprinkle ice water gradually over the mixture, tossing with a fork. Shape into a ball; roll, between sheets of waxed paper, into an 11-inch circle. Refrigerate until ready to use. Fit the pastry into a 9-inch pie plate. If it is crumbly, press gently against the pie plate to repair breaks. Form a neat rim around edge of pie plate; do not crimp. Set aside until ready to fill and bake.

STREUSEL TOPPING
⅔ cup sifted all-purpose flour
⅓ cup light brown sugar, firmly packed
⅓ cup butter or margarine

In a small bowl, combine the flour and sugar. Cut in the butter, with pastry blender or two knives, until the mixture is like coarse cornmeal. Refrigerate until ready to use.

PEAR PIE FILLING
¼ cup granulated sugar
¼ teaspoon ginger
4 teaspoons flour
5 ripe Bartlett pears (about 2 pounds)
4 teaspoons lemon juice
½ cup light corn syrup (optional)*

Preheat oven to 375 degrees.

Combine sugar, ginger and flour; sprinkle about a third of the mixture over the bottom of the pie shell. Peel and core the pears; slice thinly into a bowl. Arrange half of the pears in the shell; top with a third of the sugar mixture. Arrange remaining pears; top with remaining sugar mixture. Drizzle lemon juice and ¼ cup corn syrup over the top. Cover with streusel topping. Drizzle the other ¼ cup of corn syrup over the streusel topping, if desired. Bake 40–50 minutes, or until pears are tender.

*By drizzling the last ¼ cup of syrup over the streusel topping the pie gets a very moist and crunchy topping. Just a little different from your dry type topping. It also gets a very beautiful glaze. This was discovered by mistake and the fair judges thought it added the most delightful touch.

BLUE RIBBON WINNER, ILLINOIS STATE FAIR

VIOLA BAILEY — YORK, PENNSYLVANIA

Thanks to Viola Bailey we have been able to record a Pennsylvania Dutch favorite for posterity. Viola's Shoo Fly Pie, a long-time family favorite, has been winning blue ribbons in Pennsylvania for almost twenty years.

Viola and Reed Bailey are retired from farming these days. But Viola remains active selling donuts at the Eastern Farmer's Market, raising collies and winning blue ribbons for her wonderful cooking skills.

Viola mostly bakes from memory and we are pleased that her Shoo Fly Pie is recorded here for the first time.

SHOO FLY PIE

2 pie pans lined with your favorite crust

CRUMB MIXTURE
2½ cups flour
1 cup granulated sugar
Pinch of salt
1 teaspoon baking powder
½ cup butter and lard mixed or (shortening may be substituted for lard)

Mix above ingredients together.

FILLING
1 pint molasses
1 pint hot water

Pinch of salt
2 eggs
1 teaspoon baking soda

Mix above ingredients together.

Place two-thirds of the crumbs into pie crusts. Pour in filling. Sprinkle remaining crumbs on top. Place in preheated 425-degree oven for 10 minutes. Reduce oven to 300 degrees for 35 mintues. Cool and cover with aluminum foil. If desired let sit for covered 24 hours for moister pie.

BLUE RIBBON WINNER, YORK INTER–STATE FAIR

DOROTHY HALTIWANGER — WEST COLUMBIA, SOUTH CAROLINA

The Southern Pecan Pie recipe that we have chosen has been a regular winner at the South Carolina State Fair for years. Dorothy Haltiwanger developed the recipe herself, "getting a little bit from here and a little bit from there." She has been a regular contestant for almost twenty-four years and competes most often in the canning categories. We think you'll agree that her skills really come together in this pecan pie recipe that she has provided.

SOUTHERN PECAN PIE

1 9-inch pie shell
1 cup sugar
2 Tablespoons margarine
¼ teaspoon salt
1 Tablespoon flour
3 eggs
1 cup white corn syrup
1 teaspoon vanilla
1 cup chopped pecans

Cream the sugar, salt, flour and margarine together. Add eggs and mix well. Add syrup and vanilla and mix well. Prick the pie shell and bake at 350 degrees for about 4 minutes. Add chopped pecans to the pie shell, then pour in the filling. Bake at 350 degrees for about 50 minutes. Check after about 15 minutes. If the pie crust edges are getting too brown, you may cover the pie with a piece of aluminum foil in which you have cut out a circle 2½ inches in diameter.

BLUE RIBBON WINNER, SOUTH CAROLINA STATE FAIR

PAT HEATH — NEW KENT, VIRGINIA

CHOCOLATE CHESS PIE
Yield: 6 to 8 servings

- 2 cups sugar
- 2 Tablespoons cornstarch
- 4 eggs
- 1 can (8 oz.) chocolate-flavored syrup
- ¼ cup milk
- ¼ cup butter, melted
- 1 unbaked pie shell (recipe below)

Combine the sugar, cornstarch, eggs, chocolate-flavored syrup, milk and butter in a bowl. Beat until smooth, using an electric mixer at medium speed. Pour into an unbaked pie shell. Bake in 350-degree oven 55 minutes or until center is set. Cool on rack.

CRUST
- 2¼ cups sifted flour
- 1 Tablespoon sugar
- 1 teaspoon salt
- ¾ cup shortening

1 egg yolk, beaten
¼ cup milk
1 Tablespoon lemon juice

Combine the flour, sugar and salt in a bowl. Cut in the shortening until fine crumbs form, using a pastry blender. Blend together the egg yolk, milk and lemon juice in a small bowl. Add egg yolk mixture to the dry ingredients, tossing with a fork, until dough forms. Press dough firmly into a ball. Roll out on a lightly floured surface. Makes pastry for two (single) 8-inch or 9-inch pie crusts. Unused crust may be frozen.

BLUE RIBBON WINNER, VIRGINIA STATE FAIR

GRACE STOUT — LOCKBOURNE, OHIO

Grace Stout has been collecting blue ribbons at the Ohio State Fair for almost twenty-five years. The Apple Crumb Pie that she provided has been a blue ribbon winner for the past two years.

APPLE CRUMB PIE

5 to 7 tart apples
¾ to 1 cup sugar
2 Tablespoons flour
½ to 1 teaspoon cinnamon
Dash of nutmeg
Dash of salt
1 9-inch pie crust (recipe below)
2 Tablespoons butter
Crumb topping (recipe below)

Pare the apples and slice thin. Combine the sugar, flour, spices and salt; mix with apples. Line a 9-inch pie plate with pastry, fill with apple mixture and dot with butter. Sprinkle with the crumb topping. Bake at 400 degrees for 50 minutes or until done.

9-INCH PIE CRUST
1 cup flour
½ teaspoon salt
⅓ cup shortening (lard)
2 Tablespoons water

Cut shortening into the dry ingredients with a pastry blender or two knives. Sprinkle with water and work into a ball. Roll out on a lightly floured surface.

CRUMB TOPPING
½ cup quick oats
½ cup flour
½ cup brown sugar
⅓ cup butter

Mix together the first three ingredients. Cut in the butter until crumbly.

BLUE RIBBON WINNER, OHIO STATE FAIR

JOYCE GARDNER — SYRACUSE, NEW YORK

Many of our blue ribbon winners become totally involved in the state fair each year. The Gardner family of Syracuse, New York, are a good example.

Robert Gardner spends his entire vacation at the fair from 8 a.m. in the morning until 10 p.m. at night. His primary interest is horticulture and he often enjoys competing in the rose competition.

As a child, the Gardner's daughter, Jill, regularly competed in the equestrian competition as a 4-H member. In 1982 she demonstrated her culinary skills by taking six awards in the homemade jelly contest.

Joyce Gardner is a versatile contestant, usually winning awards for latch-hook rugs, apple-head dolls and hand painted items. In the past two years she has won blue ribbons for both apple and blueberry pies. "Neither of these were 'special' recipes," according to Mrs. Gardner, "just the kind of pies we make for the family to have for dessert."

That's what we think makes them so special and so we are pleased to offer you the chance to try Joyce's special Blueberry Pie.

BLUEBERRY PIE

1 cup unsugared, frozen blueberries
1 cup canned blueberries
1 cup sugar
3 Tablespoons tapioca
9-inch pie crust (recipe follows)
  Butter
  Lemon juice

Measure berries and set aside, reserving ¾ cup of blueberry juice. In a saucepan, combine the blueberry juice, sugar and tapioca. Stir constantly over low heat until thickened. Put berries into the pie shell. Cover evenly with thickened syrup. Dot with butter; squirt with lemon juice. Cut crust in strips for lattice top. Bake at 350 degrees for about 30 minutes or until brown.

PIE CRUST
1 cup shortening
3 cups flour
1 teaspoon salt
½ cup water

Cut shortening, flour and salt together with a pastry blender or two knives until mealy. Mix in ½ cup of water until the dough forms a ball. Roll out on a lightly floured surface. Cut one pie crust. Cut remaining dough into strips for lattice top.

BLUE RIBBON WINNER, NEW YORK STATE FAIR

CHOCOLATE MINT PRALINE PECAN PIE

PIE CRUST
- 2 cups sifted all-purpose flour
- ½ teaspoon salt
- ⅓ cup butter
- ⅓ cup shortening
- 6 Tablespoons ice cold water

Place the flour and salt in a mixing bowl and stir to combine. Cut in ⅓ cup of butter with a pastry blender until it is the size and texture of cornmeal. Next, add the shortening and cut it in until the mixture is the size of small green peas. Sprinkle the ice water over the mixture and stir it quickly with a fork. Gather the dough together in a ball. Place on a saucer and refrigerate a few minutes. This will make enough dough for two 9-inch one-crust pies. Roll out the dough into a large circle and place into a 9-inch pie pan. Trim the edges about 1 inch larger all around. Fold the dough double around the edge and flute edges. Prick the bottom of the dough with a fork to let steam escape as it cooks. Place the dough-lined pie pan in a preheated 425 degree oven and cook for about 15 minutes until it is lightly browned. Remove from oven and let cool to room temperature.

FILLING
- 1 envelope unflavored gelatin
- ¼ cup water
- ⅓ cup crème de menthe liqueur
- ¾ cup brown sugar
- 6 ounces chocolate chips
- 4 eggs, separated
- ¼ teaspoon salt

1 cup heavy cream (for whipping)
⅓ cup chopped pecans

In a saucepan mix the gelatin, water, ¼ cup of sugar and crème de menthe and place it over low heat. Stir until it is mixed well and the sugar and gelatin are dissolved. Now add the chocolate chips and stir until they melt. Remove from heat and stir in the egg yolks one at a time, beating after each addition. Cool. Place the egg whites in a mixing bowl, add the salt and beat at high speed until stiff peaks form. Gradually beat in the remaining ½ cup of brown sugar until the meringue is very stiff. Now fold the egg whites into the chocolate-gelatin mixture. Next, whip the cup of heavy cream and fold it into the chocolate mixture. Fold in the chopped pecans. Pile this mixture into the cooled pie shell and spread evenly. Prepare the pralined pecans halves (below) and place them on the surface of the pie filling in concentric circles, beginning at the edge of the filling next to the crust. One dollop of whipped cream may be placed on the center of the pie surface.

PRALINED PECAN HALVES
1 cup sugar
½ teaspoon baking soda
½ cup cream (half and half)
1 Tablespoon butter
1½ cups pecan halves

In a deep saucepan, mix the sugar and soda together well. Add the cream and stir well. Place over medium heat and bring to a rolling boil. As the mixture foams up the heat may be reduced some. Continue cooking and stirring occasionally until the soft-ball stage is reached (234 degrees Fahrenheit). The mixture, by this time, will have taken on a rich caramel color. Remove the pan from the heat and stir in the tablespoon of butter until it melts. Immediately add the pecan halves. Beat the mixture with a spoon until the pecans are well coated and it thickens. Pour or spoon the coated pecans onto a piece of buttered foil and quickly separate each pecan half with a spoon. If some stick together they may be broken apart when cool enough to handle. Select the prettiest pecan halves for decorating the pie and use the rest as a candy!

BLUE RIBBON WINNER, BEST OF SHOW, TEXAS STATE FAIR

MARJORY MORSE — GREAT FALLS, MONTANA

FRESH CHERRY PIE

   1½ cups sugar
   ⅓ cup flour
   ⅛ teaspoon salt
   3 drops almond extract
   4 cups pitted tart cherries
   2 Tablespoons butter
9-inch pie shell

Combine the sugar, flour and salt. Sprinkle 4 tablespoons on the bottom crust. Add almond extract to the cherries and toss with the sugar and flour mixture. Mix thoroughly. Turn into a pastry-lined 9-inch pie pan. Make a lattice top and flute the edges. Bake in hot oven (375 degrees) for approximately 45 minutes.

BLUE RIBBON WINNER, MONTANA STATE FAIR

CONNIE SPRENKLE — YORK, PENNSYLVANIA

Choosing an apple pie winner was perhaps one of the most difficult tasks. We received so many wonderful apple pie recipes that we could probably devote an entire book to this all-American favorite. But only one could be selected to appear here, and that honor goes to Connie Sprenkle of York, Pennsylvania. Her recipe took top honors at the York Inter–State Fair, a leading exposition in that state.

Two people influenced Connie's cooking skills . . . her mother, Gloria Wolf, and her Home Ec teacher, Frances Dietz. Mrs. Dietz was recently acclaimed by Woman's Day *magazine for having converted a favorite hobby (cooking) into a successful business. Connie is following in her footsteps. She is presently packaging and selling her fantastic apple pie seasoning in local food stores. If you're ever in the York area, look for the "Blue Ribbon Apple Pie Seasoning" label. If you're not, you can get the same results by trying Connie's very special apple pie recipe.*

APPLE PIE

SUPER FLAKY PIE CRUST
(This is enough for two crusts.)
2⅔ cup flour
  2 teaspoons salt
 ½ cup water
  1 cup shortening

Cut the shortening into a mixture of the flour, salt, and water by using two table knives. Place one knife between the thumb and first finger and the other knife between the first and second fingers. Cut into the flour mixture until the crumbs are about the size of peas. (Pastry blenders and forks make crumbs too small; therefore the crust is not as tender and flaky.) With your hand, press the dough into a ball against the side of the bowl. Place the ball on a floured board and place a bowl, upside-down, over the top of it. Let the dough "rest" for at least 5 minutes. Roll dough as thin as you can and still be able to handle it. For the very quickest, easiest, and best results, use a pastry cloth and rolling pin sleeve. Spray a pie pan with vegetable cooking spray. Put the dough into the pan. Cut the edge of the crust, with a knife, even with the edge of the pie pan.

The key to good, tender, flaky crust is to not overwork or handle the dough too much.

FILLING
¼ cup margarine
 8 medium-size apples (Summer Rambo, if available)

¼ cup flour
5 Tablespoons sugar
6 Tablespoons brown sugar
1 Tablespoon cinnamon

Cut ¼ cup of margarine into 10 equal slices. For seasoning, mix together the flour, sugars and cinnamon. Peel and slice 8 medium-size apples. Slices should be about ¼ inch thick. Place 4 sliced apples in the crust. Top with half the seasoning mixture and 5 slices margarine. Put remaining 4 apples, sliced, on top and use the remainder of the seasoning and margarine. Wet (with water on finger) the edge of the crust. Carefully place the top crust over apples. Cut even with pan edge. Pinch the edges together to seal the pie. (The damp edge on the crust helps to seal the edge better.) Prick holes in the top crust to allow steam to escape during baking. Bake pie at 425 degrees for 15 minutes. Reduce heat to 350 degrees and continue baking for 45 minutes. Cool before cutting.

BLUE RIBBON WINNER, YORK INTER–STATE FAIR

MARIE WEYER — LOUISVILLE, KENTUCKY

Marie Weyer spends her winters in Cape Coral, Florida, where she competes in the Breeze Recipe Contest. But when summer rolls around she returns to Louisville, where she competes at the Kentucky State Fair.

Marie's Banana Split Pie took a blue ribbon by winning first place in the "Favorite Dessert" division.

BANANA SPLIT PIE

2 cups crushed graham crackers
1½ cups butter
1 pound powdered sugar
2 eggs

1 teaspoon vanilla
3 to 4 medium bananas, sliced
1 small can (6½ oz.) crushed pineapple
  Whipped cream or dessert topping

Blend the graham crackers crumbs with ½ cup of butter. Press into the bottom of a 9×12-inch pan. Bake the crust at 350 degrees for 15 minutes. Meanwhile, combine the remaining butter with the sugar and eggs. Beat 15 minutes. Add vanilla and mix well. Pour the filling into the crust, then cover with a layer of bananas and the crushed pineapple. Top with whipped cream or dessert topping. Decorate with red sugar or maraschino cherries, if desired.

BLUE RIBBON WINNER, KENTUCKY STATE FAIR

EVA WIESNER — SYRACUSE, NEW YORK

COCONUT CUSTARD PIE

CRUST
1 cup flour
½ teaspoon salt
⅛ teaspoon baking powder
⅓ cup plus 1 Tablespoon shortening
2 Tablespoons ice water

Sift the flour, salt and baking powder. Cut in the shortening. Sprinkle in water and mix with a fork until all the flour is moistened. Roll out the dough and fit into an 8-inch pie pan. Trim and flute the edges and refrigerate for one hour.

CUSTARD FILLING
3 eggs
½ cup sugar

¼ teaspoon salt
1 cup milk, scalded
1 cup heavy cream, scalded
1 teaspoon vanilla
1 cup shredded coconut

Beat the eggs slightly with a rotary beater. Add the remaining ingredients and pour into the prepared pie crust. Bake at 450 degrees for 15 minutes, reduce heat to 350 degrees and bake for 10 to 15 minutes more. Bake until a knife inserted 1 inch from the side of the filling comes out clean.

BLUE RIBBON WINNER, NEW YORK STATE FAIR

JOY STARKEY — CHARLES CITY, VIRGINIA

BUTTERMILK COCONUT PIE

6 eggs
½ cup (1 stick) butter or margarine, melted
1 cup buttermilk (shake well)
2 cups sugar
1 cup coconut, heaping
2 pie shells

Mix the first five ingredients together well. Pour into two prepared 8-inch pie shells or one 10-inch shell. Bake at 350 degrees for about 30 minutes or until the pie is done.

BLUE RIBBON WINNER, VIRGINIA STATE FAIR

STRAWBERRY–RHUBARB PIE

¼ cup enriched flour
1½ cups sugar
¼ teaspoon salt
2 cups fresh strawberries (whole)
3 cups fresh rhubarb (diced)
9-inch pie crust, plus crust for lattice (your recipe)

Combine the flour, sugar and salt. Add the strawberries and rhubarb and combine thoroughly. Put into a 9-inch pastry-lined pan (unbaked). Dot with 1 tablespoon of butter. Place lattice strips over the filling. Seal and flute. Bake in hot oven (450 degrees) for 10 minutes, then at 350 degrees for 50–55 minutes.

BLUE RIBBON WINNER, KENTUCKY STATE FAIR

GINA WALDNER — LOUISVILLE, KENTUCKY

Gina Waldner is a freshman at Spalding College in Louisville where she is an art and communications major. Her interest in state fair competition began three years ago when her good friends down the street convinced her to enter. Since then she has won ribbons in such diverse categories as bread, art and tropical fish. That last category, quite unusual in state fair competition, was won by Gina's fourteen-inch pet goldfish which she raises in her backyard pond.

Gina credits her pie baking skills to her grandmother Helen Walker. The following Marvelous Pie recipe, the product of Gina's skills, was a blue ribbon winner at the Kentucky State Fair.

MARVELOUS PIE

- ¼ cup (½ stick) butter, melted
- 1 cup sugar
- ½ cup white syrup
- ½ cup coconut
- ½ cup crushed pineapple, drained
- 1 teaspoon lemon juice
- 3 eggs, beaten
- ¼ teaspoon salt
- 1 unbaked 9-inch pie crust

Mix the first four ingredients together thoroughly, and pour into the pie crust. Bake in 300-degree oven for 45 minutes or until light brown on top.

BLUE RIBBON WINNER, KENTUCKY STATE FAIR

CAROL KERN — LOUISVILLE, KENTUCKY
BETTY CONNIFF — LOUISVILLE, KENTUCKY

Carol Kern and Betty Conniff are great cooks, but we have Joe Conniff to thank for these great recipes. A few years ago Joe convinced his wife, Betty, to enter some of her baked goods in the Kentucky State Fair. She did and began winning ribbons immediately.

Betty enjoyed the experience so much that she convinced her sister Carol to compete alongside her.

Joe, meanwhile, is sitting pretty. His wife and sister-in-law provide a steady stream of blue ribbon baking for his enjoyment.

LEMON MERINGUE PIE

   7 Tablespoons cornstarch
1¼ cups sugar
  ¼ teaspoon salt
  2 cups water
  3 eggs, separated
  ¼ teaspoon lemon extract
  1 Tablespoon grated lemon rind
  ⅓ cup lemon juice
  6 Tablespoons sugar
  1 baked 9-inch pie shell

Mix the cornstarch, sugar and salt in a 1-quart saucepan. Add water slowly and mix until smooth. Cook on medium heat until the mixture is thick, stirring constantly. Turn heat to low, and cook until the mixture is very thick and smooth, stirring constantly. Stir a small amount of the cornstarch mixture into slightly beaten egg yolks. Return to the saucepan and cook for 3 to 5 minutes, stirring constantly. Remove from heat. Add the butter, lemon extract, lemon rind and juice; blend. Cool to room temperature. Pour the filling into a baked 9-inch pie shell. Beat the egg whites until foamy. Beat in sugar gradually and continue beating until stiff. Spread lightly on the pie filling in the shell. Spread the meringue out to the edge of the pie shell to make a complete seal. Bake in 325-degree oven for 15–20 minutes.

BLUE RIBBON WINNER, KENTUCKY STATE FAIR

PEACH PIE

5 cups sliced fresh peaches (8 or 9 medium peaches)
1 teaspoon lemon juice
¼ cup apricot or peach jam
¾ cup brown sugar
¼ cup flour
¼ teaspoon cinnamon
2 Tablespoons butter
  Pastry for 9-inch two-crust pie

Mix the peaches, lemon juice and jam together. Mix the sugar, flour and cinnamon together and stir into the peaches. Turn into a pastry-lined pie dish and dot with butter. Cover with the top crust with slits cut in it, or use a lattice crust top. Seal and flute the edge. Brush the top crust with milk and sprinkle with sugar. Bake in 425-degree oven for 35–45 minutes, or until crust is brown and juice bubbles through the slits or lattice.

BLUE RIBBON WINNER, KENTUCKY STATE FAIR

CHRIS HULSEY — BLOOMINGTON, ILLINOIS

The Grand Champion of the 1982 Illinois State Fair was Chris Hulsey of Bloomington. Chris entered four categories and scored well in each. But it was her Mystery Pecan Pie that won the pastry competition and then went on to win top honors at the fair by winning the Grand Championship Bake-off.

Chris learned how to bake when she was five years old, helping her grandmother make cookies. She was a 4–H member for nine years and currently gets a lot of practice baking for her children, her husband, Ray, and her parents, Glenn and Diane Miller.

The Mystery Pecan Pie has its origins in Oklahoma. She obtained the original recipe from her sister-in-law in Tulsa, but added her own "mystery ingredient," cream cheese.

Chris was thrilled with her victory and well she should be: it is one of the most prestigious cooking events in the country. Although she is now precluded from competing at the Illinois State Fair, she is still interested in state fair competition. When she does compete again, the Oklahoma State Fair could be her next stop.

PECAN MYSTERY PIE

PASTRY
   1 cup all-purpose flour
   ½ teaspoon salt
   ⅓ cup shortening
   3 to 4 Tablespoons cold water

Measure the flour, salt and shortening into a large mixer bowl; blend on medium speed until the particles are the size of small peas. Sprinkle cold water over the flour mixture, mixing on low speed and adding 1 tablespoon of water at a time until the dough is just moist enough to stick together. Form dough into a ball. Wrap in wax paper and refrigerate for 15 minutes or until slightly chilled. Makes one 9-inch pie crust.

FILLING
   1 package (8 oz.) cream cheese, softened
   ⅓ cup sugar
   ¼ teaspoon salt
   1 teaspoon vanilla
   1 egg
   1¼ cups chopped pecans

TOPPING
   3 eggs
   ½ cup sugar
   1 cup light corn syrup
   1 teaspoon vanilla

In a small mixing bowl, combine the cream cheese, sugar, salt, vanilla and 1 egg. Blend well at medium speed. Spread in the bottom of the unbaked pastry shell. Sprinkle with pecans.

For the topping, beat the eggs, then add the rest of the ingredients. Gently pour over the pecans. Bake at 375 degrees for 35–40 minutes until the center is firm to the touch. Serve when cool.

BLUE RIBBON WINNER, ILLINOIS STATE FAIR

CECILIA SYPAL — BRAINARD, NEBRASKA

RHUBARB PIE

Pastry for 2-crust pie
3 cups rhubarb (cut in ½-inch pieces)
1 cup sugar
2 Tablespoons tapioca
Dash of salt
1½ Tablespoons butter
Cream

Line a 9-inch pie pan with pastry. Mix together the rhubarb, sugar, tapioca and salt, place in the pie pan and dot with butter. Use the remaining crust to make a lattice top and flute the edges. Brush the crust with cream and sprinkle with sugar. Bake at 400 degrees for 10 minutes, then reduce temperature to 375 degrees and bake for 20–25 minutes.

BLUE RIBBON WINNER, NEBRASKA STATE FAIR

JANA GUNN — SALEM, OREGON

Who is the "greatest cook" in Oregon? If winning the Grand Sweepstakes Award at the Oregon State Fair qualifies a person for that title,

Jana Gunn gets the crown. To win the Sweepstakes Jana had sixty entries in everything from dried food to candy. And because she considers pies her specialty, she entered nineteen of her best in the category. When the fair ended Jana went home with thirty-five ribbons and the coveted Grand Sweepstakes Award.

Fifteen years ago, when her husband Robert was in law school, Jana entered the fair just to see how good her cooking was. She was a good cook then, but is an even better cook now. Maybe that's because she finds cooking and caring for her husband and eight children so fulfilling. Jana feels homemaking can be a gratifying career. Cooking gives her "the chance to express myself and achieve the success and recognition everyone needs." But to Jana Gunn the family always comes first: "They're the top priority in my book."

CHOCOLATE ANGEL PIE

    Meringue layer (recipe below)
1 baked 9-inch pie shell
1 package (6 oz.) semisweet chocolate pieces, melted and cooled
2 egg yolks, beaten (reserve whites for meringue)
¼ cup water
1 cup heavy cream
¼ cup sugar
¼ teaspoon ground cinnamon

Prepare the meringue layer. Spread it over the bottom and up the sides of the baked pie shell. Bake in 325 degree oven for 15–18 minutes, or until golden brown. Cool on rack. Combine the cooled chocolate, egg yolks and water; beat well with a rotary beater or wire whisk. Spread 3 tablespoons of chocolate mixture over meringue layer. Whip the heavy cream in a bowl until it begins to thicken, using an electric mixer at high speed. Gradually add the sugar and cinnamon, beating until stiff peaks form. Spread half of the cream mixture over the chocolate layer. Fold the remaining chocolate mixture into the remaining cream mixture. Spread evenly over the cream layer. Cover and refrigerate for 4 hours or until set.

MERINGUE LAYER
2 egg whites
½ teaspoon vinegar
¼ teaspoon salt
¼ teaspoon ground cinnamon
½ cup sugar

Combine the egg whites, vinegar, salt and ground cinnamon in a bowl. Beat with an electric mixer at high speed until foamy. Gradually add the sugar, beating until stiff, glossy peaks form.

BLUE RIBBON WINNER, OREGON STATE FAIR

BANANA CREAM PIE

Baked 9-inch pie shell
3 Tablespoons sugar
6 Tablespoons flour
¼ teaspoon salt
2 cups milk
2 eggs, separated
3 to 4 cups bananas
1½ teaspoons vanilla
1 Tablespoon butter
4 Tablespoons sugar
1 cup whipping cream, sweetened to taste

Combine 3 tablespoons of sugar, flour and salt in the top of a double boiler. Add the milk and slightly beaten egg yolks; stir until smooth. Cook over boiling water until thickened, stirring constantly. Cover and cook 10 minutes longer. Remove from heat. Add the vanilla and butter. Beat the egg whites until foamy, add 4 tablespoons of sugar gradually and beat until stiff. Fold in the hot mixture. Cool. Slice bananas on the pie shell, then put on a layer of cream filling. Alternate with bananas and filling until the shell is full. Top with sweetened whipped cream and garnish with bananas.

BLUE RIBBON WINNER, OREGON STATE FAIR

LEMON FLUFF PIE

    Baked 9-inch pie shell
4 eggs, separated
    Grated peel of 1 lemon
¼ cup fresh lemon juice
3 Tablespoons water
1 cup sugar

Separate the eggs, putting the whites in a mixing bowl and the yolks in the top of a double boiler. Beat the yolks until thick. Gradually stir in the lemon peel and juice, water and ½ cup of the sugar. Cook over hot water until thickened, stirring constantly. Remove from hot water. Beat the egg whites until stiff; beat in the remaining ½ cup of sugar (1 tablespoon at a time). Continue beating until the whites are glossy and pile well. Fold half the whites into the warm yolk mixture; when evenly blended, empty into the pie shell, smoothing the surface. Spoon the remaining meringue to make a crown around edge of the pie (make sure it touches the crust). Bake in slow oven (325 degrees) long enough to brown the meringue lightly, about 15 minutes.

BLUE RIBBON WINNER, OREGON STATE FAIR

NEVER FAIL PIE CRUST
Yield: 2 or 3 single crusts depending upon thickness rolled

  2½ cups flour
   1 cup shortening
  ½ teaspoon salt
   1 egg
   1 Tablespoon vinegar
  ¼ cup cold water

Blend together the flour, shortening and salt until the mixture resembles small peas. Slightly beat the egg and blend in vinegar and water. Combine the liquid with the flour mixture until thoroughly blended.

BLUE RIBBON WINNER, OREGON STATE FAIR

GEORGE AND TERRY MIZE — GILLESPIE, ILLINOIS

George Mize works at a steel mill. He also bakes a mean Chocolate Crinkle Cookie. If you think George is worried that the guys at the mill will find out about his culinary skills, you're wrong. George often bakes cookies for them and many of them ask him to prepare special baked goods for their wives' birthdays and for other special occasions.

George's wife, Terry, is also a skilled cook and she enjoys competing against him at the Illinois State Fair. In fact, a few years back, George and Terry were both in the finals for Best Cookie at the Fair. George's Chocolate Crinkle Cookie won.

But Terry has also had her moments in the spotlight. Two years ago she took the blue ribbon for a special event sponsored by the Hershey Chocolate Company. She also took top honors for Best Cake at the Macoupin County Fair for five consecutive years.

Below is George's blue ribbon recipe for Blackberry Surprise Pie, his famous Chocolate Crinkle Cookie can be found on page 246. Terry's Chocolate Chew Bars and her Orange Ice-Box Cookies are on pages 246–247.

BLACKBERRY SURPRISE PIE

PASTRY
  3 cups flour
  1 cup vegetable oil
  ½ cup milk or buttermilk

FILLING
  2 quarts blackberries, or 1 quart blackberries and 1 quart black
     raspberries
1½ cups sugar
2½ Tablespoons instant tapioca

Blend the pastry ingredients with large spoon in cutting motions.
Do not knead with your hands. Press the pastry into a 9×13-inch
pan with fingers. Do not roll with a pin. Pour in the filling, then
crumble the remaining pastry into a topping (crumble crust) and
then fold the sides of the pastry down onto the filling. Bake at
325–350 degrees until the filling is thoroughly cooked, usually
45 minutes to one hour, depending on the ripeness of berries.
The secret here is the oil in the pastry. It allows one to bake the
filling longer and more slowly without fear of burning the crust.
When the filling is done, turn up heat to 425 degrees to brown.
Usually only a few minutes are necessary. These instructions
apply to any fruit-filling pie.

BLUE RIBBON WINNER, ILLINOIS STATE FAIR

LILLIE LIPPS — O'KEENE, OKLAHOMA

*Born on the Fourth of July, Lillie Lipps has always been a real "fire-
cracker." This former All-Tournament Star Forward is still active as a*

member of the basketball boosters, the senior citizens club, the Baptist Church, the Home Demonstration Club and the Women's Missionary Society. While Lillie, now seventy-two years old, no longer takes center court herself, the basketball tradition has passed down to her grandchildren. Five of them recently competed in O'Keene's basketball tournament and Lillie sat in the stands from 2 p.m. until after 11 p.m. rooting for and giving tips to her grandchildren. Her No-Weep Custard Pie won the Grand Championship against 214 entries. She was also reserve Grand Champion in the Blue Ribbon Chef contest and won almost fifty ribbons in state fair competition in 1982. A self-acknowledged "fairaholic," Lillie really wanted to share her blue ribbon pie with our readers because "so many people have trouble with custard" and because "sharing is what it's all about."

HALF AND HALF AND HALF PIE CRUST

    1   cup flour
    ¼   teaspoon salt
    ½   cup shortening
    ¼   cup cold water
    1   teaspoon vinegar

Combine the flour and salt and mix in the shortening. Add water and vinegar and knead in a ball, then roll out on a floured board to fit a 8- or 9-inch pie pan. After you once make the crust you don't need to hunt for the recipe, just remember to start or measure out the flour first with salt, then measure half as much shortening as flour and half as much liquid as shortening. It keeps well refrigerated for 2–3 weeks, and freezes well for 4 months.

NO–WEEP CUSTARD PIE

    1 Half and Half and Half Pie Crust (recipe above)
    2½ cups milk, scalded
    4 whole eggs
    ¼ teaspoon salt
    1 teaspoon vanilla
    ½ cup sugar
       Nutmeg

Roll out the pie dough and put in a 9-inch pie pan, brush with melted oleo on the bottom and sides of the crust to prevent a soggy crust.

Scald the milk. Beat the eggs slightly with the salt, vanilla and sugar. Gradually mix the milk with the egg mixture. Pour into the unbaked pie crust, and sprinkle the top with nutmeg. Bake at 450 degrees for 10 minutes. Reduce to 350 degrees and bake an additional 20–30 minutes, or until set in center.

BLUE RIBBON WINNER, OKLAHOMA STATE FAIR

ELEANOR MCLAUGHLIN — BANGOR, MAINE

Eleanor McLaughlin had lots of company growing up on a farm in Prentiss, Maine. She had five brothers and ten sisters.

Today, Eleanor and her husband, Ivory, reside in Bangor, where they are regular competitors at the Bangor State Fair. Her interest in state fairs traces to her childhood . . . her father and her grandfather were officials at the Springfield Fair near Prentiss. Over the years she has won blue ribbons in a wide range of categories, including rug making, quilting and almost every food contest imaginable. We are pleased that she has agreed to share her blue ribbon recipe for Mince Pie. Eleanor often prepares it with her own homemade filling made with deer meat but suggests that commercially prepared mincemeat can be readily substituted.

MINCE PIE

Pastry for 9-inch two-crust pie
1 quart homemade or commercially prepared mincemeat
½ cup sugar
1 teaspoon salt
3 teaspoons butter
½ cup molasses

Prepare pastry for a 9-inch two-crust pie. Mix the mincemeat with the sugar, salt and molasses. Adjust salt to taste if using commercially prepared mincemeat. Pour the ingredients into a lined pie pan and dot with butter. Cover with the top crust, and bake in 350-degree oven for 30 minutes.

BLUE RIBBON WINNER, BANGOR STATE FAIR

JEAN TASSANO — SONORA, CALIFORNIA

Jean and Jim Tassano run their own business, the Foothill Sierra Pest Control, in Sonora, California. Jean first entered a county fair competition in 1969 and "got the bug." In 1975, she upgraded to state fair competion and now competes regularly at the California State Fair, Tuolumne County Fair, Amador County Fair, Calaveras County Fair (beware of pesky jumping frogs) and at the Los Angeles County Fair. To date, Jean has won more than three thousand ribbons, including twelve hundred blues.

Her Raspberry Pie recipe has won a blue ribbon at every one of those fairs. Jean admits it is a little difficult to make, but is well worth the effort. She emphasizes the importance of using only fresh raspberries.

RASPBERRY PIE

    4 to 5 cups fresh raspberries
    ¾ cup sugar
    2 Tablespoons cornstarch
    2 to 3 drops almond extract
    1 to 2 Tablespoons lemon juice
       Pastry dough for 9-inch double crust

In a large pan combine the raspberries, sugar, cornstarch, extract
and lemon juice. Heat slowly over low heat. Stir gently until the
juice flows and the mixture begins to thicken. Remove from heat
and let cool. Roll the dough out for the bottom crust and fit into a
9-inch pan. Pour in the raspberry mixture. Dot with butter. Roll
out the top crust and put over the pie. Flute the edges. Bake in
425-degree oven for 10 minutes, reduce heat to 375 degrees and
bake for an additional 30 minutes or until crust is done. The pie
may need to be covered for the last 10 minutes.

BLUE RIBBON WINNER, CALIFORNIA STATE FAIR

6

COOKIES

SUNNY HICKEY — MIAMISBURG, OHIO

If you drop in at the Hickey farm you never know if you'll be asked to deliver a calf, clear a field or test a recipe. If luck is with you, you might be asked to sample the cookies. Sunny Hickey has been entering the Ohio State Fair for fifteen years and has averaged thirty ribbons each time, in everything from sewing to canning. "I'm hung up on state fair competition," says Sunny. "It's amazing the people I see there. They've watched my children grow up and I've watched theirs." This year Sunny not only topped fifty-one entries in the cookie competition, her original recipe went on to win the national Archway Cookie Contest. Sunny attributes her great success to her strong family relationships and her belief in the basics of good homestyle cooking. Winning the Archway Cookie Contest ended "ten years of trying to win that contest." It's a true accomplishment for this blue ribbon winner from Ohio.

GREEK MAZURKAS
Yield: 3½ dozen large cookies

  1 can (12 oz.) poppy seed filling
  4 teaspoons lemon juice
  1 cup butter
1½ cup sugar
  1 teaspoon vanilla
  2 teaspoons lemon extract
  1 Tablespoon grated lemon peel

3 egg yolks
1¼ teaspoons soda
¾ cup buttermilk (shake before pouring)
3½ cups flour
2 teaspoons baking powder

ICING
3 cups sifted confectioners sugar
2 Tablespoons butter, softened
2 teaspoons lemon extract
1 teaspoon grated lemon peel
2 Tablespoons milk

In a medium bowl, combine the poppy seed filling and lemon juice. Set aside while preparing cookie batter. Cream the butter; add the next five ingredients and beat well. Stir the soda into the buttermilk; then add to the creamed mixture. Stir the flour and baking powder together. Add to the mixture and beat. Place 1 level tablespoon of the cookie batter on a greased cookie sheet. Place 1 teaspoon of the poppy seed filling in the middle. Drop another teaspoon of batter over the filling, spreading to cover the filling. Repeat with the remaining batter. Bake in 350-degree oven for 10–12 minutes. Remove from oven; cool on wire racks. Prepare the icing in a medium-size bowl, by mixing the confectioners sugar and butter and then adding the remaining ingredients. Frost the cookies and sprinkle them with poppy seeds for decoration.

BLUE RIBBON WINNER, OHIO STATE FAIR

JAM THUMBPRINTS
Yield: About 3 dozen cookies

- ⅔ cup butter
- ⅓ cup sugar
- 2 eggs, separated
- 1 teaspoon vanilla
- ½ teaspoon salt
- 1½ cups flour
- ¾ cup finely chopped nuts
- Strawberry preserves

Cream together the butter and sugar until fluffy. Add the egg yolks, vanilla and ½ teaspoon salt. Beat well, gradually adding the flour and mixing well. Shape into ¾-inch balls; dip into the slightly beaten egg whites, then roll in the chopped nuts. Press down the center of each cookie with thumb. Bake in 350-degree oven for 10 minutes. Cool. Just before serving, fill the centers of the cookies with strawberry preserves.

BLUE RIBBON WINNER, IOWA STATE FAIR

GINGERBREAD BOYS
Yield: About 1½ dozen cookies

- ⅓ cup brown sugar
- ⅓ cup butter
- 1 egg
- ½ teaspoon vanilla
- ⅔ cup molasses

2¾ cups flour
1 teaspoon soda
1 teaspoon salt
2 teaspoons cinnamon
1 teaspoon ginger

Cream the brown sugar and butter. Add the egg, vanilla and molasses; mix well. Sift the dry ingredients together and add to the mixture. Chill. Roll the dough ¼ inch thick on a lightly floured board. Cut with a gingerbread-boy cutter. Bake at 350 degrees for about 8–10 minutes. When cooled, decorate as desired.

BLUE RIBBON WINNER, IOWA STATE FAIR

LEMON CHEESE PRESSED COOKIE
Yield: 4 dozen cookies

1 cup butter
1 package (3 oz.) cream cheese
1 cup sugar
1 egg
1 teaspoon lemon juice
1 teaspoon grated lemon rind
2½ cups flour
1 teaspoon baking powder

Blend the butter and cream cheese. Add the sugar; cream thoroughly. Add the egg, lemon juice and lemon rind; blend well. Blend the flour and baking powder. Add to the cream cheese mixture. Mix thoroughly. Chill the dough for 30 minutes. Force the dough through a cookie press onto an ungreased baking sheet. Bake at 350 degrees for 8–10 minutes, or until slightly browned.

BLUE RIBBON WINNER, IOWA STATE FAIR

FROSTED BON BON
Yield: About 2 dozen cookies

1 cup chopped dates
1 cup powdered sugar
1 Tablespoon butter
1 cup peanut butter
1 cup finely chopped pecans
2 cups Rice Krispies
   Chocolate chips
   Pecan halves

Mix all the ingredients, except the chocloate chips and pecans, together well. Form into 1-inch balls. Melt your coating of the chocolate chips. Dip the cookies. Place half a pecan on top of each cookie.

BLUE RIBBON WINNER, IOWA STATE FAIR

BUTTERSCOTCH BARS
Yield: 3 dozen bars

½ cup butter or margarine
2 cups brown sugar
2 eggs
1 teaspoon vanilla
2 cups sifted all-purpose flour
2 teaspoons baking powder
¼ teaspoon salt
1 cup shredded coconut
1 cup chopped walnuts

In a saucepan combine the butter and brown sugar; cook over low heat until bubbly, stirring constantly. Cool. Add the eggs to the cooled mixture, one at a time, beating well after each addition. Add vanilla. Sift together the dry ingredients; add with the coconut and nuts to the brown sugar mixture; mix thoroughly. Spread in a greased 15½×10½×1-inch jelly roll pan. Bake in moderate oven (350 degrees) for about 25 minutes or until done. Cut in bars while warm. Remove from the pan when almost cool.

BLUE RIBBON WINNER, IOWA STATE FAIR

VIRGINIA BENAVIDEZ — CORRALES, NEW MEXICO

Although Virginia Benavidez has been winning blue ribbons for four years, she takes special pride in the one for her Biscochitos. This traditional Christmas cookie is made "by everyone in New Mexico" and her recipe took several years to perfect. Virginia loves to cook and experiments with foods from all cultures. She finds preparing special dishes for her family "a joy because they appreciate everything I make."

BISCOCHITOS
Yield: 5 to 6 dozen cookies

> 1½ cups sugar
> 1 pound pure lard (no substitutes)
> 3 eggs
> 1 ounce wine, brandy or whiskey
> 7 cups flour
> 3 teaspoons baking powder
> ½ teaspoon salt
> 1 Tablespoon anise seed, crushed
> Sugar and cinnamon topping (recipe follows)

Cream the lard and add the sugar. Then cream again. Break in the eggs, one at a time, beating into the creamed mixture. Mix in the wine. Add the flour, baking powder, salt and crushed anise seeds. Refrigerate overnight. On a floured surface roll out ¼ inch thick. Cut into fancy shapes. Dip the tops of the cookies in sugar and cinnamon topping. Bake at 350 degrees for about 12 minutes or until light brown.

TOPPING
½ cup sugar
1 Tablespoon cinnamon

Blend sugar and cinnamon together in a mixing bowl.

BLUE RIBBON WINNER, NEW MEXICO STATE FAIR

FRAN NEAVOLL — SALEM, OREGON

VIENNESE WALNUT COOKIES
Yield: 1 to 1½ dozen cookies

½ cup butter
⅓ cup granulated sugar
¼ teaspoon salt
¾ teaspoon pure vanilla
1 egg yolk
1¼ cups all-purpose sifted flour
⅓ cup ground walnuts

Cream the butter, sugar, salt and vanilla together with an electric mixer until creamy. Add the egg yolk and beat well. Blend in the flour and walnuts. Divide the dough into fourths and wrap in wax paper. Chill for 30 minutes. Roll ⅛ or ¼ inch thick between sheets of lightly floured wax paper. Remove wax paper. Cut with 1½-inch round cookie cutter. Bake on an ungreased cookie sheet (Teflon preferred) at 350 degrees for 8–10 minutes or until lightly browned. Remove from the cookie sheet at once. Cool. Place two cookies together with the following icing:

ICING
2 cups sifted powdered sugar
2 Tablespoons butter, melted
½ teaspoon pure vanilla
Whipping cream
Pink food coloring
Walnut halves

Mix together the powdered sugar, butter and vanilla. Add sufficient cream to make a spreading consistency and blend well with an electric mixer. Add a small drop of pink food coloring. Fill icing between two cookies. Using a decorator tube #30, put a swirl of icing on top and place a walnut half in the center of the icing.

BLUE RIBBON WINNER, OREGON STATE FAIR

SUGAR COOKIES
Yield: 6 dozen cookies

1 cup butter
2 cups granulated sugar
2 eggs
4¼ cups flour
1 teaspoon salt
1½ teaspoons baking powder
1 teaspoon soda
¼ cup milk
1 teaspoon pure vanilla

Cream the butter and sugar together with an electric mixer. Add vanilla. Add the eggs and beat until fluffy. Sift the flour. Measure and add salt, soda and baking powder. Add the sifted dry ingredients alternately with milk. Stir until dough is smooth. Divide the dough into fourths and wrap in wax paper. Refrigerate overnight. Using a small amount of dough, roll out to ⅛- or ¼-inch thickness between sheets of floured wax paper. Remove wax paper. Cut with a cookie cutter. Place 1 inch apart on a greased cookie sheet (Teflon preferred). Bake at 400 degrees for 5 minutes. Frost with the following Butter Cream Icing:

BUTTER CREAM ICING
1 pound sifted powdered sugar
¼ teaspoon salt
¼ cup milk
1 teaspoon white vanilla
⅓ cup butter, softened

Beat all ingredients until smooth. If too stiff, beat in a few drops of milk. You can shape this dough into lollipop cookies by rolling it ¼ inch thick and inserting a popsicle stick. Then decorate them and write names and slogans on them in icing. The cookies can be wrapped in a small plastic bag and tied with a yarn bow. They are a big hit at bazaars and with children. You can even make Cookie-Grams. Cut the cookie very large, about 8 inches (either round or heart-shaped). Decorate the cookies for the occasion, Happy Birthday or Happy Valentine's Day, etc. Also use this recipe to make a cookie tree. Use a small cookie cutter to make the shape of stars, snowflakes, and bells. Before baking, cut a small hole in top of cookie for fastening to tree. Decorate the cookies. Fasten the cookies with a toothpick to a cone-shaped Styrofoam, which has been covered with plastic wrap. Decorate with ribbon bows between cookies.

BLUE RIBBON WINNER, OREGON STATE FAIR

FLAVIA HARRIS — FALLON, NEVADA

These "Hello Dolly" Cookies were a triple winner at the Nevada State Fair. The blue ribbon actually went to Flavia Harris, who qualified for the competition by winning her local county fair. But Flavia's recipe was given to her twenty years ago by her good friend and neighbor, *Zona Murdock.*

On the day of the fair Flavia couldn't attend, so another friend, *Bonnie Gardner,* acted as her representative. It may be a mystery to you who actually won . . . but not to Flavia. She split the prize money three ways and all three winners celebrated.

"HELLO DOLLY" COOKIES
Yield: About 2 dozen cookies

    3 Tablespoons butter, melted
    1 cup finely crushed graham crackers
    1 cup chocolate chips
    1 cup sweetened coconut
    1 cup chopped nuts
    1 can (15 oz.) sweetened condensed milk

Heat a 9×13-inch pan to melt butter. Add the graham cracker crumbs amd pat out on the bottom of the pan. Mix the other ingredients together in bowl, except the milk, and sprinkle over the graham crackers. Dribble milk evenly over the top. Bake at 350 degrees for 30 minutes.

BLUE RIBBON WINNER, NEVADA STATE FAIR

PHYLLIS PRALL — MITCHELLVILLE, IOWA

MICROWAVE NUT BARS
Yield: 16 bars

    2 Tablespoons butter
    1 cup brown sugar

1 cup chopped nuts
⅓ cup flour
⅛ teaspoon baking soda
⅛ teaspoon salt
2 eggs, beaten
1 teaspoon vanilla
  Confectioners sugar

In an 8×8-inch pan melt the butter. In a bowl, stir together the sugar, nuts, flour, soda and salt. Add the eggs and vanilla. Carefully pour the nut mixture over the melted butter, but don't stir it. Cook 6–7 minutes in a microwave oven on high until done. Cookies will appear moist in the center. Remove from oven and let stand for 2 minutes. Sift confectioners sugar over the top and cut into bars.

BLUE RIBBON WINNER, IOWA STATE FAIR

KIM AND KANDICE MORSE — GREAT FALLS, MONTANA

SPICY GINGER COOKIES
Yield: 6 to 7 dozen cookies

¾ cup butter
1 cup sugar
1 teaspoon vanilla
1 egg
¼ cup molasses
2¼ cups sifted flour
2 teaspoons baking soda
1 teaspoon salt
1 teaspoon cinnamon
¾ teaspoon ginger
½ teaspoon ground cloves
  Sugar

Cream together the butter and sugar until light and fluffy. Add the vanilla, egg and molasses. Beat well. In another bowl sift together the flour, baking soda, salt, cinnamon, ginger and cloves. Add gradually to the creamed mixture. Chill several hours in refrigerator. Shape into balls ¾ inch in diameter. If the dough seems sticky, mix in an additional ¼ cup of flour. Roll in sugar and place 2 inches apart on a buttered baking sheet. Bake at 375 degrees for 7–8 minutes. Cool on a wire rack.

BLUE RIBBON WINNER, MONTANA STATE FAIR

DOLLY BUEHLER — LOUISVILLE, KENTUCKY

Charlie and Edna ("Dolly") Buehler are retired now . . . they have been married forty-three years and have raised two fine sons in Louisville, Kentucky. Dolly wishes that today's marriages would last as long and be as happy as theirs. Of course Charlie and Dolly have a lot in common. He's an electrician and she's an electrifying cook.

It took Dolly an awful long time to enter a state fair competition. She first entered in 1979 at the age of sixty-four. That year she entered three cookie recipes and walked off with three blue ribbons. We think you'll enjoy her Rolled Oat Cookies, a blue ribbon winner at the 1982 Kentucky State Fair.

ROLLED OAT COOKIES
Yield: 4 dozen cookies

¾ cup margarine, softened
1 cup brown sugar
½ cup granulated sugar
1 egg
¼ cup milk
1 teaspoon pure vanilla
1 teaspoon salt
1 teaspoon cinnamon

2 cups unsifted flour
½ teaspoon baking soda
½ teaspoon nutmeg
3 cups uncooked rolled oats (regular)
1 cup white raisins
   Currant jelly

Beat well the margarine, sugars, egg, milk, and vanilla. Sift together the flour, salt and soda. Add to the margarine mixture, mixing well. Blend in rolled oats, and raisins. Drop by teaspoonful onto greased cookie sheets. With your finger make a dent in each cookie and fill with small amount of currant jelly. If the cookie dough sticks to your finger, dip your finger lightly in flour. Bake in moderate oven (350 degrees) for 12–15 minutes.

BLUE RIBBON WINNER, KENTUCKY STATE FAIR

CHRISTI AND TRACY GARBER — ALBUQUERQUE, NEW MEXICO

We spent a lot of time deciding which Chocolate Chip Cookie recipe to include. It's an all-American favorite and it had to be special. Among the many we received was one that came from a very special family in Albuquerque, New Mexico.

Christi Garber won a blue ribbon for this cookie at the 1982 New Mexico State Fair. She is thirteen years old.

Last year Christi's sister Tracy won a blue ribbon and a rosette for best cookie, using the same recipe. Tracy was only ten years old at the time.

Christi plays the violin, Tracy plays the flute . . . musical talents they obviously inherited from their guitar-, banjo- and piano-playing father, Frank. But Mom also contributed to their well-rounded backgrounds. Gail Garber is a regular contestant in the crafts division, where she specializes in sewing and quilting.

CHOCOLATE CHIP COOKIES
Yield: About 3 to 4 dozen cookies

- ¾ cup vegetable shortening
- ½ cup sugar
- ¼ cup brown sugar
- 1 egg
- 1 teaspoon vanilla
- 1½ to 2 cups flour
- ¾ teaspoon salt
- ½ teaspoon soda
- 6 ounces chocolate chips
- ½ cup nuts (optional)

Cream ½ cup of the shortening, the sugar, eggs and vanilla until very light and fluffy. Add the extra ¼ cup of shortening and mix well. Mix in 1 cup of the flour and the other dry ingredients, except for the chocolate chips and nuts. Add the remaining flour a little at a time until the dough is no longer wet and sticky. Add the chocolate chips. Roll a heaping teaspoonful of the dough into a ball. This way the cookies will all be perfectly round. Bake on greased cookie sheet at 350 degrees for 10–15 minutes.

BLUE RIBBON WINNER, NEW MEXICO STATE FAIR

CAROL KERN — LOUISVILLE, KENTUCKY

MEXICAN WEDDING CAKES
Yield: About 4 dozen cookies

- 1 cup butter, softened
- ½ cup powdered sugar
- ¼ teaspoon salt

2 teaspoons vanilla
2 cups unsifted flour
2 cups finely chopped pecans

Preheat oven to 325 degrees. Mix the butter, powdered sugar, and salt and vanilla together. Blend in the flour and pecans until the dough holds together. Shape into crescents or 1-inch balls. Place 1 inch apart on an ungreased baking sheet. Bake 15–20 minutes, or until set but not brown. Cool slightly, then roll in powdered sugar. Cool completely and roll again in powdered sugar.

BLUE RIBBON WINNER, KENTUCKY STATE FAIR

FERN HARMON — GRANGER, IOWA

HONEY–LEMON SPECIALS
Yield: 4 dozen cookies

½ cup (1 stick) butter or margarine
½ cup sugar
½ cup honey
1 egg
1 teaspoon grated lemon rind
2 cups sifted flour
¼ teaspoon salt
1 teaspoon baking powder
1 cup wheat germ

Beat the butter or margarine, sugar and honey until fluffy with an electric mixer in a large bowl. Add the egg and lemon rind; beat. Stir the flour, salt, baking powder, ½ cup of wheat germ into the butter-sugar mixture. Refrigerate for at least one hour. Shape the dough into 1-inch balls; roll in the remaining wheat germ. Place on ungreased cookie sheets. Flatten slightly with your finger. Bake at 350 degrees for 8–10 minutes, or until edges are lightly browned. Remove with a spatula to wire racks to cool. Store in a covered container.

BLUE RIBBON WINNER, IOWA STATE FAIR

JULIA BRINKLEY — CARY, NORTH CAROLINA

DATE BARS
Yield: 2 dozen bars

  1 cup all-purpose flour
  ½ cup brown sugar, firmly packed
  ½ cup margarine

FILLING
  1 cup chopped dates
  ½ cup sugar
  ½ cup margarine
  1 egg, well beaten
  2 cups Rice Krispies cereal
  1 cup chopped nuts
  1 teaspoon vanilla

FROSTING
  2 cups powdered sugar
  2 to 3 teaspoons milk, if desired
  ½ teaspoon vanilla
  1 package (3 oz.) cream cheese, softened

Heat oven to 375 degrees. Combine the first three ingredients; mix until crumbly. Press into an ungreased 11×7-inch or 9-inch square pan. Bake at 375 degrees for 10–12 minutes or until golden brown. In a medium saucepan, combine the dates, sugar, and margarine. Cook over medium heat until the mixture boils, stirring constantly; simmer 3 minutes. Blend about ¼ cup of the hot mixture into the beaten egg; return the egg mixture to the saucepan. Cook just until mixture bubbles, stirring constantly. Remove from heat; stir in Rice Krispies cereal, nuts and vanilla. Spread over the baked crust; cool completely. Combine the frosting ingredients; beat at low speed until smooth. Spread over the filling.

BLUE RIBBON WINNER, NORTH CAROLINA STATE FAIR

ANNA J. STONE — CIRCLEVILLE, OHIO

RAISIN DATE COOKIES
Yield: About 6 to 7 dozen cookies

7 cups all-purpose flour
1 cup chopped walnuts
1 cup chopped dates
1 cup chopped raisins
1 teaspoon soda
½ teaspoon salt
1 teaspoon cinnamon
1 pound margarine, melted
2 cups brown sugar
1 cup white sugar
3 eggs, beaten
2 teaspoons vanilla

Put 4 cups of flour in a bowl and set aside. In another, larger bowl put 3 cups of flour. To this add the walnuts, dates and raisins. Be sure each is coated with flour. Add the soda, salt and cinnamon to the flour and fruit mixture. In a mixer bowl cream the melted margarine and brown and white sugars. Add 3 beaten eggs. Beat well. Add the fruit and flour mixture. Blend. Add the vanilla and the remaining 4 cups of flour. Mix well. Divide into three equal quantities. Shape into rolls and wrap in plastic wrap. Store in refrigerator for 2 or 3 days and then freeze. Aging 2 weeks before baking gives a better-tasting cookie. Cut in ¼-inch slices. Bake at 350 degrees for 12 minutes or until slightly brown around the edges. Do not let get brown all over or the cookie will be hard.

Hint: Chop the raisins, dates and nuts with ½ cup of the flour in a food processor: this does an excellent job in a few seconds.

BLUE RIBBON WINNER, OHIO STATE FAIR

CATHY YOUNG — LOUISVILLE, KENTUCKY

OLD–FASHIONED SUGAR COOKIES
Yield: About 7 to 8 dozen cookies

    1 cup vegetable oil
    1 cup butter
    1 cup granulated sugar
    1 cup powdered sugar
    1 teaspoon vanilla
    2 eggs
    1 teaspoon soda
 4½ cups flour, sifted
  ½ teaspoon salt
    1 teaspoon cream of tartar

Thoroughly cream the oil, butter and both sugars. Add the vanilla and eggs. Sift the dry ingredients in and blend well. Chill the dough before shaping. Roll 2 teaspoons of dough into a ball. Roll the ball in granulated sugar. Place on a greased cookie sheet.

Cross each ball with a fork. Bake at 375 degrees for about 8–10 minutes. Will keep in refrigerator for several days.

BLUE RIBBON WINNER, KENTUCKY STATE FAIR

JOY STARKEY — CHARLES CITY, VIRGINIA

DREAM BARS
Yield: 1½ to 2 dozen bars

½ cup butter
½ cup brown sugar
1 cup flour

Mix the above ingredients until crumbly. Pat into a 9×13-inch pan. Bake at 350 degrees for about 10 minutes, until lightly brown.

TOPPING
1 cup brown sugar
1 teaspoon vanilla
½ teaspoon baking powder
1 cup coconut
2 eggs
2 Tablespoons flour
¼ teaspoon salt
½ to 1 cup chopped nuts

Combine the above ingredients well and pour over the baked mixture. Bake again at 350 degrees for 20–25 minutes, until brown. Cut into bars.

BLUE RIBBON WINNER, VIRGINIA STATE FAIR

If you think you have to be a professional cook or a home economist to win a blue ribbon at a state fair, meet Betty Morris of Roanoke, Virginia. Although Betty grew up near the fairgrounds in Fairlea, West Virginia, and attended regularly as a child, she had never before been tempted to enter a single event. In 1982 she decided to enter her favorite cookie recipes in one of the most prestigious events at the West Virginia State Fair, the Governor's Cookie Jar. To enter, a contestant must submit at least nine different cookies in a plain one-gallon cookie jar. The blue ribbon winner is introduced to the governor of the state on Governor's Day at the fair and presents the prize winning assortment.

Mrs. Morris and her family drove over two hours from Roanoke in neighboring Virginia to enter the contest. Although she was off enjoying the other attractions at the fair when the blue ribbon was awarded, her son Mike was present to observe the honors. He soon relayed the good news to his mother and the family celebrated Mrs. Morris's wonderful achievement of winning the coveted blue ribbon for the Governor's Cookie Jar on her first attempt. Below are Mrs. Morris's eleven prize winning recipes which you can enjoy individually or as an assortment as they were presented at the 1982 West Virginia State Fair.

GOVERNOR'S COOKIE JAR

To give you an idea of what it takes to win a Governor's Cookie Jar contest, read the following entry instructions for the West Virginia Fair:

"Jar of fancy assorted cookies made from different kinds of batters and doughs. These should be a variety of color and may be decorated if desired. The container MUST be a one gallon clear glass jar with wide mouth and lid so that the jar may be tightly sealed. The jar may be decorated if desired but extra 'attention getters' will not be permitted. Jar must be filled and contain not less than nine (9) kinds of cookies. Bring one of each kind of cookie in a small box so that the judge will not need to open the jar. First prize cookie jar will be presented to Governor John D. Rockefeller on Governor's Day by the winning exhibitor. 1st prize $25.00; 2nd prize $20.00; 3rd $15.00."

CHERRY COCONUT COOKIES
Yield: 3 to 4 dozen cookies

> 2½ cups flour
> 1 teaspoon baking powder
> ½ teaspoon salt
> ¾ cup shortening
> ½ cup maraschino cherries, finely chopped
> 1 cup sugar
> 1 egg
> ¼ cup milk
> 1 teaspoon vanilla
> Coconut

Sift together the flour, baking powder and salt. In another bowl, mix together the shortening and the sugar. Add the egg and beat. Stir in milk and vanilla. Add the flour mixture and beat well. Stir in maraschino cherries. Shape into balls and roll in the coconut. Place on a cookie sheet about 2 inches apart. Bake on oven rack placed slightly below the center of the 350-degree oven for 12 minutes or until lightly browned. Remove from baking sheet at once.

CHOCOLATE BUTTERSWEETS
Yield: About 1½ dozen cookies

½ cup butter
½ cup confectioners sugar
¼ teaspoon salt
1 teaspoon vanilla
1 to 1¼ cups flour (not self-rising)

Cream the butter, add the sugar, salt and vanilla. Cream together thoroughly. Gradually add the flour. Shape into balls. Bake on an ungreased cookie sheet at 350 degrees for 12–15 minutes until delicately browned at the edges. Fill while warm, frost when cool.

CREAMY FILLING
1 package (3 oz.) cream cheese, softened
1 cup confectioners sugar
2 Tablespoons flour
1 teaspoon vanilla
½ cup nuts
½ cup coconut

Soften the cream cheese. Blend in the confectioners sugar, flour and vanilla. Cream well. Stir in the nuts and coconut.

CHOCOLATE FROSTING
½ cup chocolate chips
2 Tablespoons water
2 Tablespoons butter
½ cup confectioners sugar

Combine the chocolate chips, water and butter in a small saucepan. Cook over low heat, stirring occasionally, until the chips are melted. Remove from heat and add the confectioners sugar. Beat until smooth.

GALLETS
Yield: About 7 dozen cookies

1½ cups butter
1 pound brown sugar
3 Tablespoons white sugar
1 Tablespoon honey
6 eggs
4 cups flour
1 teaspoon vanilla

Cream the butter; add the sugars and cream well. Add the honey, then the eggs, then the flour and vanilla. Chill the batter for 2 hours, or overnight. Bake on a gallet iron.

LEMON SUGAR COOKIES
Yield: About 18 dozen cookies

2 cups milk
2 heaping tablespoons pulverized bakers ammonia
2 cups butter, or 2 cups shortening plus ½ teaspoon salt
4 cups sugar
5 eggs
1 teaspoon oil of lemon
12 cups flour, plus additional flour as needed
Egg whites

Dissolve the bakers ammonia in milk. Add all the other ingredients except the flour. Add 12 cups of flour and mix well. Gradually add more flour, a little at a time, until the dough is stiff enough to be rolled ½ inch thick. Try to keep the dough soft by adding as little additional flour as possible. Cut cookies, brush tops with egg white and prick with fork. Bake at 375 degrees for 10–15 minutes.

FROSTED DROP COOKIES
Yield: 3 to 4 dozen cookies

    2 cups sifted flour
    1 teaspoon baking powder
    ½ teaspoon vanilla
    ¼ cup milk
    ¾ cup butter
    1 cup confectioners sugar
    1 egg, separated

Sift together the flour and baking powder. In a separate bowl add vanilla to milk. In another bowl cream the butter and sugar together for 2 minutes. Add the egg yolk and continue beating for 1 minute. Beat the egg white until stiff and set aside. Add the flour and the milk mixtures alternately to the creamed butter and sugar. Begin with one-third of the flour mixture, then one-half of the milk mixture, etc., working quickly to avoid overbeating. Fold in the beaten egg white. Drop onto a buttered cookie sheet and bake at 375 degrees for 15 minutes. Frost as soon as removed from oven.

    FROSTING
    1½ cups confectioners sugar
    ½ teaspoon vanilla
    3 Tablespoons cream

Combine the ingredients and beat at high speed for 2 minutes.

HOLIDAY FRUIT DROPS
Yield: About 8 dozen cookies

    1   cup shortening
    2   cups brown sugar, firmly packed
    2   eggs
    ½   cup buttermilk or water
    3½ cups all-purpose flour
    1   teaspoon baking soda
    1   teaspoon salt
    1½ cups broken pecans
    2   cups candied cherries, halved
    2   cups chopped dates

Mix the shortening, sugar and eggs well. Stir in the buttermilk. Measure the flour by dipping method or by sifting. Blend the dry ingredients, and beat in. Stir in the pecans, cherries and dates. Chill for at least one hour. Drop the dough by rounded teaspoons about 2 inches apart on a lightly greased cookie sheet. Place a pecan half on each cookie, if desired. Bake at 400 degrees for 8–10 minutes or until almost no imprint remains when lightly touched.

OLD–FASHIONED OATMEAL COOKIES
Yield: 6 to 7 dozen cookies

    1   cup raisins
    1   cup water
    ¾   cup shortening
    1½ cups sugar
    2   eggs
    1   teaspoon vanilla
    2½ cups all-purpose flour

½ teaspoon baking powder
1 teaspoon baking soda
1 teaspoon salt
1 teaspoon cinnamon
½ teaspoon cloves
2 cups rolled oats
½ cup chopped nuts

Simmer the raisins in water over low heat for 20–30 minutes until plump. Strain the raisin liquid into a measuring cup and add enough water to make ½ cup. Mix together the shortening, sugar, eggs and vanilla. Add the raisin liquid. Stir together the flour, baking powder, baking soda, salt and spices; blend in. Add the rolled oats, nuts and raisins. Drop the dough by rounded teaspoons about 2 inches apart on an ungreased baking sheet. Bake at 400 degrees for 8–10 minutes, or until lightly browned.

PECAN TARTS
Yield: About 1 dozen tarts

6 ounces cream cheese
1 cup butter
2 cups flour
Pecan filling (recipe below)

Melt the cream cheese and butter together over low heat. Add the flour and chill at least one hour or overnight. Press the dough into small cupcake pans. Fill two-thirds full with the filling. Bake in 325-degree oven for 30–35 minutes.

FILLING
2½ cups brown sugar
3 eggs
3 Tablespoons butter
2½ cups pecans

2 teaspooons vanilla
¼ teaspoon salt

Combine all ingredients.

PFEFFERNUESSE
Yield: About 4½ dozen cookies

    ¾ cup light molasses
    ½ cup butter or margarine
    2 eggs, beaten
    4¼ cups sifted all-purpose flour
    ½ cup granulated sugar
    1¼ teaspoons baking soda
    1½ teaspoons cinnamon
    ½ teaspoon cloves
    ½ teaspoon nutmeg
       Dash of pepper
       Confectioners sugar

In a saucepan, combine the molasses and butter. Cook and stir until the butter melts. Cool to room temperature. Add the eggs. Sift together the flour, sugar, baking soda, cinnamon, cloves, nutmeg and pepper. Add to the molasses mixture and beat well. Chill for several hours or overnight. Shape the dough into 1-inch balls. Bake on a greased cookie sheet at 375 degrees for 12 minutes. Cool; roll in confectioners sugar.

SKILLET COOKIES
Yield: About 2 dozen cookies

    ½ cup butter or margarine
    8 ounces chopped dates

2 eggs
1 cup sugar
1 teaspoon vanilla
2 cups Rice Krispies cereal
½ cup nuts
Coconut

Melt the butter in a skillet. Add the dates. Beat the eggs and sugar together and add to the dates and butter. Cook over low heat for 8 minutes or until thick. In a mixing bowl, combine the Rice Krispies, nuts and vanilla. Stir in the butter mixture. Cool. Shape into balls and roll in coconut.

SWEET ALMOND POCKETS
Yield: About 3 dozen cookies

2¼ cups all-purpose flour
¼ cup confectioners sugar
1 cup butter or margarine, softened
6 ounces cream cheese, softened
1 teaspoon grated lemon peel
1 teaspoon lemon juice
Filling (recipe below)

Lightly spoon the flour into a measuring cup; level off. In a large bowl combine all the ingredients and blend to form a soft dough. Chill, covered, for about 30 minutes. Divide the pastry into four parts. On a floured surface, roll out each into a 9-inch square. Cut into 3-inch squares. Place 1 rounded teaspoon of the filling in the center of each square. Fold the pastry in half; seal the edges with a fork. Bake at 350 degrees on ungreased cookie sheets for 18–22 minutes, until the edges are lightly browned. Sprinkle with sugar, if desired.

FILLING

1 can (12 oz.) almond cake and pastry filling
1 cup coconut

Combine ingredients.

BLUE RIBBON WINNER, WEST VIRGINIA STATE FAIR

DEBBIE NELSON — IRMO, SOUTH CAROLINA

Toccoa, Georgia, lost one of its foremost cooks when Debbie Nelson moved north to Charleston and later to Irmo, South Carolina. Georgia's loss was South Carolina's gain and, as a result, competition at the South Carolina State Fair has increased during the past few years.

Debbie first entered the contest in 1980 and began winning blue ribbons immediately. She has been consistent, winning two blues every year she entered . . . for pound cakes, cookies, pies and the Brownie recipe that follows.

Debbie's husband, Gary, is an environmental engineer for the state of Georgia. They have one daughter, Casey Elizabeth, and expect another child any day.

BROWNIES
Yield: About 3 dozen squares

1½ cups all-purpose flour
1 teaspoon baking powder
1 teaspoon salt
1 cup (2 sticks) butter, softened to room temperature
2 cups sugar
4 eggs (room temperature)
½ cup plus 2 Tablespoons cocoa
1 teaspoon vanilla
1 cup chopped nuts

Sift the flour, baking powder and salt together. Add the remaining ingredients and combine. Place in a buttered 9×13-inch pan. Bake in 350-degree oven for 30 minutes. Ingredients may be halved and baked in buttered 8×8×2-inch pan for same amount of time. Do not overcook.

BLUE RIBBON WINNER, SOUTH CAROLINA STATE FAIR

LORI ROBB — ALBUQUERQUE, NEW MEXICO

At fifteen, Lori Robb is a sophomore at Sandia High School. She lives in Albuquerque with her parents, Mary and Mike Robb, and a seventeen-year-old brother, Dan. Lori is an up-and-coming ballerina. She's also on the swim team and is a volunteer candy striper at the Presbyterian Hospital in Albuquerque.

Years ago she decided that she would like to compete at the New Mexico State Fair. This year she picked up a blue ribbon for her Fudge Brownie recipe, which follows.

FUDGE BROWNIE
Yield: 16 squares

   ½ cup butter or margarine
   1 cup sugar
   1 teaspoon vanilla
   2 eggs
   2 1-ounce squares unsweetened chocolate, melted
   ½ cup sifted all-purpose flour
   ½ cup chopped walnuts

Preheat oven 325 degrees. Cream the butter, sugar, and vanilla; beat in the eggs. Blend in the melted chocolate. Stir in the flour and nuts. Bake in greased 8×8×2-inch pan at 325 degrees for 30–35 minutes. Cool.

BLUE RIBBON WINNER, NEW MEXICO STATE FAIR

VALERIE SAKAI — CLARKSBURG, CALIFORNIA

Valerie Sakai drew on the best of her Chinese, Japanese and Spanish heritage to pick up a blue ribbon for her all-American oatmeal cookie recipe at the California State Fair. When we spoke to her on Christmas Eve she was not only preparing for the holidays, but also for her wedding.

Valerie is employed by the Department of Education and is involved in Child Nutrition Services, a natural field considering her culinary skills.

Valerie has been competing at the California State Fair since 1975 and has won over fifty ribbons. She especially enjoys participating in the fair's Cooking Shed Demonstration Kitchen, where winners demonstrate how to prepare their blue ribbon recipes.

OATMEAL COOKIES
Yield: About 5 dozen cookies

¾	cup butter
¾	cup sugar
¾	cup brown sugar
2	eggs
1	teaspoon vanilla
1	cup flour
½	teaspoon soda
¼	teaspoon salt
½	teaspoon baking powder
2¼	cups quick oats
½	cup finely chopped nuts

Cream the butter, both sugars and eggs together well and add the vanilla. In another bowl mix the dry ingredients together and gradually add to the creamed mixture. Shape into 1-inch balls and place about 3 inches apart on a greased cookie sheet. Bake at 350 degrees for approximately 8 minutes. Cool.

BLUE RIBBON WINNER, CALIFORNIA STATE FAIR

PEGGY BRADEN — HARRISONVILLE, MISSOURI

Peggy Braden is a kindergarten teacher in Harrisonville, Missouri. She grew up near the state fair in Sedalia and finally decided last year to participate in the cooking contest. She won a blue ribbon on her first try and took the top prize for the prestigious First Lady's Cookie event.

Peggy has selected her recipe for Pecan Tassies, which was one of the six recipes that won a blue ribbon for the First Lady's Cookies at the 1982 Missouri State Fair.

PECAN TASSIES
Yield: 2 dozen cookies

½ cup butter
1 package (3 oz.) cream cheese, softened
1 cup flour
¾ cup brown sugar, firmly packed
1 egg
1 teaspoon vanilla
¾ cup chopped pecans

Combine the butter and cream cheese; add the flour and mix well. Chill. Combine the brown sugar, egg and vanilla; stir in the nuts. Divide the dough into 24 balls. Press into miniature muffin pans. Fill each cup three-fourths full with the brown sugar mixture. Bake at 325 degrees for 25–30 minutes. Cool in pan for 5 minutes before removing.

BLUE RIBBON WINNER, MISSOURI STATE FAIR

APRICOT–RAISIN BARS
Yield: 36 bars

½   cup butter
1¼ cups sugar
½   teaspoon salt
1   Tablespoon grated lemon rind
1   cup sifted flour
1   cup bran flakes with raisins
1   package (8 oz.) cream cheese
2   eggs
2   teaspoon lemon juice
½   teaspoon baking powder
¾   cup chopped dried apricots
¾   cup chopped raisins

Cream the butter and ½ cup of the sugar; add the salt, lemon rind, flour and bran flakes. Blend. Press the dough into the bottom of a greased 13×9½-inch pan. Combine the cream cheese, the remaining ¾ cup of sugar, eggs, lemon juice and baking powder; blend until smooth. Add the raisins and apricots; blend well. Spread over the crust. Bake at 350 degrees for 30–35 minutes. Cool; cut into bars. Can be frozen for 6 months.

BLUE RIBBON WINNER, FLEMINGTON (N.J.) FAIR

LUCILLE MARTONE — SYRACUSE, NEW YORK

The Dey Brothers Department Store in Syracuse, New York, recognizes an outstanding employee when they see one. Lucille Martone won a blue ribbon for her Molasses Sparkle Cookies at the New York State Fair and Dey Brothers immediately asked her to demonstrate the recipe using the new convection oven that they sell. What better endorsement could there be?

Lucille has been using the recipe for many years, but it has been a family secret until a few years ago when her daughter Mary Anne convinced her to enter the fair.

MOLASSES SPARKLE COOKIES
Yield: About 4 dozen cookies

    1   cup shortening
    ¾   cup sugar
    ¼   cup molasses
    1   egg
    2   cups flour
    2   teaspoons baking soda
    1   teaspoon ginger
    1   teaspoon cinnamon
    ½   teaspoon powdered cloves
    ½   teaspoon salt

Cream together the shortening and sugar. Add the eggs and molasses and mix together. Sift together the dry ingredients. Stir into the molasses mixture and blend well. Shape the dough into golfball-size nuggets. Dip the tops in sugar. Bake in 350-degree oven for 12 minutes.

BLUE RIBBON WINNER, NEW YORK STATE FAIR

SUSAN STONEMAN — RICHMOND, VIRGINIA

Susan Stoneman comes from a true state fair family. Both her father and grandfather were on the Board of Directors of the Virginia State Fair. That background may have kindled Susan's interest in the fair, but it didn't provide an advantage in the culinary competition. Her success in that category is truly her own doing.

Susan first competed in 1964 at the age of eleven and was very successful in her first showing. Over the years she has accumulated seventy-three ribbons, including forty-two blues. In 1982 she won a total of eight blue ribbons, including two special awards for the State Fair Cookie Jar. The two recipes that Susan has provided were included in those special awards.

A graduate of the University of Georgia, Susan is presently a legal assistant specializing in tax law in Richmond, Virginia.

VALENTINE SHORTBREAD
Yield: About 2 dozen cookies

¾ cup butter, softened
¼ cup sugar
2 cups all-purpose flour

Preheat oven to 350 degrees. Cream the butter and sugar. Work in the flour. If the dough is crumbly, mix in 1 to 2 tablespoons additional soft butter. Roll dough to ¼-inch thickness on a lightly floured cloth-covered board. Cut into heart shapes (or any other shape desired) with a cutter. Place ½ inch apart on an ungreased baking sheet. Bake about 20 minutes or until set. Immediately remove from the baking sheet.

ICING FOR VALENTINE SHORTBREAD
1 small package frozen strawberries, thawed
1 pound confectioners sugar

Mix enough strawberries and sugar to make a thick paste. Spread on the cooled shortbread.

BLUE RIBBON WINNER, VIRGINIA STATE FAIR

DELUXE SUGAR COOKIES

Yield: About 5 dozen cookies

- 1 cup butter or margarine, softened
- 1½ cups confectioners sugar
- 1 egg
- 1 teaspoon vanilla extract
- ½ teaspoon almond extract
- 2½ cups all-purpose flour
- 1 teaspoon soda
- 1 teaspoon cream of tartar
- Granulated sugar

Mix thoroughly the butter, confectioners sugar, egg, vanilla and almond extract. Blend in the flour, soda and cream of tartar. Cover; chill 2 to 3 hours.

Preheat oven to 375 degrees. Divide the dough in half. Roll each half ³/₁₆ inch thick on a lightly floured cloth-covered board. Cut into desired shapes; sprinkle with granulated sugar. Place on a lightly greased baking sheet. Bake 7–8 minutes or until light brown on edge.

BLUE RIBBON WINNER, VIRGINIA STATE FAIR

K. ELAINE RIPPEE — SPARKS, NEVADA

Elaine Rippee's great-great-great-grandmother was a princess of the royal blood in England. When she renounced her title and married a commoner, Victoria ascended to the throne in her place.

Elaine learned her cooking skills from her Swiss Grandma Ence and her English Grandma Bradshaw. She enjoys cooking and baking along with her other hobbies, which include poetry and, naturally, genealogy. She plans on winning additional blue ribbons at the Nevada State Fair and hopes to write a book on her British ancestors and the history of their descendants.

GLAZED LEMON SQUARES
Yield: 64 squares

1 cup Bisquick baking mix
2 Tablespoons powdered sugar
2 Tablespoons firm margarine or butter
¾ cup granulated sugar
¼ cup flaked coconut
1 Tablespoon Bisquick baking mix
2 eggs
2 Tablespoons lemon juice
2 teaspoons grated lemon peel
½ cup powdered sugar
1½ Tablespoons lemon juice

Preheat oven to 350 degrees. Mix 1 cup of the baking mix and the powdered sugar. Cut in the margarine. Press in an ungreased square pan, 8×8×2 inches. Bake until light brown, about 5 minutes. Mix the remaining ingredients except the powdered sugar and lemon juice; pour over the baked layer. Bake until set, about 25 minutes. Loosen edges from sides of pan while warm. Mix the powdered sugar and lemon juice until smooth; spread on the warm square. Cool completely; cut into 1-inch squares.

BLUE RIBBON WINNER, NEVADA STATE FAIR

JIMMY'S GRANOLA COOKIES
Yield: About 5 dozen cookies

¾ cup butter
1 cup brown sugar
½ cup granulated sugar
1 egg
¼ cup water
1 teaspoon vanilla
1 teaspoon butter flavoring
3 cups Quaker 100% Granola cereal (with dates and raisins), slightly crushed
1¼ cups all-purpose flour
1 teaspoon salt
½ teaspoon allspice
1 teaspoon cinnamon
1 cup golden raisins
1 cup coconut
1 cup chopped nuts
½ cup chopped dates (optional)

Mix the butter, sugars, egg, water, and flavorings thoroughly. Stir in the remaining ingredients. If dough looks too shiny, add another couple tablespoons of flour. Drop the dough by rounded spoonfuls about 2 inches apart on an ungreased cookie sheet. Bake at 350 degrees until slight imprint remains when touched, about 11–13 minutes. Cool before removing from the baking sheet. Store in a tightly covered container (If you can keep them that long!)

BLUE RIBBON WINNER, CALIFORNIA STATE FAIR

POLKA–DOT MACAROONS
Yield: About 2½ dozen cookies

- 2 egg whites
- ⅛ teaspoon salt
- ⅛ teaspoon cream of tartar
- 1 teaspoon vanilla (or almond or coconut extract)
- ¾ cup sugar
- 1 package (6 oz.) Nestlés Chocolate Chips
- ½ cup chopped pecans or walnuts
- ½ cup flaked coconut

Beat the egg whites, salt, cream of tartar and flavoring until soft peaks form. Add the sugar gradually, beating until peaks are stiff. Fold in the chocolate chips, nuts, and coconut. Cover a cookie sheet with parchment (not waxed) paper. Drop the mixture by rounded teaspoonfuls. Bake in slow oven (300 degrees) for about 20–25 minutes until just starting to turn golden.

BLUE RIBBON WINNER, CALIFORNIA STATE FAIR

CHOCOLATE CHEW BARS
Yield: About 2 to 3 dozen bars

- 3 cups rolled oats
- 1 cup Bakers Coconut

1   teaspoon cherry extract
1   cup finely chopped pecans
1   cup butter, melted
½   cup sugar
1   package (6 oz.) semisweet chocolate pieces
¾   cup peanut butter

Preheat oven to 350 degrees. In large bowl, blend the first six ingredients until crumbly. Press the mixture into an ungreased 9×13-inch pan. Bake for 15–20 minutes or until lightly golden brown. In a small saucepan, combine the chocolate pieces and peanut butter. Cook until melted. Spread over baked rectangle. Chill and cut into bars.

BLUE RIBBON WINNER, ILLINOIS STATE FAIR

GEORGE MIZE — GILLESPIE, ILLINOIS

CHOCOLATE CRINKLES
Yield: About 6 dozen cookies

½   cup vegetable oil
4   ounces Nestlé Choco Bake
2   cups granulated sugar
4   eggs
2   teaspoons vanilla
2   teaspoons baking powder
1¾ cup flour
½   teaspoon salt
1   cup confectioners sugar

Mix together the oil, chocolate and granulated sugar. Blend in the eggs one at a time. Add the vanilla. Sift the flour, baking powder, and salt into the oil mixture. Chill several hours or overnight.

Preheat oven to 350 degrees. Drop by teaspoons onto the confectioners sugar. Roll in the sugar, and shape into balls. Place 2 inches apart on a greased sheet. Bake 10–12 minutes. Don't overbake.

BLUE RIBBON WINNER, ILLINOIS STATE FAIR

TERRY MIZE — GILLESPIE, ILLINOIS

TERRY'S ORANGE ICE–BOX COOKIES
Yield: About 5 dozen cookies

   1 cup butter
   ½ cup sugar
   ½ cup brown sugar
   1 egg
   3 Tablespoons orange juice
   2¼ cups sifted flour
   ½ teaspoon salt
   ½ teaspoon soda
   1 Tablespoon grated orange rind
   ½ cup blanched almonds
   ¼ cup flour

Cream the butter and add the white sugar. Add the brown sugar and mix. Add the egg; beat well. Add the orange juice. Sift the flour, salt, soda, and add to mixture. Coat the orange rind and nuts with ¼ cup of flour. Add to the dough and mix well. Form into a roll, wrap in wax paper and chill for 3 hours. Cut into thin slices and bake on a greased cookie sheet at 400 degrees for about 6–7 minutes. Don't let them get too brown.

BLUE RIBBON WINNER, ILLINOIS STATE FAIR

ROCKS

 2 cups butter
 3 cups packed brown sugar
 6 eggs
 2 teaspoons vanilla
 2 teaspoons cinnamon
 ½ teaspoon cloves or 1 teaspoon allspice
 6 cups sifted flour
 2 teaspoons soda
 3 cups chopped nuts
 4 cups raisins

Cream the butter and sugar. Add the eggs and beat well. Add the vanilla, sifted dry ingredients, nuts and raisins. Drop by teaspoonfuls onto a lightly greased baking sheet. Bake in a 350-degree oven for about 15–20 minutes.

BLUE RIBBON WINNER, WYOMING STATE FAIR

LOUANNE BEBB — GLENBURN, MAINE

TOLL HOUSE COOKIES
Yield: 3 dozen cookies

 ½ cup granulated sugar
 ¼ cup brown sugar

½ cup margarine
1 egg
1 teaspoon vanilla
1 cup sifted all-purpose flour
¾ teaspoon salt
½ teaspoon baking soda
1 package (6 oz.) semisweet chocolate chips
½ cup nuts
½ cup raisins

Cream sugars, margarine, egg, and vanilla. Combine flour, salt, and baking soda; stir into the creamed mixture. Blend in chocolate chips, nuts, and raisins. Drop from teaspoon 2 inches apart on to a greased cookie sheet. Bake at 375 degrees for 10–12 minutes. Remove from sheet immediately and place on paper towels to cool.

BLUE RIBBON WINNER, BANGOR STATE FAIR

ANDREA BRINKLEY — CARY, NORTH CAROLINA

BUTTERSCOTCH BROWNIES
Yield: 24 bars

½ cup butter, melted
1 cup brown sugar
1 egg
1 teaspoon vanilla
½ cup bread flour
1 teaspoon baking powder
½ teaspoon salt
½ cup finely chopped nuts

Melt the butter. Stir in the sugar until dissolved. Cool slightly. Beat in the egg and vanilla. Sift the flour, then resift with the baking powder and salt. Add to the butter mixture. Stir in the nuts. Bake in a greased and floured 8×8-inch pan at 350 degrees for 30 minutes.

BLUE RIBBON WINNER, NORTH CAROLINA STATE FAIR

7

CANDIES

BETTY GRIFFIN — CARY, NORTH CAROLINA

Betty Griffin entered the North Carolina State Fair "just for the heck of it," and won a blue ribbon on her first try. Married to Braxton Griffin for twenty-five years, Betty didn't learn to cook until after the wedding.

Betty and her friend Cassie Marcom (Cassie's Cheese Straws are on page 22) share secrets and recipes. Betty credits her for teaching her the art of fine home cooking. "I've learned more from Cassie than anyone. She can do anything." Betty has been making this treat for her two children for over ten years, and she willingly shares her "Old North Carolina" recipe with the rest of the country.

OLD NORTH CAROLINA PEANUT BRITTLE

   2 cups sugar
   3 cups peanuts, raw
  ⅔ cup white corn syrup
  ¼ cup water
     Dash of salt
   3 teaspoons baking soda

Using a large pot, combine sugar, peanuts, syrup, water, and salt. Cook on medium heat, stirring constantly. Cook at 290–300 degrees to hard crack stage, using a candy thermometer. When it gets to the hard crack stage, remove from heat, and stir in the baking soda. When color changes to brown, pour out as fast as you can onto a pan such as biscuit pan or pizza pan which has been greased with margarine.

BLUE RIBBON WINNER, NORTH CAROLINA STATE FAIR

RUTH S. SAMS — LOUISVILLE, KENTUCKY

Ruth Sams of Louisville has won more than a hundred ribbons in a wide range of categories at the Kentucky State Fair. Although Ruth's original interest was in textiles, it is our good fortune that she now also enjoys applying her talents in the culinary arts. In 1982 Ruth won a total of eleven ribbons plus the sweepstakes for knitting and crocheting. We think you'll enjoy trying Ruth's Kentucky Bourbon Balls, a very traditional bluegrass, blue ribbon winner.

KENTUCKY BOURBON BALLS

    1 pound powdered sugar
  ⅓ cup quality bourbon
  ⅜ cup butter
    1 pound bakers semisweet chocolate
  ½ block parafin
      Pecan halves

To make the fondant, mix the sugar, bourbon and ¼ cup of butter thoroughly with an electric mixer until very creamy. Refrigerate until hard.

In the top of double boiler, melt the chocolate, paraffin and the remaining ⅛ cup of butter. When thoroughly melted, roll the fondant into 1-inch balls and top each with a pecan half. Dip the fondant ball in the chocolate, using a toothpick as a dipper. Wrap in plastic wrap and refrigerate.

BLUE RIBBON WINNER, KENTUCKY STATE FAIR

BARRETT SHAW — LOUISVILLE, KENTUCKY

Barrett Shaw believes you should be both "traditional" and "original" in order to win a blue ribbon at a state fair. Her recipes for candied grapefruit and orange peels shows that she follows her own advice. It won a blue ribbon at the 1982 Kentucky State Fair.

In addition to cooking and creating new recipes, Barrett enjoys tap dancing and restoring a nineteenth-century cottage she owns. She is also a reporter for the Louisville Times *and holds degrees in both English and American literature. She is also working on an associate degree in the culinary arts.*

CANDIED GRAPEFRUIT PEEL

Peel from 2 grapefruit
1 cup sugar
1 cup white corn syrup
1 cup water
Additional granulated sugar for dipping
White dipping chocolate (available in candymaking supply shops)

Cut the peel from each grapefruit into 4 lengthwise sections. If the white membrane is very thick, remove some, otherwise leave intact. In a saucepan cover the peel with cold water, bring to a boil and boil for 10 minutes. Drain and repeat the process three times. Reserve 1 cup of the liquid from the second boiling.

Cut the peel into thin strips. In a saucepan combine the sugar, corn syrup and the reserved liquid. Stir over low heat until the sugar dissolves. Add the peel strips, bring to boil and boil gently, uncovered, approximately 40 minutes or until most of the syrup is absorbed. Drain in a colander.

Roll the peels, a few pieces at a time, in granulated sugar. Arrange in a single layer on a cookie sheet lined with wax paper. Let dry for a day or two. Can be used as is, or each slice can be dipped (leaving the tip showing for contrast and ease in dipping) in melted white coating chocolate. Cool on wax paper. Store in a tightly covered jar in refrigerator.

BLUE RIBBON WINNER, KENTUCKY STATE FAIR

CANDIED ORANGE PEEL

    Peel from 6 thick-skinned oranges
2 cups sugar
2 teaspoons white corn syrup
1 cup water
    Additional granulated sugar for rolling, or
    Semisweet dipping chocolate (dipping chocolate preferred over melted chocolate chips)

Follow the same procedure for Candied Grapefruit Peel (recipe above), using adjusted amounts of sugar and syrup. Do not use very thin skinned peels or the results will be too hard and dry. Decrease boiling time by 5 minutes for each boiling step in the previous recipe. Dip in semisweet chocolate.

BLUE RIBBON WINNER, KENTUCKY STATE FAIR

NANCY MOORE — CHAPEL HILL, NORTH CAROLINA

Cooking came naturally to Nancy Moore, and since the food exhibits had always been her favorite part of the fair, she decided to give it a try. Her success has earned her a dozen blue ribbons and led her into professional catering, specializing in wedding cakes.

Nancy feels cooking can be therapeutic and likes to experiment with it just for the family's pleasure. Her Own Mints, featured here, will let you share some of that pleasure.

MY OWN MINTS
Yield: 150 pieces

 ¼ cup butter, softened
 1 pound confectioners sugar
 ¼ teaspoon salt
 ¼ cup heavy cream
 5 drops peppermint oil
   Food coloring to make pastel colors as desired
   Chocolate coating (recipe follows)

Soften the butter and add all the other ingredients; mix thoroughly. Add a little more sugar or cream to make the mixture the right consistency to "pat" out with fingers to about ¼ inch in thickness. Cut the mints with a small canapé cutter. The size and shape used depends on the occasion. Place the mints on a cookie sheet; chill 30 minutes before coating with chocolate.

CHOCOLATE COATING
 1 package (6 oz.) semisweet chocolate morsels
 1 tablespoon melted paraffin

Combine the chocolate morsels and paraffin in the top of a double boiler over hot water, stirring until the chocolate is melted. Dip each mint into the chocolate mixture. Place on wax paper for cooling. Decorate each mint with a very tiny pastel flower.

BLUE RIBBON WINNNER, NORTH CAROLINA STATE FAIR

OLIVE JEAN TARBELL — CENTERVILLE, IOWA

PENUCHE CANDY

    2 cups brown sugar
    1 cup white sugar
    3 Tablespoons white syrup
    1 cup thick cream
    1 cup nut meats
    1 teaspoon vanilla

Mix the sugars, syrup, and cream together. Cook until it forms a very soft ball (234–238 degrees) when dropped in cold water. Remove from stove and let stand until it is cool. Then beat until it begins to stiffen. Add the nuts and vanilla and pour into a buttered pan. Cut into squares.

BLUE RIBBON WINNER, IOWA STATE FAIR

MARY ANN EATON — DANVERS, MASSACHUSETTS

HONEY TAFFY

    ½ cup honey
    ⅛ teaspoon salt
    ¼ cup brown sugar
    2 Tablespoons butter

Put all the ingredients in a double boiler. Beat constantly until the mixture reaches 195 degrees, approximately 25 minutes. Put in a buttered dish. Cool until it can be handled. With buttered hands, pull and knead the taffy for about 10 minutes, or until it achieves a "whitish look." Twist, cut with buttered shears and wrap individual pieces in wax paper, twisting the ends of the paper securely.

BLUE RIBBON WINNER, TOPSFIELD FAIR

ELLEN CAREY — GUTHRIE, OKLAHOMA

Oklahoma's Blue Ribbon Chef is Ellen Carey. She earned that honor by accumulating more ribbons than anyone else at the 1982 Oklahoma State Fair. Ellen has been entering the fair for over thirty-five years and has won hundreds of ribbons. She and her husband raise cattle and wheat on their Guthrie farm as they've been doing for close to forty years. Ellen is also active in the Abell Extension Homemakers Group and in the community church. She enjoys raising chickens and has a big garden for her family's own use. She also plans to continue entering her homegrown products at the Oklahoma fair for many years to come.

MEXICAN PECAN CANDY

    2 cups white sugar
    1 cup light cream
    2 Tablespoons butter
    ¼ teaspoon salt
    1 cup pecans, in whole pieces
    1 cup sugar, caramelized
    1 teaspoon vanilla

Mix 2 cups sugar, the salt, cream, butter and pecans in a heavy saucepan and cook until it forms a soft ball in cold water (236 degrees on a candy thermometer). While this first mixture cooks, place 1 cup of sugar in a heavy skillet over medium heat and let caramelize until light tan. Pour into the first mixture and cook until it reaches 238 degrees (or makes a firm ball in cold water). Add the vanilla and cool until warm. Beat until it begins to lose its gloss. Pour into an 8-inch buttered baking dish or drop by tea-spoonfuls onto wax paper. After the candy hardens you may store it in jars.

BLUE RIBBON WINNER, OKLAHOMA STATE FAIR

JUNE ROBBINS — GREAT FALLS, MONTANA

ROBBINS' NEST WEDDING MINTS

    1   package (3 oz.) cream cheese, at room temperature
    1   Tablespoon butter
        Pinch of salt
    ½   teaspoon flavoring of choice (if using extract, 3–5 drops is
        enough)
    1   pound sifted confectioners sugar
    1   to 3 drops food color of choice
        Granulated sugar

Cream everything but the food color and sugars until fluffy. Gradually add the confectioners sugar. The dough will be much like pie dough. Work with hands on a surface dusted with powdered sugar, until satiny and quite pliable. Work the coloring in. Form into four smaller balls; cover those not being worked. Roll each ball into a roll about ½ inch thick. Pinch off pieces in the size desired. Gently roll each mint into a smooth ball then shake in granulated sugar. The sugar will prevent the mint from sticking to the mold. Shape as desired. Store tightly covered and refrigerate until about one hour before use. Best at room temperature.

BLUE RIBBON WINNER, MONTANA STATE FAIR and IDAHO STATE FAIR

CASSANDRA MYERS — FLORENCE, MISSISSIPPI

CREAMY PRALINES
Yield: 26 pralines

  2½ cups sugar
   1 cup milk
  ½ cup (1 stick) butter
  1¼ cups pecans
   1 teaspoon maple flavoring

Cook the sugar and milk until a small amount forms a firm ball (244–248 degrees) when dropped in cold water. Remove from heat; add the butter and beat immediately. When the mixture begins to firm, add the pecans and maple flavoring; spoon onto wax paper. If the mixture hardens, set the pan in hot water.

BLUE RIBBON WINNER, MISSISSIPPI STATE FAIR

FLORENCE NEAVOLL — SALEM, OREGON

PEANUT–CARAMEL–MARSHMALLOW CLUSTERS

This recipe is Florence Neavoll's version of the famous Goo-Goo Clusters made in Nashville, Tennessee, by the Standard Candy Company. Goo-Goo's are a sponsor of the Grand Ole Opry, and when Florence attended a Saturday night performance there in June 1981, the announcer described how they were put together. Florence later presented a box of these to Roy Acuff, who raved about them on the Grand Ole Opry show.

STEP 1

Crack 3–4 cups of unshelled peanuts and place about ½ inch thick on a cookie sheet with borders.

STEP 2: MILK CARAMEL

 ¾ cup granulated sugar
 2 Tablespoons cold water
 1 cup white corn syrup
 4 Tablespoons butter
 ¾ cup evaporated milk
 ½ teaspoon salt
 1 teaspoon pure vanilla

Place the sugar, water and syrup into a pan and cook on medium heat while stirring constantly with a wooden spoon. When the mixture boils up, wash the sugar crystals down from the side of the pan, and also from the spoon, with wet paper towel. Stir in the butter. When the mixture boils, add the evaporated milk very slowly, a little at a time, stirring constantly. Stir the mixture constantly to prevent scorching and cook to a firm state (about 15–18 minutes). Test caramel in cold water by placing a pan in the sink and keeping cold water slowly running into pan; dip a tablespoon of the caramel in the cold water, and in a few seconds take the caramel off the spoon and roll it into a ball. The caramel should form a ball and feel fairly firm. If the caramel does not form a ball, cook a few minutes more, stirring constantly. The caramel should be golden brown in color. If the mixture appears too hard, add 2 tablespoons of hot water, stir and boil up again and test. Add the vanilla and salt. Let it cool slightly in pan. Place teaspoonfuls of caramel on the bed of peanuts, about 1 inch apart. Some nuts will be left over but this amount of nuts is needed to bed the caramel. If the caramel should get too stiff, simply reheat it. Form candy into round pieces working nuts around the side.

STEP 3: MARSHMALLOW FILLING

 ⅓ cup cold water
 2 packages unflavored gelatin

1¼ cups granulated sugar
⅓ cup additional water
1 cup white corn syrup
1 teaspoon pure vanilla

Place ⅓ cup of cold water into a cup and add the gelatin. Stir just until the gelatin is wet. Set aside. Put the sugar and the rest of the water into a pan. Boil up once to dissolve the sugar. Wash down the sides of the pot with wet paper towel and boil up one more time. Take from heat and pour the mixture into a deep bowl. Add the corn syrup and the dissolved gelatin. Mix well. Beat with an electric mixer at medium speed for about 20 minutes. Add the vanilla. Place a spoonful of the mixture on top of the caramel, working quickly and keeping the top smooth as possible and covering all areas of the caramel. There will be remaining marshmallow mixture left over for other uses. Very lightly dust the top of the marshmallow topping with flour and let dry. Shake off excess flour, trying to keep it out of the nuts. Form the candy into round pieces. When it feels dry, dip in melted milk chocolate.

Note: The above marshmallow recipe won the blue ribbon in the Marshmallow category at the 1981 Oregon State Fair. The same recipe can be used for heart-shaped Valentine candy. The caramel recipe took second award in the 1976 Oregon State Fair. And the two recipes combined took the blue ribbon at the 1981 Oregon State Fair, in the Miscellaneous category, entitled Peanut-Caramel-Marshmallow Clusters.

BLUE RIBBON WINNER, OREGON STATE FAIR

DONNA MYLES — RENICK, WEST VIRGINIA

If you want a good corn dog at the West Virginia State Fair, stop by Lew Myles's Pronto Pup concession. We can vouch for the food because Lew has a good cook working for him, his daughter-in-law Donna Myles.

When Donna is not cooking for Lew you can find her winning blue ribbons in the cooking competition. She's been competing at the fair for about sixteen years and, last year, convinced her husband, Mike, to enter the photography contest for the first time.

Donna is a graduate of Berea College in Kentucky. When she is not making corn dogs or winning blue ribbons she is an engineering assistant for Brackenrich and Associates, a consulting company in the mining industry. If that background isn't varied enough, you should know that Donna also excels at needlework, quilting and sewing.

STRAWBERRY CANDY

    1 can (14 oz.) sweetened condensed milk
    1 package (14 oz.) flaked coconut (5⅓ cups)
    1 package (6 oz.) strawberry-flavored gelatin
    1 cup chopped pecans
    1 teaspoon almond extract
       Red food coloring

In a large bowl combine the milk, coconut, pecans, extract, ⅓ cup of gelatin and enough color to tint a strawbery shade (if desired). Chill until firm enough to handle. Form strawberries, using about ½ tablespoon for each. Sprinkle the remaining gelatin on wax paper. Roll each strawberry in gelatin to coat. To be extra decorative, make butter cream icing tinted green; using a pastry bag with an open star tip, pipe a small amount onto the top of each berry. Store the candy in a covered container at room temperature or in the refrigerator.

BLUE RIBBON WINNER, WEST VIRGINIA STATE FAIR

HONEY CRISPY BARS
Yield: 24 bars

  6 Tablespoons butter
  ½ cup honey
  6 cups Rice Krispies cereal
  5 cups miniature marshmallows
  ½ cup peanut butter

Heat 3 tablespoons of butter and ¼ cup of honey over low heat until the butter is melted. Remove from heat and stir in the cereal. Spread the mixture into a buttered 9×13-inch baking dish and bake at 350 degrees for 10 minutes. Melt the remaining butter with the marshmallows. Add the peanut butter and the remaining honey. Combine with the cooked cereal mixture and press into a buttered pan. Cut into small squares.

BLUE RIBBON WINNER, WYOMING STATE FAIR

WHEAT GERM AND HONEY CANDY ROLL
Yield: Approximately 2 dozen

  1½ cups dry powdered milk
  ½ cup raw wheat germ (plus wheat germ used for rolling)
  1 cup peanut butter
  1 cup honey

Mix all the ingredients and roll into walnut-sized balls. Roll in wheat germ until well coated. Chill. Store in refrigerator.

BLUE RIBBON WINNER, WYOMING STATE FAIR

CARLA WARNER — NEW ALBANY, INDIANA

Divinity is not easy to make, but this blue ribbon recipe from Carla Warner has never failed. Carla explains that she is a very accurate cook and never improvises, so we strongly suggest that you stay close to her directions.

Carla began making Divinity shortly after she got married . . . Her husband "was so thin" in those days and it was "the only sweet he would eat." Over the years she has received so many raves that she finally decided to enter the state fair in neighboring Kentucky. Her husband repaid her for the years of treats by bringing her entry to the fair on the day of the contest. He reported back that her entry was greeted with oohs and ahs but Carla had to wait until Sunday to find out that she had actually won a blue ribbon. A real thrill, Carla admits, since it was her first try in a state fair competition.

When not competing at the state fair, Carla is a director of the Louisville Health Fair. Her husband, Tony, is the Director of the University Center at Indiana University Southeast. He has demonstrated his pleasure with her cooking skills and his pride in her victory by framing her blue ribbon and an accompanying newspaper article about her victory. A very sweet thing to do.

BLUE RIBBON DIVINITY
Yield: Approximately 40 pieces

2½ cups granulated sugar
½ cup light corn syrup
¼ teaspoon salt
½ cup water
2 egg whites (room temperature)
1 teaspoon vanilla
Pecan halves

In a 2-quart saucepan, combine the sugar, corn syrup, ¼ teaspoon of salt and ½ cup of water. Cook to hard ball stage (260 degrees), stirring only until the sugar dissolves. Beat the egg whites until stiff peaks form. Gradually pour the syrup over the egg whites, beating for 5–7 minutes on high speed until the candy loses its shine and holds its shape. Quickly drop by teaspoon onto wax paper and press a pecan half into the center of each.

BLUE RIBBON WINNER, KENTUCKY STATE FAIR

8

CONDIMENTS and PRESERVED FOODS

PHYLLIS TONTRUP — TIMONIUM, MARYLAND

Awakening to the aroma of freshly baked bread, cakes and pies at her grandparents' North Carolina farm is one of Phyllis Tontrup's earliest and fondest memories. Through the years Phyllis spent hours in the kitchens of both her grandmothers, kneading bread, making pies and learning many of their recipes. Those memories, along with her mother's encouragement and her husband, Ted's, willingness to help in the kitchen are surely the reason Phyllis equates home cooking with love and family. This former 4–H member makes her Granny's Relish, along with her preserves and yeast breads, as Christmas presents for her special friends.

GRANNY'S RELISH
Yield: 8 pints

- 12 medium onions (4 cups ground)
- 1 medium head of cabbage (4 cups ground)
- 10 green tomatoes (4 cups ground)
- 12 green peppers
- 6 sweet red peppers
- ½ cup coarse salt
- 6 cups sugar
- 2 Tablespoons mustard seed
- 1 Tablespoon celery seed

1½ teaspoons turmeric (optional)
4 cups cider vinegar
2 cups water

Grind the vegetables, using a coarse blade. Sprinkle with salt and let stand overnight. Rinse and drain. Combine the remaining ingredients and pour over the vegetables. Heat to boiling and simmer for 3 minutes. Seal in hot sterilized jars.

BLUE RIBBON WINNER, MARYLAND STATE FAIR

OLIVE JEAN TARBELL — CENTERVILLE, IOWA

APPLE CHUTNEY
Yield: 6½ pints

2 quarts chopped apples
4 cups brown sugar
2 quarts vinegar
1 clove garlic
1 onion
3 sweet red peppers
1 Tablespoon salt
1 pod hot pepper
2 pounds seeded raisins
2 Tablespoons white mustard seed
2 Tablespoons black mustard seed
2 Tablespoons ginger

Cook the apples, sugar, vinegar, garlic, onion and peppers together until a sauce is formed. Add the raisins and spices and simmer for 30 minutes. Let stand overnight. Heat to boiling. Pour into hot jars and seal at once.

BLUE RIBBON WINNER, IOWA STATE FAIR

AURELIA PETERS — SEDALIA, MISSOURI

It has been a truly golden year for the Peters family. They celebrated fifty years of marriage and won a total of ten ribbons at the Missouri State Fair. Although they had never entered the fair before, Earl was convinced that his wife's cooking was as good as anything he had seen entered in competition. His judgment proved to be correct because Aurelia won three blue ribbons in this first year of competition.

GOOD OLE HOMEMADE SAUERKRAUT
Yield: About 5–6 pints

    5 pounds firm cabbage
    2 Tablespoons pickling salt

Remove the outer leaves from mature heads of cabbage. Quarter the heads and slice off cores. Shred the cabbage finely and put 5 pounds cabbage and 2 tablespoons of salt into a large pan. Mix with hands and pack gently into a crock with a potato masher. This will form brine to cover. Repeat until the crock is nearly full. Cover with a clean cloth, a plate and weigh down. Place the crock in a warm spot to cure for 10 to 12 days. Shorter fermentation at warmer temperatures produces a sweeter sauerkraut; longer fermentation at cooler temperatures produces a much tarter sauerkraut. It is important to check the sauerkraut every day or two and skim off any mold or scum that has formed, otherwise the mold can lower the lactic acid concentration below the point necessary for preservation. When the sauerkraut has been cured, pack it into clean canning jars (about 5 one-pint jars), adding sauerkuaut and brine to within ½ inch of the top. Put on caps, screwing bands tightly. Process in water bath for 15 minutes.

BLUE RIBBON WINNER, MISSOURI STATE FAIR

CHOW–CHOW RELISH
Yield: About 4 pints

        1   quart chopped cabbage (about 1 small head)
        3   cups chopped cauliflower (about 1 medium head)
        2   cups chopped onions
        2   cups chopped green tomatoes (about 4 medium)
        2   cups chopped sweet green peppers (about 4 medium)
        1   cup chopped sweet red peppers (about 2 medium)
        3   Tablespoons salt
    2½ cups vinegar
    1½ cups sugar
        2   teaspoons dry mustard
        1   teaspoon turmeric
    ½   teaspoon ground ginger
        2   teaspoons celery seed
        1   teaspoon mustard seed

Combine the chopped vegetables and sprinkle with salt. Let stand 4 to 6 hours in a cool place. Drain well. Combine the vinegar, sugar and spices; simmer for 10 minutes. Add the vegetables; simmer for 10 minutes. Bring to boiling, pack boiling hot into hot jars, leaving ⅛-inch head space. Process for 10 minutes with closed lids.

BLUE RIBBON WINNER, MISSISSIPPI STATE FAIR

GREEN CHILI JELLY
Yield: 2½ pints

 3 large bell peppers, chopped
 6 medium jalapeno peppers, chopped
6½ cups sugar
1½ cups white vinegar
 1 bottle liquid pectin
 2 to 3 drops green food coloring

Combine the chopped green peppers, jalapeno peppers, sugar and vinegar in a large pan and mix well. Bring to full boil for 10 minutes, stirring constantly. Remove from heat and add pectin and food coloring. Return to boil and boil for 2 minutes. Remove from heat, skim and ladle into hot sterilized jars. Process in boiling water bath for 10 minutes.

Note: Great on crackers and cheese or toast. Also this can be melted down at a later date for use as a sweet and sour sauce which is great over meatballs for cocktail food.

BLUE RIBBON WINNER, NEW MEXICO STATE FAIR

PICKLED BEETS

1½ cups sugar
 2 cups water
 1 cup vinegar

1 teaspoon salt
Scant teaspoon pepper
3 quarts diced cooked beets

Combine the first five ingredients and let boil. Add cooked diced beets and let simmer for 15 minutes. Do not boil. Put in jars and seal. Process in boiling water bath for 10 minutes.

BLUE RIBBON WINNER, OHIO STATE FAIR

MARCY DALE — SIERRA VISTA, ARIZONA

Marcy takes her cooking very seriously, and well she should. She had the opportunity to take cooking lessons in Italy, France and Germany while her husband was in the service.

Marcy is a real estate broker in Sierra Vista, Arizona. One day last year she brought some homemade jelly to the office to celebrate her recent sale of a house. Her co-workers were so impressed that they convinced her to enter the Douglas County Fair. She did and walked off with four blue ribbons.

On the day she went out to the county fair she stopped by a booth sponsored by the Arizona State Fair. Her co-workers were again encouraging her to move up in competition but she was reluctant because the state fair is about three and a half hours away. Fortunately the state fair representatives were willing to stop by her office the next day to pick up her entries. Fortunately for us, because both her Chili Sauce and Prickly Pear Jelly (page 289) managed to win blue ribbons.

In addition to being a gourmet cook Marcy also likes to collect cookbooks. Her current library includes 1500 books, soon to be 1501. The newest addition will contain two of her own special recipes from Sierra Vista, Arizona.

CHILI SAUCE
Yield: About 1–1½ pints

4 pounds fresh tomatoes, chopped
2 medium onions, chopped

2 medium bell peppers, chopped
4 large garlic cloves, minced
1 Tablespoon salt
2 yellow hot peppers, unpeeled and chopped
4 to 6 jalapeno peppers unpeeled and chopped
¾ cup white vinegar
½ teaspoon sugar
2 teaspoons oregano
2 teaspoons monosodium glutinate (MSG)

Place all the ingredients in a large pan and simmer for 45 minutes, uncovered. If too spicy, add some tomato sauce. If not spicy enough, add some crushed hot peppers or cayenne. Can be used for dips but is also a great burger topping.

BLUE RIBBON WINNER, ARIZONA STATE FAIR

LAEL ARRASMITH — AMES, IOWA

APPLE BUTTER
Yield: 5 pints

2 dozen apples, quartered
2 quarts sweet cider
3 cups sugar
1½ teaspoons ground cinnamon
½ teaspoon ground cloves

Cook the apples in the cider until tender. Press through a sieve or food mill; measure 3 quarts of apple pulp. Cook the pulp until thick enough to round up in a spoon. As the pulp thickens, stir frequently to prevent sticking. Add the sugar and spices. Cook slowly, stirring frequently until thick, 1 to 2 hours. Pour hot into hot jars, leaving ¼-inch head space. Adjust caps. Process pints and quarts in boiling water bath for 10 minutes. When cool, test for seal. Remove bands and store.

BLUE RIBBON WINNER, IOWA STATE FAIR

SHIRLEY SCHNURMAN — RICHMOND, VIRGINIA

Every summer Shirley Schnurman would visit her grandparents' farm in Varina, Virginia. Those were memorable years and Shirley recalls watching as Grandmother Purks canned fruits and vegetables and baked home- made biscuits for breakfast.

In 1979 a friend encouraged Shirley to enter the Virginia State Fair. The experiences of her childhood, and the perfection of those cooking skills, have enabled her to accumulate fourteen ribbons in three short years. She is especially proud of her first blue ribbon and of the special state fair award she received in 1982, for her Best of Three Pickles which follows.

Shirley's interest in the fair has spread to her husband and son, both named Michael. Michael senior has won multiple ribbons in the agricul- tural produce category and their son, a 4–H member, has won red ribbons for his macaroon cookies.

GRINDER RELISH
Yield: 5½ pints

```
12  cucumbers
 2  medium large onions
 1  stalk celery
 2  Tablespoons salt
 1  pint vinegar
 3  cups sugar
 1  teaspoon mustard seed
 1  teaspoon celery seed
½  teaspoon turmeric
 5  to 6 red hot peppers (1 whole in each jar)
```

Grind the cucumbers, onions and celery. (This can be done in a meat grinder or food processor) Add the salt and cover with water. Soak overnight. Drain. Put the remaining ingredients (excluding the hot peppers) in a large pan and boil for 3–4 minutes. Add the cucumber mixture and heat, but do not boil. Pack hot into jars, inserting 1 whole hot pepper in the center of each jar. Seal. Process in boiling water bath for 15 minutes.

BLUE RIBBON WINNER, VIRGINIA STATE FAIR

SUPER FAST AND EASY PICKLED SQUASH
Yield: 4 pints

> 4 cups thinly sliced yellow squash
> 4 cups thinly sliced zucchini squash
> 3 cups thinly sliced onions
> 1 Tablespoon salt
> 2 cups vinegar
> 3½ cups sugar
> 1 teaspoon celery seed
> 1 teaspoon mustard seed
> ½ teaspoon turmeric
> 3 to 4 red hot peppers, sliced and seeded (optional)

In a large container, combine the squashes, onions and hot peppers. Sprinkle with salt, cover with water and let stand for 1 hour. Drain. Combine the vinegar, sugar and spices in a large pan and bring to a boil; add the squash mixture. Do not boil. Pack hot and seal at once. Process in boiling water bath for 15 minutes.

The red, green and yellow vegetables in this recipe give you a beautiful jar of pickles. If you like "chunk" pickles, you can cut the squash into chunks and quarter the onions instead of slicing them.

BLUE RIBBON WINNER, VIRGINIA STATE FAIR

KRISPY LUNCH PICKLES
Yield: 6–8 pints

25 to 30 cucumbers
8 large onions
2 large sweet peppers
½ cup salt
5 cups vinegar
5 cups sugar
1 Tablespoon mustard seed
1 Tablespoon celery seed
1 teaspoon turmeric
Red hot peppers (optional)

Slice the cucumbers and onions very thin. Chop the sweet peppers. Combine and add salt. Let stand for 3 hours and drain. Combine the vinegar, sugar and spices in a large pan. Bring to a boil and add the drained cucumber mixture. Heat but do not boil. Pack hot in jars. Before placing lids on jars, insert 1 or 2 red hot peppers in the center of each jar. Seal. Process in boiling water bath for 15 minutes.

BLUE RIBBON WINNER, VIRGINIA STATE FAIR

MARGARET HEER — DOUGLAS, NORTH DAKOTA

Competition at the North Dakota State Fair will likely be more intense next year. Margaret Heer is expecting her grandchildren from Montana to be visiting her farm in Douglas, North Dakota, and that will likely mean three generations of Heers at the fairgrounds.

Margaret has been competing at the fair for as long as she can remember. She is also a 4–H leader and has been a part of that organization for twenty-one years.

Margaret's husband, Art, is a retired farmer but he still helps his son harvest their 760 acres of wheat and oats. The Heers have raised four children. Their oldest, Betty, lives in Montana, Robert is a CPA in Colo-

rado and the two youngest, Richard and Dennis, remain in the area. Richard manages the Heer farm and Dennis has his own body shop in a nearby town.

ZUCCHINI RELISH
Yield: 6–8 pints

10	cups unpeeled zucchini, ground
4	cups ground onions
3	cups ground green peppers
3	Tablespoons salt
2¼	cups vinegar
1	teaspoon celery salt
1	teaspoon turmeric
1	can chopped pimento
4½	cups sugar
1½	teaspoon black pepper
3	Tablespoons cornstarch

Soak the zucchini, onions and green pepper in the 3 tablespoons of salt overnight. Drain and rinse in clear, cold water. Bring the other ingredients to boil, add the vegetables, bring to boil, seal in jars. Process in boiling water bath for 5 minutes.

BLUE RIBBON WINNER, NORTH DAKOTA STATE FAIR

JOAN SIMPSON — HOUSTON, DELAWARE

For Joan Simpson, the Delaware State Fair was love at first sight. Back in 1969 she was helping her cousin tend his cattle in the fair's cattle barn when Bill Simpson walked in. He saw her, she saw him and they've been a state fair family ever since. In more ways than one, we might add, because Bill's father, George, is the General Manager of the Delaware State Fair.

Joan and Bill now live in Houston, Delaware, where they farm five hundred acres. Their primary crop has been soybeans and corn but they are currently shifting to other vegetables and hay. They have four children, George (seven), Tim (six), Kevin (four) and Loretta (two).

Joan's initial interest in state fair competition began when she was a child and participated as a 4–H member. She now looks forward to the day when her children will be old enough to join 4–H and begin participating on their own.

PICKLED ONIONS
Yield: 4 pints

    4   quarts garden scallions or onions, sliced
    3   cloves garlic
    ⅓   cup salt
    5   cups sugar
    1½ teaspoons celery seed
    1½ teaspoons dry mustard
    2   Tablespoons mustard seed
    3   cups vinegar

Slice the onions thinly, add whole garlic cloves and salt and cover with cracked ice. Mix gently, keeping the slices intact. Let stand for 3 hours. Drain off water, then combine the remaining ingredients and pour over the onion mixture. Heat just to boiling. Seal in hot sterilized jars, process in boiling water bath for 5 minutes. A little yellow food coloring may be added to make a prettier color.

BLUE RIBBON WINNER, DELAWARE STATE FAIR

MARLEE BRICE — SHOREVIEW, MINNESOTA

The Brices have lived in Minnesota for about eleven years and have often attended the Minnesota State Fair. Even though Marlee has been canning fruits and vegetables for most of those years, she was never tempted to enter the state fair competition.

In 1980, a friend decided to enter a painting at the state fair and asked

Marlee to come along. She did, and brought her best canned goods with her. That first year she took fourth place for a cucumber relish and gained enough incentive to continue competing ever since.

In 1981 she took her first blue ribbon for the Prepared Pumpkin recipe that follows. The recipe became a two-time winner by picking up an additional blue ribbon at the 1982 state fair.

Marlee's husband, Bill, is a geological engineer and they have one daughter, Lindsay, who is six years of age. Marlee expects to compete again this year but there will be a distraction. The Brices are expecting their second child in March.

PREPARED PUMPKIN

Wash one fresh pumpkin and cut into eighths, remove seeds and strings. Steam pieces until soft, and cool. Remove pumpkin from skin with a large spoon. Blend in a food processor until smoothly pureed. Pack into hot sterilized pint jars and seal.

Use pressure canner at 10 pounds pressure for 55 minutes; count time when gauge starts to jiggle, and let canner cool down completely before removing lid.

Note: When packing pumpkin puree into jars, rotate a butter knife through until all air bubbles are gone.

BLUE RIBBON WINNER, MINNESOTA STATE FAIR

CAROLYN E. JENDREK — BALTIMORE, MARYLAND

BEEF JERKY

1½ pounds very lean beef round. Slice this ⅛ inch thick. You can either buy it like steak roll or freeze a roast and slice it partially frozen. I usually make it in strips 1 inch by 4 inches by ⅛ inch.

MARINADE

¼ cup soy sauce
1 Tablespoon Worcestershire sauce
¼ teaspoon black pepper
¼ teaspoon garlic powder
½ teaspoon onion powder
⅛ teaspoon nutmeg
⅛ teaspoon ginger

Combine all the ingredients. Lay the meat strips in the marinade and refrigerate overnight. Make sure all the strips are covered with marinade. Dry at 115 degrees for about 8 hours.

BLUE RIBBON WINNER, MARYLAND STATE FAIR

CAROLYN MAKK — LOUISVILLE, KENTUCKY

Carolyn Makk took up pickling in 1976 out of necessity. The previous year the Makks bought a 300-acre farm in Louisville and Carolyn planted about fifty hills of squash, which yielded enough squash to feed the entire city. Waste not, want not. Carolyn decided to take up pickling to preserve the fruits of her harvest. The following year, with the encouragement of her children, she decided to enter the Kentucky State Fair. In that first year she won the Sweepstakes for the most points in the category.

Carolyn's husband, Laszlo, is a former Hungarian freedom fighter who left his native Hungary in 1956. He completed his medical education here and is now Chief Pathologist at St. Anthony Hospital in Louisville. The Makks have four sons: Laszlo junior, Steve, Chris and Andrew.

Carolyn has learned her lesson about squash farming. The family now concentrates on corn, soybeans, tobacco and alfalfa. In addition they also raise Maine–Anjou cattle and Arabian horses.

BREAD AND BUTTER PICKLES
Yield: 8 pints

  4 quarts sliced, unpared cucumbers
  6 medium white onions, sliced
  1 green pepper, cut in strips
  1 sweet red pepper, cut in strips
  ⅓ cup salt
  ¼ teaspoon garlic powder or 3 cloves garlic, minced
  3 cups white vinegar
  5 cups sugar
  2 Tablespoons mustard seed
  1½ teaspoons turmeric
  1½ teaspoons celery seed

Combine the vegetables and salt. Cover well with ice cubes and mix thoroughly. Let stand for 3 hours. (Ice makes the pickles crisp.) Drain well and combine the other ingredients. Pour over the vegetables and bring to a boil. Do not cook further. Ladle hot pickles into hot, sterilized jars and seal. Let stand a month or so before using.

BLUE RIBBON WINNER, SWEEPSTAKES WINNER, KENTUCKY STATE FAIR

MRS. MAKK'S PICKLED BEETS
Yield: 5 pints

  5 pounds beets, 1–3 inches in diameter
    Salt
  2 cups white vinegar
  2 cups sugar

Wash the beets; leave roots, but trim stems to 2 inches. Cover with boiling water and boil just 20 minutes. Dip in cold water.

Skins should slip right off at this point. Slice the larger beets and leave the little ones whole. Pack in hot jars, leaving ½-inch head space. Add ½ teaspoon salt per pint jar. Meanwhile, boil the vinegar and sugar together, pour over the beets and leave ½-inch head room. Adjust lids and process in a boiling water bath for 30 minutes.

BLUE RIBBON WINNER, KENTUCKY STATE FAIR

WATERMELON PICKLES
Yield: About 6 pints

- 1 large watermelon
- 2 Tablespoons slaked lime
  Water
- 6 cups sugar
- 2 cups white vinegar
  Few drops green food coloring
- 1 teaspoon whole cloves
- 1 large stick cinnamon, broken
- 6 to 8 star anise (from an Oriental market or gourmet grocery)

After everyone has enjoyed eating the watermelon, chunk up the rind and trim the green skin and pink fruit from each chunk. Cut the remaining white rind into squares about 1 inch on a side and about ½ inch thick.

Dissolve slaked lime in 2 quarts of cool water. Put the pieces of rind in a plastic bowl or bucket and cover with the lime solution. Let stand at room temperature overnight.

Next day drain and rinse. Simmer in fresh water until tender, about 25 minutes. The rind will absorb syrup better if simmered first.

Make syrup by combining 2 cups of water with the sugar, vinegar, food coloring, cloves and cinnamon. There should be enough syrup to cover the rind. If there is not, prepare additional syrup following the same proportions.

Bring the syrup and rind to a boil, being careful it does not scorch. As soon as the syrup reaches a boil, turn it off and leave it overnight at room temperature.

Next morning, drain the rind and reserve the syrup. Boil the syrup until it's slightly thick, or about 10 minutes at a rolling boil. Pack the rind in hot jars; cover with the thickened syrup, leaving ½-inch head space. Put a star anise in the top of each jar. Adjust lids and process in a hot water bath for 5 minutes.

The watermelon rind should never be more than 1 inch square and ½ inch thick, according to Mrs. Makk. This allows the pickles to become properly translucent before the syrup burns.

She also recommends simmering the rind in water before boiling in the syrup. This tenderizes the produce and helps the syrup flavors quickly penetrate into the rind.

BLUE RIBBON WINNER, KENTUCKY STATE FAIR

GRETA DISE — GLEN ROCK, PENNSYLVANIA

Greta Dise entered the York Inter-State Fair because her sister-in-law talked her into it. The judges agreed with her sister-in-law and awarded Greta the blue ribbon on her first entry. Between juggling a career, raising her nine-year-old daughter and being a homemaker Greta has found time to grow her own produce. Her husband, having been raised on a farm, preferred homegrown vegetables. Greta learned the necessary skills well enough to win eleven ribbons in her first year of competition.

PEPPER RELISH
Yield: About 5 pints

- 2 dozen peppers (green and red)
- 7 medium onions
- 1½ Tablespoons mustard seed
- 2 Tablespoons salt
- 1½ cups water

1½ cups vinegar
3 cups sugar

Grind the peppers and onions. Boil everything together in a kettle for 20 minutes. Jar and seal.

BLUE RIBBON WINNER, YORK INTER–STATE FAIR

DELLA DOWNS — MURRAY, UTAH

When we spoke to Della Downs, she and her husband, Leeroy, were celebrating their thirty-ninth wedding anniversary. They have always enjoyed doing things together, whether it was washing dishes or pouring cement. And they have poured a lot of cement in their lifetime.

Twenty-seven years ago the freeway cut through their valley in Utah and displaced their home. Fifteen years later the city extended a road to the other side of town and, you guessed it, the Downses' home was again in its path.

When they saw it coming they began building another home, working evenings, weekends and holidays to get it completed. Their sons did the blueprints and they did almost all the work themselves.

Della has been competing at the Utah State Fair for several years and has "a bushel of ribbons" to show for her efforts. She enters a wide range of canned and dried fruits and vegetables as well as poultry, jams, jellies and sauces. She even enters three kinds of homemade soap which she and Leeroy no doubt use to wash dishes when they're not pouring cement.

MUSTARD PICKLES
Yield: About 4 quarts

4 quarts small cucumbers, cut into small pieces
1 large cauliflower, cut into small flowerets
2 green bell peppers, cut into small pieces
2 sweet red peppers, cut into small pieces
1 quart small white pickling onions, peeled
1 cup salt

1 cup flour
6 Tablespoons powdered mustard
1 quart white vinegar
2 teaspoons turmeric
3 cups brown sugar
3 Tablespoons prepared mustard

Sprinkle the vegetables with 1 cup of salt. Cover with boiling water and let sit several hours or overnight. Make a paste with the flour, powdered mustard and a small amount of vinegar. Heat the remaining vinegar with the other ingredients; add the paste, stirring constantly. Drain and add the vegetables. Cook and stir for 15 minutes. Pack in hot, sterilized jars and seal.

BLUE RIBBON WINNER, UTAH STATE FAIR

ELIZABETH BEAUGARD — FLEMINGTON, NEW JERSEY

How far can a good cook go? In the case of Elizabeth Beaugard, the answer is all the way to Paris.

Elizabeth and her husband, Dr. Peter Beaugard, decided that city life was a bit too much and moved their family to a more rural setting in Flemington, New Jersey. They bought a small eight-acre farm and began raising sheep, goats, chickens and geese and an abundance of garden-fresh vegetables.

As she settled into her new life-style, Elizabeth took up cooking in a serious way. She began entering her recipes and winning blue ribbons at the Flemington Fair in New Jersey. She readily admits that the Beaugards have become a real country family and that state fairs have become an important part of their lives.

Elizabeth also entered an original recipe in a contest sponsored by Leroux Liqueurs in Cuisine magazine. In July 1982 she learned that her recipe was one of sixty-five finalists being forwarded to L'Ecole de Cuisine La Varenne in Paris for final judging. In August she learned that her pot roast cooked in licorice liqueur was one of the five grand prize winners.

The prize included five days of cooking lessons at the famous French school, airfare, hotel accommodations at the Paris–Sheraton Hotel plus $500 in spending money. Rights to the winning recipe were signed over to the contest sponsors and, of course, cannot be published here. We are for-

tunate, however, to have two of Elizabeth's blue ribbon winers from the Flemington Fair.

ELIZABETH BEAUGARD'S JARDINIERE

The most important thing to remember when preparing Jardiniere is to choose the vegetables according to color and size. Packing the jar is the most difficult step; easiest to use are Ball freezer jars or wide mouth canning jars. The whole effect is achieved by careful and imaginative packing.

Possible vegetables to use are:
RAW: cucumber, zucchini, sliced green tomatoes, green cherry tomatoes, green and red bell peppers, Jerusalem artichokes.
BLANCHED: quartered onion, immature red onions and/or shallots, okra, cabbage, pimiento peppers.
PARBOILED: whole white onions, small eggplants, cauliflower, broccoli, carrots, wax beans, green beans.

FOR EACH QUART OF VINEGAR USE:
½ cup salt
1 cup sugar
3 Tablespoons mixed pickling spice

Combine the vinegar, salt and sugar in a saucepan. Tie the spices in a square of cheesecloth, or put into a tea infuser, and add. Bring to a boil; remove spices. Pour the mixture over the vegetables layered in jars. Seal. Process pints for 10 minutes, quarts for 15 minutes, in a boiling water bath.

BLUE RIBBON WINNER, FLEMINGTON (N.J.) STATE FAIR

MANGO CHUTNEY
Yield: 6 half pints

1 cup distilled white vinegar
3¼ cups sugar
6 cups green mango slices (about 10 medium)
1½ cups seedless raisins
¼ cup chopped candied ginger (or use ¼ cup freshly grated ginger root)
2 chili peppers (seeds removed), finely chopped
1 clove garlic, finely chopped
⅓ cup sliced onion
½ teapoon salt

Boil the vinegar and sugar for 5 minutes. Add the remaining ingredients; cook for about ½ hour, until thick and of desired consistency.

Ladle into hot jars and seal. Process in boiling water for five minutes.

BLUE RIBBON WINNER, FLEMINGTON (N.J.) FAIR

9

JAMS, JELLIES and PRESERVES

JAMES TROUSDALE — LOUISVILLE, KENTUCKY

James Trousdale proves that men can be big winners too at state fairs. In fact, a friend's mother, an eighty-year-old contestant, read about the many blue ribbons that he had won with his jams, jellies and preserves. She told her son to tell Jim to "stop that," reflecting, perhaps, a bias against men in the competition, but also the fact that she had come in second to him in the Crabapple Jelly contest.

Jim's interest in jams and jellies goes back to his childhood memories of his mother. But his education in chemical engineering also played a major role. We can assure you, however, that you won't need a degree in chemistry to make delicious jams and jellies with the two blue ribbon recipes that Jim has provided.

BLACKBERRY JAM
Yield: Approximately 8 cups

2   quarts blackberries (or enough to make 5½ cups prepared berries)
7   cups sugar
1   packet less 1 Tablespoon, powdered fruit pectin

Wash the berries and thoroughly crush, removing seeds from half of the berries by sieving. Stir the fruit pectin into the prepared berries. In a 6- to 8-quart pan (preferably stainless steel) bring the fruit and pectin mixture to a full boil, stirring constantly.

When the berry mixture has come to a full boil remove from heat and add sugar, stirring in completely to prevent burning and sticking to the pan. Return to heat. Stirring constantly, return to full rolling boil. Boil for 1 minute and remove from heat. Skim foam from the surface and ladle into hot sterilized jars. Seal at once.

BLUE RIBBON WINNER, KENTUCKY STATE FAIR

STRAWBERRY JELLY
Yield: Approximately 6 cups

2½ quarts strawberries (or enough to make 3¾ cups prepared juice)
5 cups sugar
1 packet powdered fruit pectin

Wash the berries throughly and remove caps. Crush the berries, place in a dampened jelly bag and allow the juice to drip. Never squeeze the bag, as this will cause the jelly to be cloudy because of the inclusion of pulp. Measure the juice into a 6- to 8-quart pan (preferrably stainless steel) and add the fruit pectin. Bring the mixture to a full boil, stirring constantly. Remove from heat and add the sugar, stirring in completely to prevent burning and sticking to the pan. Return to heat. Stirring constantly, return to full rolling boil. Boil for 1 minute and remove from heat. Skim foam from the surface and ladle into hot sterilized jars. Seal at once.

BLUE RIBBON WINNER, KENTUCKY STATE FAIR

PRICKLY PEAR JELLY
Yield: 6 half-pints or 4 pints or 4 12-ounce jars

This recipe can be prepared only by those who have access to the juice of the prickly pear cactus. To our knowledge it is not sold commercially and is predominantly found in the Southwest. We apologize to those who do not have access to it but felt the recipe was so unique and distinctive that we had to record it for the enjoyment of those who do.

TO MAKE JUICE
Pick the fruits from prickly pear cactus with rubber gloves and tongs. Rinse real well with water. Fill a 12-quart pot with fruit. Put in 5 cups of water. Cover the pot and bring to boil. Roll for 10 minutes, then mash with a potato masher. Boil for another 10 minutes. Press through a sieve and pour through a jelly bag. Pour 3¼ cups of prickly pear juice into 1-quart containers. Refrigerate or freeze. This makes four batches of juice.

FOR JELLY
  ⅔ cup fresh lemon juice (fresh only)
3¼ cups of prickly pear juice
  1 box Sure Jell
  5 cups sugar

Put the lemon juice, prickly pear juice and Sure Jell in a 5- or 6-quart pot. Cook on medium-high heat until it comes to a rolling boil. Add the sugar all at one time. Boil for 5½ minutes on high heat. Remove from heat. Let sit until foam rises. Remove foam with a metal spoon. Pour into sterilized jars and seal. You do not need to use paraffin.

If the jelly is too thin, put jelly into large pan and add ¼ cup of sugar. Mix ¼ cup of water with 4 teaspoons of Sure Jell per quart of jelly. Bring to boil. Add to the jelly mixture. Bring to boil and boil for 30 seconds. Put back into jars.

LENA FORBIS — LOUISVILLE, KENTUCKY

Lena Forbis also proves that first-timers can be winners in state fair cooking competitions. She took a blue ribbon on her first try in the jelly competition at the Kentucky State Fair.

At Derby time we always think of Kentucky mint juleps. Here's a Kentucky Mint Jelly that your entire family can enjoy all year round.

KENTUCKY MINT JELLY

3 cups water
1 box dry pectin
4 cups sugar
  Lime green paste food coloring
6 drops peppermint oil

Bring the water and pectin to full boil over high heat, stirring constantly. Add the sugar all at once. Stir and bring to full rolling boil (a boil that cannot be stirred down). Boil hard for 1 minute, stirring constantly, and add several drops of green food coloring and 6 drops of peppermint oil. Stir. Remove from heat. Skim off foam with a large metal spoon. Immediately ladle into hot jars, leaving ½-inch head space, and cover with melted paraffin.

JOE KNIGHT — DES MOINES, IOWA

Like all of us, Joe Knight loves a state fair. He has attended the Iowa State Fair almost every year for the last fifty-five years.

His specialty is jam and he finds the cooking competition to be a "good way to find out what the other fellow is doing." You don't do it for the money, just for the pleasure.

Over the years he has been active as a church worker, a scout master and as a Masonic volunteer at the Veterans Hospital.

Joe has shared some of his secrets for blue ribbon jam. He uses fruit from his garden only when it is fully ripe. He then makes his jam the same day and stores it in his refrigerator until it is ready to use.

BLACKBERRY JAM

    1½ quarts blackberries
    1 box powdered pectin
    5¼ cups sugar

Crush the blackberries, sieving half of the pulp to remove some of the seeds. Measure 3 cups into a large bowl. Measure 5¼ cups (2 pounds 5 ounces) of sugar. Stir the pectin into the fruit, heat to a full rolling boil, add the sugar, again bring to a full rolling boil and boil hard for 1 minute. Skim off the foam and ladle into jars. Cover with hot lids.

BLUE RIBBON WINNER, IOWA STATE FAIR

SHIRLEY SCHNURMAN — RICHMOND, VIRGINIA

GRAPE JAM

    4 pounds concord grapes (makes 6 cups prepared grapes)
    7½ cups sugar
    1 box Sure-Jell fruit pectin

Wash and remove stems from the grapes. Slip skins and set aside. Add 1 cup of water to the pulp. Cover and simmer for 5 minutes, stirring occasionally. Sieve to remove seeds. Grind or finely chop the skins. Stir the skins into the sieved pulp. Add the pectin to the fruit. Bring to a full boil over high heat, stirring constantly. Stir in the sugar all at once. Stir and bring to a full rolling boil, boiling hard for 1 minute. Remove from heat and skim with a metal spoon. Ladle into hot jars. Cover and process in boiling water bath for 5 minutes.

BLUE RIBBON WINNER, VIRGINIA STATE FAIR

INGRID GRAY — PITTSTOWN, NEW JERSEY

Ingrid Gray became interested in canning as a child. Her Hungarian grandmother had a stone cellar full of shelves lined with canned apples and other fruits.

Her mother also made her own jellies and jams, picking her own fresh fruits from her prolific gooseberry bushes and raspberry thickets. Ingrid assisted her mother in those days and continued to make jelly when she lived on her own.

As a newlywed in Terre Haute, Indiana, she continued her hobby and "put up" over five hundred jars of different vegetables. The Grays are back in New Jersey now and are fortunate to be living on a property with established currant bushes, gooseberries, grapevines, horseradish, raspberries, apples and pears. Ingrid's husband added two large gardens which provide an abundance of vegetables.

With all that training and the availability of fresh fruit and produce, it was only natural that Ingrid began entering the Flemington Fair. On her first try in 1980 she took home seven ribbons. Last year she added sixteen more, including a blue ribbon for the following Red Raspberry Jelly.

RED RASPBERRY JELLY

    2½ quarts freshly picked berries
    4 cups raspberry juice (drained from whole berries)

> 6½ cups sugar (set aside)
> 1 box commercial fruit pectin
> Cheesecloth

Wash 2½ quarts of unblemished berries and crush. Prepare several layers of damp cheesecloth over a jelly strainer or over the top of a pitcher, using a rubber band to clamp on the cloth. Ladle crushed berries onto the cheesecloth. Do not squeeze. Measure out 4 cups of juice. Place in a large pot. Stir in the pectin, bring to boil over high heat, immediately add the sugar while stirring constantly. Bring to rolling boil, still stirring, and boil hard for 1 minute. Remove from heat and remove foam from top. Ladle the mixture into hot glasses, making sure the rims are free of drips. Screw on lids and immerse in boiling water bath for 5 minutes. Remove and cool in location free of draft. (Jelly takes a couple of days to set firmly.)

BLUE RIBBON WINNER, FLEMINGTON (N.J.) FAIR

WANDA SCHMIDT — STOCKTON, NEW JERSEY

Who is Wanda Schmidt? This question is often asked at the Flemington Fair because products bearing her name are usually adorned with a blue ribbon. This year alone Wanda took fifty-two first prizes, including thirty-six in her favorite category, canning.

This charming senior citizen lives on the homestead farm of her late parents in Stockton, New Jersey. She raises most of her own fresh fruits and vegetables, often with the help of friends and neighbors because of her rheumatoid arthritis. But it won't slow her down. She plans to participate in the fair again next year and hopes to top her previous prize-winning records.

MULBERRY JAM

> 4 cups crushed mulberries
> 1 cup crushed black raspberries

7 cups sugar
1 box Sure-Jell fruit pectin

Measure 5 cups of fruit into a saucepan. (If you wish, strain some of the fruit to remove seeds.) Add Sure-Jell; bring to a hard boil and stir in the sugar. Bring to a full rolling boil; boil hard for 1 minute. Remove from heat and skim off foam. Ladle into hot jars and seal. Process in a hot water bath for 5 minutes.

BLUE RIBBON WINNER, FLEMINGTON (N.J.) FAIR

ORANGE MARMALADE

   4 oranges
   2 lemons
2½ cups water
   ⅛ teaspoon baking soda
   1 box Sure-Jell fruit pectin
6½ cups sugar

Peel the rind from the fruits, using a vegetable peeler. Thinly slice the rind. In a saucepan, combine the rind with water and baking soda. Cover and simmer for 20 minutes. Chop the peeled oranges and lemon; add, with juice, to the cooked mixture. Cover and simmer for 10 minutes. Measure 4 cups of the mixture, return to the saucepan and add Sure-Jell. Bring to a hard boil; stir in sugar. Bring to a full rolling boil; boil hard for 1 minute. Remove from the heat and skim off foam. Ladle into hot jars and seal. Process in a hot water bath for 5 minutes.

BLUE RIBBON WINNER, FLEMINGTON (N.J.) FAIR

CRANBERRY MARMALADE

    2 medium oranges
    1 medium lemon
    3 cups water
    1 pound cranberries, fully ripe
    7 cups sugar
    1 box Sure-Jell fruit pectin

Peel the oranges and lemon; remove half of the white part of the rinds. Slice or grind the rind very finely. Add water; bring to a boil. Turn down heat and simmer, covered, for 20 minutes, stirring occasionally. Chop the peeled oranges and lemon; add with cranberries to the rind; simmer 10 minutes longer. Measure 6 cups of the mixture into a large saucepan; add the Sure-Jell and bring to a hard boil. Cook gently for 1 minute. Stir in the sugar and boil hard for 1 minute. Skim off foam and ladle into hot jars; seal. Process in a hot water bath for 5 minutes.

BLUE RIBBON WINNER, FLEMINGTON (N.J.) FAIR

PEACH–PINEAPPLE CONSERVE

    2¼ cups prepared peaches
    ⅓ cup chopped maraschino cherries
    1 can (8 oz.) pineapple
    ¼ cup chopped nuts (optional)
    7½ cups sugar
    1 package Certo fruit pectin

Peel, pit and chop the peaches; measure into a saucepan. Add the cherries, pineapple, lemon juice and nuts. Stir in the sugar and bring to a boil; boil hard for 1 minute. Remove from heat and stir in the pectin. Skim off foam, ladle into hot jars and seal. Process in a hot water bath for 5 minutes.

SERENA ELBERG — MINOT, NORTH DAKOTA

Serena Elberg proves that you can't keep a good state fair contestant down. This seventy-four-year-old contestant suffered a heart attack on her son's farm last summer and was worried that she couldn't compete. But all turned out well and when the fair began, Serena was back on her feet competing with her preserves and jellies.

Serena was born in Carpio, North Dakota, but spent much of her life in the Minot area. Her husband was a truck driver and later a farmer and Serena still enjoys the farm life. Even today she manages to drive the forty-five-mile trip out to visit her son and his family. When she's at her own place in town in Minot she enjoys working at various crafts and sells much of her handiwork at various craft sales.

STRAWBERRY PRESERVES

  5 cups strawberries
  6 cups sugar
     Juice of ½ lemon

Stir the ingredients together and let stand for 2 hours. Bring to rolling boil and boil for 7 minutes. Put into rectangular cake pan and stir or shake occasionally. Refrigerate overnight and pour into jars. Freeze until used.

FREEZER STRAWBERRY RHUBARB PRESERVES

4 cups rhubarb
3 cups sugar
1 package Wild Strawberry Jell-O

Cut the rhubarb into small pieces. Add the sugar and let stand overnight. Stir and bring to a boil. Cook for 3 minutes. Remove from heat and add the Jell-O. Put into jars and cool. Freeze until ready to use.

BLUE RIBBON WINNER, NORTH DAKOTA STATE FAIR

MARGARET GARDNER — HODGENVILLE, KENTUCKY

It took sixty-seven years and a "dare" from a friend to get Margaret Gardner to compete at the Kentucky State Fair. She didn't think she was good enough so she only took six jars. Four won ribbons, including a blue ribbon for her Peach Preserves recipe which follows.

Margaret and Floyd Gardner spent most of their years in Louisville, where he worked in a packing house and she ran a gift shop. As they neared retirement they bought a little piece of land in Hodgenville where they built their retirement home. The Gardners have two children, a son, Daniel, and a daughter, Annetta.

PEACH PRESERVES

16 cups peaches
16 cups sugar
3 Tablespoons lemon juice

Peel and cut the peaches into a large pot; add the sugar. Stir and cook until thickened. Add the lemon juice and stir. Put into jars. This recipe can be reduced proportionately.

BLUE RIBBON WINNER, KENTUCKY STATE FAIR

ELAINE WILLS — PRESTON, GEORGIA

Thirty-one years ago the Marshall family of Lizella, Georgia, was named "Bibb County's Blue Ribbon Family." In those days the four Marshall children always competed at the Georgia State Fair. But Ora Marshall, their mother, couldn't. She had taken a job as a secretary in the old "round building," the nickname in those days for the Women's Division at the fair.

Elaine Marshall later married Sanford Wills and moved to Preston, Georgia, where they are raising three sons of their own. But Elaine Marshall Wills regularly makes the eighty-five-mile return trip to Macon, Georgia, to compete at the fair and to visit her mother in nearby Lizella.

Elaine's specialties are jellies and preserves and she has won numerous blue ribbons over the years. Her talents, however, extend beyond the kitchen. She has recently enrolled in Albany Junior College where she has begun to work toward a business degree. Here again she has proven to be a prize-winner, having been named to the merit list for the first quarter.

Following are Elaine's recipes for her Plum Jelly and Pear Preserves. Also included is Elaine's recipe for a regional favorite of Scuppernong Jelly. The scuppernong grape is indigenous to the southeastern United States.

PLUM JELLY
Yield: 8½ cups

    7½ cups sugar
    5½ cups prepared plum juice
    1 box Sure-Jell

Measure the sugar and set aside. Measure the juice and pour into a 6- or 8-quart boiler. Stir the Sure-Jell into the juice and bring to a full boil over high heat, stirring constantly. Stir in all the sugar at once. Continue stirring and bring to a full boil that cannot be stirred down and boil hard for 1 minute, stirring constantly. Remove from heat. Skim off foam with a metal spoon. Pour into prepared jars, then pour hot paraffin onto hot jelly. Quickly seal jars by covering with hot lids. Screw bands on firmly.

BLUE RIBBON WINNER, GEORGIA STATE FAIR

SCUPPERNONG JELLY

Scuppernong is a grape that grows along the Scuppernong River from North Carolina to Georgia. Other grapes may be substituted.

TO MAKE JUICE
Prepare scuppernongs by washing well. Place in a large container and barely cover with water. Cook until juice starts to flow. Simmer for about 10 minutes, stirring occasionally. Let juice drip from bag.

FOR JELLY
5 cups juice
1 box Sure-Jell
7 cups sugar

Stir the Sure-Jell into the juice and bring to a full boil over high heat, stirring constantly. Stir in all the sugar at once. Continue stirring and bring to a full rolling boil that cannot be stirred down and boil hard for 1 minute, stirring constantly. Remove from heat. Skim off foam with a metal spoon. Pour into prepared jars, then pour hot paraffin onto hot jelly. Quickly seal jars by covering with hot lids. Screw bands on firmly.

BLUE RIBBON WINNER, GEORGIA STATE FAIR

PEAR PRESERVES

    Pears
    Sugar
2 lemons, sliced (if desired)

Select firm, slightly underripe pears. Peel and cut into approximately ½-inch slices. In a large pan place a layer of pears then a layer of sugar, continue these layers until the pan is three-fourths full. Cover and let set overnight. Next morning cook until the fruit has a clear, transparent appearance and the syrup is somewhat thick. Pack hot into hot jars, leaving ⅛-inch head space. Seal. Process in boiling water bath for 5 minutes.

BLUE RIBBON WINNER, GEORGIA STATE FAIR

CAROLYN JENDREK BLAIR — BALTIMORE, MARYLAND

PEACH MARMALADE
Yield: 5 8-ounce glasses

6 yellow peaches
2 oranges
½ lemon
    Sugar

Chop 6 yellow peaches. Put 2 oranges and ½ lemon in a food processor to chop. Measure this and add an equal amount of granulated sugar. Let it stand all night. The next morning boil it all for 20 minutes and pour into five 8-ounce glasses. Seal. This has a beautiful color and taste.

BLUE RIBBON WINNER, MARYLAND STATE FAIR

APRICOT JAM

    2 cups pitted mashed apricots, fresh
    1½ cups sugar
    2 Tablespoons lemon juice

Boil the ingredients rapidly until they reach the jelling point, stirring so the mixture does not burn, about 20–30 minutes. Pour into hot, sterilized glasses.

BLUE RIBBON WINNER, MARYLAND STATE FAIR

GRAPE CONSERVE
Yield: About 6 jars

    4 cups blue concord grapes
    4 cups sugar
    ½ cup chopped walnuts
       Juice of ½ orange
       Rind from ½ orange

Cook the grapes for 30 minutes. Separate the skins into another pan. Put the pulp through a strainer when soft, to extract the seeds. Add the strained pulp to the skins and cook very slowly for about 30 minutes. Add 4 cups of sugar. Cook 30 minutes. Add the walnuts, juice and orange rind. Cook about 30 minutes longer. Pour into hot sterilized jars.

BLUE RIBBON WINNER, MARYLAND STATE FAIR

TUTTI–FRUITTI JAM
Yield: 9 half-pint jars

    1 cup diced fresh peaches
    1 cup diced fresh pears
    1 cup sliced fresh strawberries
    1 can crushed pineapple
    1 can mandarin oranges
    3 Tablespoons frozen orange juice concentrate
    2 Tablespoons lemon juice
    2 teaspoons rum extract
 1½ packages Sure-jell pectin
    1 Tablespoon margarine
    6 cups sugar

The fruit, juice and extract should measure 6–6½ cups. Place the prepared fruits, extract and juices in a large kettle. Add the pectin and margarine (reduces foaming). Bring to full boil and mix well. Add the sugar all at once, bring to full boil while stirring constantly and boil for 2 minutes. Remove from heat and stir for 2–3 minutes before ladling into jars. Stirring prevents the fruit from floating. Pour into hot, sterilized canning jars and seal. Leave jars undisturbed until set, approximately 24 hours.

BLUE RIBBON WINNER, CALIFORNIA STATE FAIR

CHARLENE WARREN — ALBUQUERQUE, NEW MEXICO

EASY STRAWBERRY JAM

    4 cups crushed strawberries (about 2 quarts)
    7 cups sugar
    ½ bottle liquid pectin

Measure the crushed strawberries into a kettle. Add the sugar and
stir well. Place on high heat and, stirring constantly, bring quickly
to a full boil with bubbles over the entire surface. Boil hard for 1
minute, stirring constantly. Remove from heat and stir in the pectin. Skim. Fill hot jars, seal and process in boiling water bath for
10 minutes.

BLUE RIBBON WINNER, NEW MEXICO STATE FAIR

VIRGINIA CONDREY — MONTEVALLO, ALABAMA

*Virginia Condrey started canning only seven years ago. That first year she
also decided to compete at the Shelby County Fair. She entered twelve
jars and won seven ribbons on her first try. Three years ago Virginia decided to try her luck against tougher competition at the Alabama State
Fair. Her winning streak continued and now she can't resist the state fair.
She travels to Birmingham every year just to be part of "fairyland" in the
Family Craft Center. Canning has given her a sense of achievement and
gives her a chance to be creative. Creativity runs in the Condrey family.
Her daughter Charlotte is an accomplished artist and has won many
awards and citations for her paintings. Achievement also runs in the fam-
ily. Son Richard has a Ph.D. and is an assistant professor at Louisiana
State while son Stephen has his masters degree in public administration.
Sampling Virginia's Fig Conserve will transport you to "fairyland" and
let you understand why her daughter Charlotte was moved to paint a por-
trait of some of her mother's fine canned goods entitled "Mother's
Jewels."*

JAMS, JELLIES AND PRESERVES / 303

FIG CONSERVE

    2 pounds figs (or 1 quart canned figs)
    ½ pound raisins
    3 cups sugar
    1 orange (pulp and thinly sliced or finely ground peel)
    ½ cup chopped pecans

Fresh figs should first be treated with a soda bath. This is done in the following way: sprinkle 2 pounds of firm ripe figs with ⅓ cup of baking soda. Cover with 2 quarts of boiling water and let stand for 5 minutes. Drain and rinse in two baths of clean cold water. Cut the figs and raisins into small pieces. Combine all the ingredients except the nuts and cook until thick and transparent (about 1 hour). Add the nuts 5 minutes before removing from heat. Pack in hot pint standard canning jars. Adjust lids. Process in a boiling water bath canner (212 degrees) for 10 minutes.

BLUE RIBBON WINNER, ALABAMA STATE FAIR

LOUANNE BEBB — GLENBURN, MAINE

PENNSYLVANIA DUTCH APPLE BUTTER
Yield: 4 pints

    2 quarts apple cider or water
  3½ pounds cooking apples
    3 cups sugar
    2 teaspoons ground allspice
    2 teaspoons ground cloves
    ¼ teaspoon salt

Boil cider or water for 15 minutes. Add the apples, cut into eighths. Cook until tender. Force through a food mill to remove peels and seeds. Return to kettle; add the sugar, spices and salt. Simmer slowly until thick, stirring frequently to prevent burning. Pour into sterilized jars. Place in boiling water bath. Water should cover jars 1 to 2 inches. Cover and boil 5 minutes. Remove jars from canner.

BLUE RIBBON WINNER, BANGOR STATE FAIR

BLUEBERRY JAM
Yield: 4 pints

   1½ quarts blueberries
   7 cups sugar
   2 Tablespoons lemon juice
   1 pouch liquid pectin

Remove stems from the blueberries. Crush the fruit one layer at a time.

In a Dutch oven measure 4½ cups of the prepared berries (add water if measure is short). Stir in lemon juice, and add sugar. Over high heat, bring to a full rolling boil that cannot be stirred down. Boil hard for 1 minute, stirring constantly. Remove from heat. At once stir in the pectin. Skim off foam with a large metal spoon. Immediately ladle into hot sterilized jars, leaving ¼-inch space at top. Place in boiling water bath. Water should cover jars 1 to 2 inches. Cover and boil for 5 minutes. Remove from canner.

BLUE RIBBON WINNER, BANGOR STATE FAIR

RHUBARB CONSERVE
Yield: 3 pints

> 2 quarts rhubarb
> ¾ cups water
> Red food coloring
> 5½ cups sugar
> 1 pouch liquid pectin

Trim (don't peel) the rhubarb. Thinly slice stalks. Put the water and rhubarb in a large Dutch oven, cover and simmer for 2 minutes or until soft. Add the food coloring. Measure out 3 cups of the prepared rhubarb, and add the sugar. Over high heat bring to full rolling boil that cannot be stirred down. Boil hard for 1 minute, stirring constantly. Remove from heat. At once stir in the pectin. Skim off foam with a large metal spoon. Immediately ladle into hot sterilized jars, leaving ¼-inch space at top. Place in boiling water bath. Water should cover jars 1 to 2 inches. Cover and boil for 15 minutes. Remove from canner.

BLUE RIBBON WINNER, BANGOR STATE FAIR

PEACH CONSERVE
Yield: 4 pints

> 4 cups peeled and chopped peaches
> ¼ cup lemon juice
> 7½ cups sugar
> 1 pouch liquid pectin

Place the peaches, lemon juice and sugar in a large pot and bring to full boil that cannot be stirred down. Boil hard for 1 full minute, stirring constantly. Remove from heat. At once, stir in the pectin and skim off foam with a large metal spoon. Immediately ladle into hot sterilized jars, leaving ¼-inch space at top. Put cover on and place in boiling water bath. Water should cover tops of jars. Cover pot and boil for 5 minutes.

BLUE RIBBON WINNER, BANGOR STATE FAIR

10

STATE FAIR INFORMATION

ALABAMA

The Alabama State Fair, "Alabama's Greatest Event," is held annually in Birmingham. At the direction of the Alabama State Fair Authority, the Alabama State Fair includes a wide variety of agricultural, educational arts and crafts competitions and exhibits.

Entertainment has included performers like the group Alabama, and a high-flying helicopter aerobatics show. All rides and entertainment within the fair, after the gate charge, are available free to visitors. The fair usually begins on the first Thursday in October. For more information call 205-786-8100.

ALASKA

The Alaska State Fair is held annually in late August and early September in Palmer, Alaska. Approximately a quarter of a million people enjoy a wide range of events at the fair's eighty-acre fairgrounds. For more information call 907-745-4827.

ARIZONA

The Arizona State Fair, held in late fall in Phoenix, is a celebration of Western spirit. In addition to rides and entertainment, the state takes great pride in its cultural heritage. Cowboys and Native Americans are to be expected in the state that is home of Tombstone, but you may be surprised by the variety in competitions like homemaking arts, beadwork, basketry, weaving, quilting and Ojo de Dios (God's Eye) crafts. All seem typically reminiscent of the first Arizona settlers, but categories such as Swedish weaving, cutwork and bobbin lace remind us that homemade doesn't always mean Early American. Special emphasis is given to Arizona industries from dairy cattle to wool and from beekeeping to wheat. For more information call 602-252-6771.

ARKANSAS

The Arkansas State Fair and Livestock Show is held annually in October in Little Rock, Arkansas. The fair attracts almost 300,000 visitors each year. For more information call 501-372-8341.

CALIFORNIA

Sunny California has hosted a state fair since 1853, only four years after the Gold Rush. Naturally the fair has grown since then, and in 1982, the California State Fair underwent quite a face-lift. Held at the Cal Expo grounds in Sacramento since 1968, this late summer event now includes even more family attractions like horseracing, carnival rides, monorail rides, pony rides and a petting zoo. The entertainment in the arena ranges from concerts to rodeos.

The heart of the California State Fair is the showcasing of the state's major industries and agriculture in the new California building. Special emphasis is given to the fine wines produced in the state and visitors may enjoy the winetasting exhibits. Many home arts, agriculture and crafts compeititions and judgings are now open to the public.

The fair usually begins during the last week of August, and in 1982 became one of the first Western state fairs to institute one-price admission. For more information call 916-263-3049.

COLORADO

The Colorado Fair is so old that it was a fair before Colorado was a state. Established in 1872, four years before Colorado was admitted to the Union, the Colorado State Fair takes pride not only in displaying the best in agriculture, crafts and home arts but also in celebrating the rich cultural heritage of the state. Thus, the special attractions at this state fair include the traditional Fiesta Day (for a taste of Old Mexico), an Indian Village (saluting Native Americans) and a top-quality rodeo. In addition to the typical state fair competitions, there are the more unusual offerings, like the "Blind Man's Tractor Driving Contest," "Butter Churning Contest," "Fiddlin' Contest" and "Rooster Crowing Contest" to entertain fairgoers. Held on the State Fairgrounds since 1901, the fair generally takes place the last week of August and ends on Labor Day. For more information call 719-561-8484.

CONNECTICUT

The two largest fairs in Connecticut are the Durham Agricultural Fair, held in late September, and the Woodstock Fair, which takes place around Labor Day. For more information about the Woodstock Fair call 860-928-3246.

DELAWARE

Delaware, the "first state," holds its annual fair during the last full week in July, in Harrington. In addition to the livestock, there are many features to entertain visitors. Harness racing, an antique auto show and the fireworks display are popular events at a number of state fairs, but Delaware has a few of its own surprises. There are Ice Cream Making and Pretty Animal contests. There is a wool and spinning demonstration and the Annual Country Music Talent Contest where you will hear everything from bluegrass to country rock. The biggest surprise of all, however, is a contest in tribute to the large Delmarva (Delaware, Maryland and Virginia) poultry industry. With a great sense of humor, the Delaware State Fair is proud to host the annual Chicken Flying Contest to see which chicken can fly the farthest, thus escaping the skillet. Or as they like to say at the fair, "It's Fly or Fry." For more information call 302-398-3269.

FLORIDA

The Florida State Fair is held each year in February, in Tampa, Florida. Attendance is about 370,000. For more information call 813-621-7821.

GEORGIA

The Georgia State Fair has changed a lot since its inception in 1851. In those days, jackrabbit racing was one of the attractions and many lengthy speeches were delivered by competing orators. The total of premiums offered was $153.90. In contrast the 1981 fair offered premiums of over $39,000. Visitors will enjoy the many competitions, the Carnival and Midway and other entertainment offerings. The fair is held each October, in Macon. For more information call 912-746-7184.

IDAHO

The Eastern Idaho State Fair is held in September, in Blackfoot, and the Western Idaho Fair is held in late August through early September, in Boise. Both attract well over 200,000 visitors each year. For more information call the Eastern Idaho State Fair, 208-785-2480, or the Western Idaho Fair, 208-376-3247.

ILLINOIS

The beginnings of the Illinois State Fair go back 130 years. In those days, the Illinois State Agricultural Society voted to hold their first fair, for which they charged an admission of only twenty-five cents. Premiums were offered in such quaint categories as best ox-yoke and best portable grist mill.

Springfield is now the permanent home of this summer event and the prices have gone up, but you can still see the latest innovations in farming and livestock equipment. This state fair offers quite a variety of contests and displays, including the unusual Heinhold pig races, instituted by Heinhold Hog Markets, Inc. "to prove that pigs are not slow, dimwitted or lazy." The annual Hog and Husband Calling contest provides plenty of laughs for participants and observers alike. Visitors should also enjoy the Bee Culture Display, one of the largest bee and honey shows in the nation. For more information call 217-782-0770.

INDIANA

Indiana State Fair is held annually in late Augusut in Indianapolis. This fair attracts over one million visitors each year and has a 238-acre fairground. For more information call 317-927-7500.

IOWA

The ten-day extravaganza known as the Iowa State Fair, held in mid August, is truly a people's fair. The fair offers diversified events such as auto and car racing, concerts, stageshows, fireworks, a Midway, and many special activities.

The fair is home for the 20-acre Farm Machinery Show, the largest art show in the state, entertainment superstars such as Dolly Parton, the Oak Ridge Boys, Alabama and many others. A visit to Heritage Village, an impressive tribute to Iowa's pioneer past, is a must.

As one of the oldest and largest exhibitions in the country, the Iowa State Fair provides a wonderful celebration of Iowa's best. For more information call 515-262-3111.

KANSAS

Kansas is America's heartland and the accent at the Kansas State Fair is on the produce and livestock that help to feed the nation. Many kinds of grain, from alfalfa to wheat, are judged and there are contests for beef, swine, goats and sheep. Homemade foods and crafts are to be expected at most state fairs, but few have "Antiques" displays and judging. Visitors have an especially large variety of entertainment to choose from, including events like stock car and motorcycle races and performers like Alabama, the Beach Boys, Willie Nelson and the Statler Brothers.

The fair is held each September in Hutchinson on the 280-acre state fairgrounds. For more information call 316-669-3600.

KENTUCKY

It is difficult to think of Kentucky without thinking "bluegrass." "Bluegrass" conjures up the sight of horses and the sound of music and you are sure to find both at the Kentucky State Fair held each summer in Louisville. The state's finest horses and best equestrians compete for prizes each year and it would be almost impossible to keep your feet from stomping at the Open Championship Fiddle Contest, where prizes are offered to the youngest and oldest fiddlers, to the one who has come the farthest and, of course, to the best. There are Country Ham, Pipe Smoking, Rooster Crowing and Tobacco Spitting contests interspersed with the colorful and exciting Marching Band, Flag and Rifle and Cheerleading competitions. For a pay-one-price admission, you are able to share the fun of the state fair, the "Pride of Kentucky." For more information call 502-367-5180.

LOUISIANA

The exciting Lousiana State Fair takes place during the last week in October. For more than seventy-five years, this fair has showcased the state's agricultural, industrial, cultural and educational programs.

Maintaining its tradition that each day of the fair should be a feature day, the 1982 fair provided events such as an educational show, "Pride in Tobacco," a 4–H talent contest, and National Year of the Handicapped Day, plus a Parade of Bands, helicopter rides, a rodeo, football, nightly fireworks displays and guest appearances by artists such as Pat Boone. For more information call 318-635-1361.

BANGOR STATE FAIR (MAINE)

The Bangor State Fair is the largest fair in the state of Maine. Carnival attractions, agricultural and horticultural exhibits and entertainment like Brenda Lee and "The Greatest Show on Wheels" highlight the Bangor State Fair held for ten days during late July and early August each year. Visitors also enjoy Harness Racing, Horse and Oxen Pulling and Arm Wrestling championships. Not to be missed is the annual Harold Carter Memorial Fiddle Contest.

Held since 1849, the Bangor State Fair is often called the "Agricultural Showcase of the Northeast," because it preserves the traditions of animal husbandry and events that epitomized America's earliest fairs. For more information call 207-947-5555.

MARYLAND

The Maryland State Fair, which begins each year during the week before Labor Day, at Timonium, includes an unusually wide variety of home arts, farm and garden competitions. There are good-sized weaving and spinning contests, including one that presents a particular challenge to spinners. Last year, spinners were required to spontaneously design and create, in under an hour, a novelty yarn. (Rumpelstiltskin, where are you?) You can find quince and dewberry jellies and preserves here and judging for the best maple products. Other state fairs have honey and beeswax competitions, but Maryland is one of the few with Mead (honey) wine contests. Fair officials also select winners in the Christmas Tree category. For more information call 410-252-0200.

MASSACHUSETTS

The Topsfield Fair in Massachusetts is one of America's oldest fairs. Begun in 1818, this fair leans primarily toward food and agriculture. Massachusetts grown Christmas trees, competitive sheepdog trials and Horse, Oxen and Pony Pulling contests lend a New England touch to the atmosphere. There are Mead, Candle and Honey competitions and an unusual contest offering awards for Beekeeping Antiques, Bee Buttons, Bee Jewelry and other bee-related items. The fair is held each October.

Another major fair in Massachusetts is the Eastern States Exposition held in mid-September in West Springfield. Attendance at this important event has exceeded one million visitors in recent years. For more information call the Topsfield Fair, 617-887-5000, or the Eastern States Exposition, 413-737-2443.

MICHIGAN

Michigan Exposition and Fairgrounds is held in Detroit in late August and early September. Also the Ionia Free Fair, held in Ionia in early August, and the Saginaw Fair, in Saginaw in mid-September, are part of the fair tradition in Michigan. For more information call Michigan Exposition and Fairgrounds, 313-369-8250, or the Ionia Free Fair, 616-527-1310.

MINNESOTA

Diversity characterizes the people of Minnesota and has marked the Minnesota State Fair since its origin in 1859. In 1906 an equal rights turnabout resulted in men entering the cake baking and needlework competitions, with the first prize in embroidery going for the first time to a member of the not so fair sex.

The 1927 fair, for example, celebrated Lindbergh's flight to Paris with an exhibit of the latest airships and performances by Gladys Ray, an aerial acrobat. That same year John Philip Sousa's band entertained fairgoers with a march he had been commissioned to compose for the University of Minnesota. During his visit Sousa was made an honorary Blackfoot Indian. Nineteen thirty-nine found the fair commemorating the one hundredth anniversary of the arrival of the first Percheron horse in America with the National Percheron Show. Ten years later, the fair celebrated the centennial of the creation of the Minnesota Territory with historical exhibits. In 1962, the fair honored the space age with numerous displays and films. From bake-offs to blast-offs. the Minnesota State Fair provides fairgoers with a variety of fun and entertainment each year in St. Paul. The fair usually begins in late August. For more information call 612-642-2200.

MISSISSIPPI

The Mississippi State Fair is the show window for Mississippi's progress during the preceding calendar year. Naturally there are many livestock, arts and crafts, educational, health and other exhibits each fall at the state fairgrounds in Jackson. Local craftsmen and women compete with their best braided rugs, cane bottoming, woodworking, leather and weaving. The Stockdog trials select the best in herding and sheepdogs. Among the more unusual events are the Pretty Cow Contest and the Deep South Horse Pulling Contest. Visitors will not want to miss the especially lush and lovely floral exhibits where the abundance of roses and dahlias, bromeliads and orchids, chysanthemums and camellias laden the air with the scents of the South. For more information call 601-961-4000.

MISSOURI

When the Missouri Legislature passed a bill in 1899 mandating the establishment of a state fair, many cities were anxious to be chosen as the fair's permanent location. Sedalia was chosen and the fairground construction began on land donated by the Van Riper family. Interestingly, the land had originally been set aside by this family as a location for the state capitol. The first official fair was held in 1901 and has been held continuously, except for two war years, ever since. On the fairgrounds is "one of the best mile dirt tracks in the country" and a half-mile oval. These tracks are the sites of the fair's popular harness and automobile races.

In addition to the large livestock and agriculture competitions, visitors may enjoy the Jumping Mule Show, music contests and the Coon Dog Water Race. The fair takes place each year during the third week in August. For more information call 660-530-5600.

MONTANA

Great Falls, Montana, is the home of the midsummer Montana State Fair. Held annually since 1931, the fair not only entertains visitors with exhibits, horse racing, rodeo, carnival and top-name shows but also includes such unusual special events as sheep-dressing contests and competitive tobacco spitting.

Many state fairs crown a fair young lady as Queen and the Montana State Fair is no exception. But in 1981, this fair added, in celebration of their history, a very special feature: Pioneer Day at the fair, during which officials ceremoniously crown the "Montana Pioneer Queen," a woman nominated by letter for the length and quality of her service to her home, community and state. Thus, among the competitors the first year were the first white child born in Great Falls, a septuagenarian Native American and the winner, Ora Schultz, an octotgenarian whose parents were early homesteaders in Montana.

Montana traditions and resources are highlighted in a wide variety of competitions, ranging from homemade aprons to Montana-grown wool. For more information call 406-727-8900.

NEBRASKA

For 114 years the Nebraska State Fair has attracted the state's finest grains, produce and livestock for judging. Farmers have also benefited from the many educational exhibits and lectures. Visitors enjoy the great variety of events offered at the fair. There are music contests and Medieval Jousting and dancing exhibits, Danish Dancing and Country Music, Wine and Beer Making competitions and discussions on topics like "Computers in Agriculture." The whole family should enjoy the fine entertainment provided by such stars as Kenny Rogers, Air Supply, Steve Martin and Alabama. The fair takes place on the Lincoln fairgrounds each fall for ten days beginning the Friday before Labor Day. For more information call 402-474-5371.

NEVADA

In what was once the "blue sky" country of the Washae and Paiute Indians, Nevada residents and visitors gather each September to enjoy the exhibits and competitions that reflect their rich cultural heritage. Carnival rides and Quick Draw Charlie, the

Reno Banjo Club and the Memorial Horse Show and competitions from leather craft to rocketry combine with livestock and agriculture to provide a panoramic display of Nevada's history and industry. The fair is held in conjunction with the fine Reno Rose Society Show. Entertainment includes performers like Juice Newton and Lonnie Kay's Country Western Group and a spectacular fireworks display. For more information call 702-688-5767.

NEW HAMPSHIRE

The largest state fair in New Hampshire is held in Deerfield in late September and early October. Another major fair of equal size is held in Rochester in mid September. For more information about the Deerfield fair call 603-463-7421, and 603-332-6585 about the Rochester fair.

NEW JERSEY

The Flemington Agricultural Fair may not be the largest fair in the country, but it is certainly one of the richest in terms of history. Held for almost 150 years, the Flemington Fair, of course, showcases the best that the "Garden State" of New Jersey has to offer in agriculture and livestock. According to fair historian, Kenneth V. Myers, in *The Flemington Fair Story*, however, the fair has not been without its problems. Dismally bad weather hurt attendance at some of the early fairs. In both 1916 and 1944, children under the age of sixteen were prohibited from attending public gatherings (such as fairs) because of infantile paralysis epidemics. In 1918, during World War I, no fair was held, although Flemington residents busied themselves collecting "six tons of peach, plum and apricot pits" to be used by the government in the manufacture of filtration systems for soldiers' gas masks. During World War II rationing and shortages closed the fair. Officials never gave up, however, and when the wars were over, the fairs were better than ever. Flemington began its Tractor Pulling Contest, in fact, due to World War II. Because of wartime machinery shortages, many farmers took to building their own tractors and the tractor pulls were instituted to test the effectiveness of the homemade machines.

Harness racing, free raffles for children (the prizes used to be ponies, now they are bicycles) and live entertainment are all old Flemington traditions, but there are always new surprises like Female Mud Wrestling and Big Wheel Races for children to attract fairgoers. The fair is held each year in Flemington during the eleven days prior to Labor Day. For more information call 201-782-2413.

NEW MEXICO

The New Mexico State Fair, which runs each September in Albuquerque, offers a wide variety of exhibits and competitions to the fairgoer. Western spirit is obvious in everything from the numerous horse shows to the Indian Village. Rodeos and horse racing, and entertainers like Juice Newton, Ronnie Milsap and Jerry Lee Lewis keep visitors entertained. There is a Sheep to Shawl exhibit celebrating the New Mexico sheep industry and numerous cattle judgings. You will see as many leather, bead, pottery, basket and Indian jewelry exhibits as you might expect, but you will also find rocketry and electronic displays. There are Fiddling and Horseshoe Pitching contests and an Antiques Contest. The Villa Hispana recreates the state's Mexican traditions and the Patriotic/Historic Exhibits honor the long, rich history of this Southwestern state. For more information call 505-265-1791.

NEW YORK

Since 1841 New Yorkers have brought their best animals, vegetables, home cooking and home crafts to the state fair. Held in the New York State Fairgrounds in Syracuse, each summer during the ten days before Labor Day, the offerings at this fair are as varied as the population and geography of the state itself. An Indian Village, a Log Cabin Arts and Crafts Village and the Pioneer Exhibit reflect the past, while Youth Activities and the Center of Progress look toward the future. The state dairy industry is represented with demonstrations of cheesemaking, a celebrity milking contest and offerings of milk, cheese, yogurt, ice cream and fudge. Not to be missed is the huge butter sculpture, annually crafted for fourteen years by William Clements. Among his past sculptures have been Square Dancers, the Cow Jumping Over the Moon, Little Miss Muffet and a Carousel. The dairy industry teamed with the ever-growing New York State wine industry (the second largest wine producer in country) for the first time in 1982, offering wine and cheese tastings to the public. There are fashion shows and silent movies, pork cook-outs and gourmet dinners, antique cars and tractor pulls, Golden Gloves boxing and the Empire State Ballet, and equine competitions from draft horses to Morgans. Live entertainment has in the past ranged from the Charlie Daniels Band to Helen O'Connell. In short, the New York State Fair offers something to suit everyone's taste. For more information call 315-487-7711.

NORTH CAROLINA

Raleigh is the scene each October for the North Carolina State Fair. Here you will find the best pears, persimmons, pecans and other agricultural offerings of the state. There is an annual fun festival for senior citizens and a barnyard for children. A special exhibit displays antique farm machinery and a Village of Yesteryear immortalizes old-fashioned skills like weaving, basketry and candle-wicking. Taxidermy and an Apprentice Bricklaying Contest are among the more unusual offerings. North Carolina is justifiably proud of the annual Folk Festival, held since 1948 to preserve and promoted the music and dance of the state's early years and to provide wholesome entertainment for the entire family. For more information call 919-821-7400.

NORTH DAKOTA

The North Dakota State Fair, held each July in Minot, combines the competition of the best of the state's agricultural products and livestock with entertainment for the whole family in celebration of the good things in North Dakota. A Pioneer Village and Rodeo revive the frontier spirit. In addition to the usual contests, there are Writing, Taxidermy, North Dakota Wool and Dairy Cook-off competitions. Performers such as Waylon Jennings, the Beach Boys and Barbara Mandrell delight fairgoers at this fair, "The Pride of North Dakota." For more information call 701-857-7620.

OHIO

In 1981, the Ohio State Fair achieved, for the first time, the distinction of being declared the world's largest fair by the International Association of Fairs and Expositions, with an attendance of 3,215,487. Ohioans attribute the growth of their fair to a number of innovations such as free grandstand entertainment and pay-one-price admission. The fair attracts top-name performers like Bob Hope, Waylan Jennings and the Beach Boys and offers a wide variety of activities to entertain visitors. There are horse and livestock shows, Sheep Shearing and Square Dance contests, Rubik's Cube and Senior Citizen Talent competitions. Regular performances in the outdoor amphitheater focus on topics like folklore and nature. One unusual feature of the fair, instituted by Governor Rhodes, is the Junior Fair Sale of Champions, where livestock raised by youthful fair competitors is auctioned for record prices. Thus, for example, Wendy's International Inc. purchased the 1981 Ohio State Fair Grand Champion Steer for $25,256 and Bob Evans Farms, Inc. purchased the 1981 Ohio State Fair Grand Champion Barrow for $13,000.

The fair is held each August on the 360-acre fairgrounds in Columbus. For more information call 614-444-FAIR.

OKLAHOMA

The State Fair of Oklahoma begins each year in Oklahoma City on the third Friday after Labor Day. During the ten-day fair, ranchers and farmers exhibit their finest animals and crops. There are many home arts and crafts competitions, many youth-oriented activities and family entertainment like the Rodeo, Ice Capades, Louise Mandrell and Jerry Reed. This state fair also sponsors a

Teacher of the Year Program and a Better Newspaper Contest. For more information call 405-948-6700.

OREGON

In 1861, in an attempt to give the state's residents a chance to exhibit and exchange home and farm products, the Oregon State Agricultural Society initiated the All Oregon Fair. Livestock, agriculture, arts and crafts, carnival and entertainment round out the modern-day Oregon State Fair.

The Oregon State Fair, held in early September, also has a particular appeal for families. This is symbolized by the addition of a new event, the Farm Family of the Year Contest. The contest seeks to focus attention on the relationship between agriculture and the family unit. For more information call 503-378-3247.

PENNSYLVANIA

Held in mid-September, the York Inter-State Fair, operated by the York County Agricultural Society, has the distinction of being one of the oldest fairs in America. It was first enacted in 1765 under a charter signed by Thomas Penn, son of William Penn. The fair continued for fifty years, conducting two fairs a year: one in the spring, the other in the fall. This privilege granted under the original charter ended in 1815.

In 1851 the fair was revised as a result of prominent citizens meeting and organizing the York County Agricultural Society. The society is responsible for the purchase of 120 acres of land, which are now known as the York Inter-State Fair Grounds.

Exhibits include livestock, home and dairy products, floral, apiary and homemade wine displays. There's even a grape-stomping contest offered for your enjoyment.

Pennsylvania also hosts the Allentown State Fair around Labor Day each year. The fair offers a wide range of family entertainment including big name stars, agricultural exhibits, championship wrestling and a Kids Day program. The Allentown Fair also features a Multi-National Festival which has become one of their most popular attractions. For more information call the York

Inter-State Fair, 717-848-2596, or the Allentown State Fair, 610-433-7541.

RHODE ISLAND

The Washington County Fair takes place in Wyoming, Rhode Island, around the second week of August. For more information call 401-539-7042.

SOUTH CAROLINA

The first South Carolina State Fair was held by the State Agricultural Society in 1856. After the fair of 1861, however, the buildings were occupied by Confederate authorities and used to manufacture munitions. In 1865, the buildings were burned by Sherman's army and no fair was held again for four years. The Agricultural Society is proud to have served as virtually the only bond between the people of South Carolina during Reconstruction days. The purpose of today's fair is "to encourage the growing of top-grade field crops and to help further the development of the livestock industry."

Special features of the fair include barnyards and zoos for the children, Senior Citizen, School and Farm Bureau Days and a Kindergarten Tour Day. There are plenty of rides and games for the whole family. The fair is held in Columbia each October. For more information call 803-799-3387.

SOUTH DAKOTA

The South Dakota State Fair is held annually in September in Huron. Attendance is approximately two hundred thousand. For more information call 605-353-7340.

TENNESSEE

Each September, the Tennessee State Fair is held in Nashville, home of the Grand Ole Opry. Midway rides, fireworks, a Flea

Market, speedway competition, a roller rink and wrestling are among the many attractions that entice fairgoers. Although fairs have been held off and on in the state for 120 years, 1906 marked the opening of the first Tennessee State Fair. With the exception of four war years, the fair has continued annually ever since. This fair claims the distinction of having hosted an appearance by film idol Rudolph Valentino. For more information call 615-862-8980.

TEXAS

Texans like to boast that they "do things in a big way," and their state fair is no exception. The State Fair of Texas is one of the largest annual expositions in the United States (based on attendance figures), and also one of the four largest annual fairs in the world. (In 1981, however, Ohio wrested away the title as the nation's largest fair.) The state fairgrounds in Dallas cover 250 acres and include a number of buildings and exhibits that are open throughout the the year, among them the Dallas Aquarium, the Dallas Health and Science Museum, the Dallas Museum of Fine Arts, the Dallas Museum of Natural History, the Texas Hall of State, the Music Hall, the permanent midway and the Cotton Bowl.

Although a number of Dallas County Fairs have been held since 1852, the first Texas State Fair took place in 1886. There were financial problems during the early days, and often the fair presidents and stockholders were forced to finance the event with personal credit. Finally, in 1903, the city of Dallas agreed to turn the fairgrounds into a park under the control of the Park Board.

Through the years, the State Fair of Texas has grown in size and scope. In addition to large livestock, food and home arts competitions, entertainment at the fair has, over the years, included such top name performers as John Philip Sousa's band, Debbie Reynolds, and Eddie Rabbit. The fair runs for seventeen days each October. For more information call 214-565-9931.

UTAH

Utah, the "Beehive State," boasts that it has the cleanest midway of any state fair in America. Beginning on the first Thursday after Labor Day in Salt Lake City, the fair has offered such popular attractions as Tammy Wynette, Pat Boone and the Disney Ice Show. There is a Rocky Mountain Rodeo and often a skydiving team. Horse cutting and log rolling events combine with fun-filled Freckle, Twin and Celebrity Look Alike contests to provide entertainment for the entire family. For more information call 801-538-STAR.

VERMONT

The largest fair in Vermont is the Champlain Valley Exposition, which is held in Essex Junction. For more information call 802-878-5545.

VIRGINIA

The Commonwealth of Virginia was home to some of our nation's most celebrated farmers, among them George Washington, Thomas Jefferson, James Monroe and Patrick Henry. Since agriculture has long been the backbone of Virginia economy, it is with great pride that Virginia residents gather each fall at the Virginia State Fair in Richmond. Livestock and produce are abundant. Vegetables, peanuts, potatoes, tobacco and honey are all judged for excellence. You will find all kinds of apples, from Golden Delicious to York Imperial. There are Hog Calling and Goat Milking contests and plenty of the famous Virginia hams and bacon. There is a Championship Auctioneer Contest and rides and entertainment for people of all ages. For more information call 804-329-4437.

WASHINGTON

Washington has a number of important fairs, including the Northwest Washington Fair in Lynden (mid-August), the Western Washington Fair in Puyallup (September) and the Central Washington Fair in Yakima (late September). For information call the Northwest Washington Fair, 360-354-4111; the Western Washington Fair, 253-841-5045; or the Central Washington Fair, 509-248-7160.

WEST VIRGINIA

Each summer, the State Fair of West Virginia showcases the best of the state's livestock and natural resources on the state fairgrounds in Lewisburg. Free harness racing, horse shows and pony-pulling contests delight spectators. West Virginia handicrafts like quilts, patchwork and embroidery share the spotlight with local products like black walnuts and home-cured country ham. New England holds no monopoly on fine maple products as attested to by competitions for best maple syrup, sugar, cakes and candy. Fair participants preserve their heritage by contesting in such old-fashioned categories as homemade soap, cottage cheese, butter and cheesemaking. Superstars like Juice Newton, Alabama, Roy Clark and Helen Reddy fill the West Virginia hills with the sound of music. For more information call 304-645-1090.

WISCONSIN

Begun in 1851, the Wisconsin State Fair has grown immensely in size and scope over the years. Through the years, there have been a number of interesting features at the fair, including spelling bees (1913), a sheep- or dog-powered churn (1900), free shower baths (1927), the collection of "scrap metal and rubber" as children's admission fees (1942), and the construction of a family fallout shelter (1959).

Today, in addition to many agriculture and livestock exhibits and competitions, there is, naturally, emphasis on the dairy and beer industries. Visitors enjoy auto racing, the Mexican Village, the Keg Put and entertainers like Kansas, Air Supply, the Beach Boys and Barbara Mandrell.

The fair takes place each August on the fair grounds in Milwaukee/West Allis. For more information call 414-266-7000.

WYOMING

You will know you are out West when you attend the Wyoming State Fair held each summer in Douglas. The thrilling rodeo performances and fine horse shows (which include western riding) help create a frontier atmosphere. There are contests in rope craft (what is a cowboy without his lasso?) and leatherworking, of course. For 70 years, sheep ranchers have brought their best products to be judged. You will see purebred sheep wool, farm flock wool, range wool and grand champion fleeces. Naturally, there is a Sheep Shearing Contest and the Ladies Sheep Lead has been created for participants to present their wool clothing along with a unique presentation of Wyoming sheep breeds. The grand parade and Rodeo on Wheels combine with grandstand entertainment like the Mel Tillis Show to lend a touch of today to yesterday's frontier. For more information call 307-358-2398.

ACKNOWLEDGMENTS

The authors gratefully acknowledge and appreciate the assistance of the following individuals. It is their dedication that ensures the continuation of the state fair tradition in America. It was their support that has made this book possible

W. L. Abernathy, South Carolina; Mrs. Robert Allgire, Maryland; Jody Basse, Tennessee; Mary Besich, Montana; Henry Brandt, Nebraska; Kirk Breed, California; Debbie Bryson, Nevada; Pope Burgess, Iowa; Dwight Butt, Oregon; Estel Callahan, Indiana; Maria Centrella, California; Gloria Chappelle, Arkansas; Bill Chiesa, Montana; Ian Cornell, California; Paul Corson, Massachusetts; Bruce Covill, Virginia; Mike Davis, Kentucky; David Drew, Nevada; Margaret Edwards, Mississippi; John Elsner, Oklahoma; John Evans, Ohio; Donna Ewing, Maryland; John Fahey, Maine; Miriam Fawcett, Wyoming; Jean Fisher, Montana; Dan Fleenor, Alabama; Purcell Foss, New Hampshire; Joann Fredericks, New York; Opal Frost, Nebraska; Wayne Gallagher, Texas; Richard Gallatin, Pennsylvania; Barney Ghio, Louisiana; James Grenier, Wisconsin; Anne Hanley, Virginia; Kathleen Hanley, Virginia; Bob Halsord, Texas; Mike Heffron, Minnesota; Mary Holloway, Missouri; John Holmes, Arkansas; Jean Hoover, Virginia; Mary Lou House, Alabama; Pat Huggins, South Carolina; Audrey Hughes, Wyoming; W. R. Humphries, New Mexico; Sid Hutchcraft, Illinois; Meg Ingold, Virginia; Charles Inman, Georgia; Gerald Iverson, North Dakota; Francis Jackson, Tennessee; Art Jones, Utah; Brenda Jordan, Virginia; Patty Kline, Illinois; Ken Kuhlman, New Jersey, Joe LaGuardia, New York; Donald Lanius, Pennsylvania; Marion Lucas, Missouri; Kate

Lynch, Washington, D.C.; Mrs. George Mahoney, Delaware; Linda Martin, Virginia; Christine Massengill, Alabama; Frank McConkey, Pennsylvania; Marilynn McHugh, Missouri; Terry McLaughlin, New York; Lewis Miller (IAFE), Missouri; Carol Mitchell, New Mexico; Howard Mosner, Maryland; Loren Nelch, Illinois; Ed Nelson, Louisiana; Bill Ogg, Wyoming; Billy Orr, Mississippi; Kay Parson, Illinois; Joe Pate, Maine; Elizabeth Peabody, Texas; Betty Lou Pearson, Colorado; Elaine Peppers, Illinois; Karen Phillips, Oklahoma; Arthur Pitzer, North Carolina; Pat Pollman, Oklahoma; Paul Putens, Nebraska; Mrs. Carl Radcliffe, Maryland; Freda Radich, California; Scottie Rechenbach, Virginia; J. Linwood Rice, Virginia; Ed Rock, West Virginia; Trish Ruesch, Virginia; Maude Ruesch, Virginia; Sandy Saunders, Oklahoma; George Scott, Colorado; Julie Shaw, Kentucky; Joan Shea, Massachusetts; Gary Simpson, Delaware; George Simpson, Delaware; Don Smith, Kentucky; Linda Smith, Kentucky; Vicki Spence, Arizona; Jean Stubblefield, Illinois; Ann Stuchenbourg, Kentucky; Kathy Swift, Iowa; Anna Taylor, Maryland; James Taylor, Iowa; Mr. & Mrs. C. L. Teachworth, Virginia; Phyllis Tontrup, Maryland; Thaxter Trafton, Arizona; Anna Troyer, Maryland; Ted Vaughan, Tennessee; Helen Wadhams, Nebraska; Barbara Walch, Massachusetts; Joanne Wasson, New Hampshire; Mrs. Wederman, Maryland; Charles Weiser, Pennsylvania; Diane Whitman, Pennsylvania; Phyllis Wiley, Maine; Bill Wiley, Massachusetts; Mrs. Wiley, Maine; Loraine Wulber, North Dakota; Lillian Young, North Carolina; Tom Young, New York.

RECIPE INDEX

Brownies (*cont.*)
Fudge, 236
Three-Layer Delights, 123–124
Butter Biscuits, 100–101
Buttermilk Coconut Pie, 191
Butterscotch
Bars, 211–212
Brownies, 250

Cakes
Angel Food, 127
Chocolate, 129–130
Grandma Arrasmith's, 127
Applesauce, 133
Banana Nut, 135–136
Black Walnut Spice, 120–121
Caramel, 162
Carrot, 121–122
Cheesecake, 118–119
Chocolate, 141
Angel, 129–130
Honey, 148
Mint Torte, 131–132
Velvet, 150–151
Cocoa Fudge, 117–118
Coconut Cream, Italian, 116–117
Devil's Food, 146–147
Honey, 157–158
Fruit Cake
Candied, Elizabeth Hall's, 112–113
Lemon, 119–120
Ruby's, 159–160
German Chocolate, 138–139
Golden Crunch Coffee Cake, 114
Golden Glow Cupcakes, 113
Lane, 134–135
Mandarin Orange, 142–143
1-2-3-4 Cake, 137–138
Orange Chiffon, 127–128
Pecan, Texas, 124–125
Pound
Million Dollar, 126
Old-Fashioned, 143
Pumpkin Nut Bundt, 144
Raspberry Whipped Cream, 151–152
Sour Cream, 149–150
Spice, Robbins' Nest, 154
Sponge, Champion, 139–140
Streusel-Filled Coffee Cake, 161
Toasted Butter Pecan, 115–116
Tropical Dream, 145–146

White, 136–137
Robbins' Nest, 152–153
Candied Fruit Cake, Elizabeth Hall's, 112–113
Candied Grapefruit Peel, 253–254
Candied Orange Peel, 254
Candies
Bourbon Balls, Kentucky, 252
Candied Grapefruit Peel, 253–254
Candied Orange Peel, 254
Divinity, Blue Ribbon, 264–265
Honey Crispy Bars, 263
Mints, My Own, 255
Mints, Robbins' Nest Wedding, 258
Peanut-Caramel-Marshmallow Clusters, 259–261
Peanut Brittle, Old North Carolina, 251–252
Pecan Candy, Mexican, 257–258
Penuche, 256
Pralines, Creamy, 259
Strawberry Candy, 262
Taffy, Honey, 256–257
Wheat Germ and Honey Roll, 263
Cantaloupe Ice Cream, 168
Captain Joe's Seafood Salad, 12–13
Caramel Cake, 162–163
Caramel Pecan Pie, 173–174
Carne Adovada Burrito Casserole, 27–29
Carrot Cake, 121–122
Cheesecake, 118–119
Cheese Straws, 22–23
Cherry Coconut Cookies, 227
Cherry Pie, Fresh, 187
Chile Bravo, 38–39
Chili, Green, 50
Chili Sauce, 271–272
Chocolate
Angel Cake, 129–130
Honey, 148
Angel Pie, 198–199
Buttersweets, 228
Cake, 141
Chess Pie, 181–182
Chew Bars, 246
Chip Cookies, 220
Crinkles, 246–247
Mint Praline Pecan Pie, 185–187
Mint Torte, 131–132

NAME INDEX